The Miegunyah Press

This is number two hundred and thirty-three in the
second numbered series of the
Miegunyah Volumes
made possible by the
Miegunyah Fund
established by bequests
under the wills of
Sir Russell and Lady Grimwade.

'Miegunyah' was the home of
Mab and Russell Grimwade
from 1911 to 1955.

The **Colonial Australian Culture Series** is a library of innovative, accessible, scholarly work that offers a compelling re-evaluation of Australia's all-too-proximate colonial past. Each title focuses on a particular cultural field, excavating often-forgotten historical sources to shed new light on aspects of our lives, practices and identities, tracing how these things transform over time.

This landmark study will be a must-have for scholars and general readers alike. Elisa deCourcy has given us the most subtle and erudite history of colonial photography yet: for the first time First Nations perspectives are centred within the larger story of photography in Australia, as she traces the unfurling of this new European technique out across the world. With precision and depth, this study tracks the ways that photography became colonial, revealing its historical power and currency. Through collaboration with First Nations peoples, deCourcy's fresh readings of Indigenous self-expression and Country contribute to a new Truth-telling agenda, and set a new direction for making photographic histories.

Professor Jane Lydon, University of Western Australia

Drawing on an extensive discursive context, including the voices of contemporary Indigenous interlocutors, *Early Photography in Colonial Australia* traces how this most crucial of mediums became colonial, in the process offering us an exemplary model of history writing. This is a book from which we could all learn much.

Professor Geoffrey Batchen, University of Oxford

This is a marvellous book that offers a complex, nuanced account of the beginnings of photography in colonial Australia. Elisa deCourcy uses a diverse range of source material, including letters, diaries, patents and other legal documents, to provide an expanded range of historical and cultural contexts for our understanding of early photographic practices. Her perspective is, however, emphatically contemporary as she addresses the blind spots and cultural absences of the past. First Nations people's encounters with photography are considered throughout. This is a book about much more than photography, but the photographs themselves have an astonishing presence and power.

Professor Emerita Helen Ennis, Australian National University

Well-researched and inventive, Elisa deCourcy's *Early Photography in Colonial Australia* shows how European migrants developed a colonial vision on unceded territories. Her book is an important contribution to rethinking the early history of photography and its imbrication in the practices and history of colonial dispossession.

Professor Steve Edwards, The Courtauld Institute of Art

Early Photography in Colonial Australia

ELISA DECOURCY

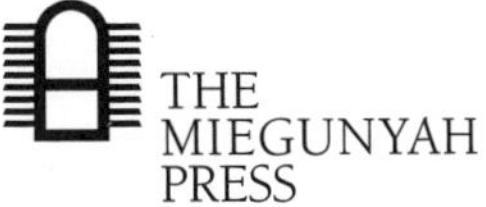

Melbourne University Publishing acknowledges the traditional owners of the unceded land on which we work, learn and live: the Wurundjeri Woiwurrung peoples of the Kulin Nation. We pay respect to elders and acknowledge the importance of Indigenous knowledge.

THE MIEGUNYAH PRESS
An imprint of Melbourne University Publishing Limited
Level 1, 715 Swanston Street, Carlton, Victoria 3053, Australia
mup-contact@unimelb.edu.au
www.mup.com.au

First published 2025

Cover design by Pfisterer + Freeman
Text design and typeset by Megan Ellis
Cover artwork: Robert Tennent (attributed), 'Banksia. The Honeysuckle of Colonists', 1849–53, salted paper print, Scottish National Portrait Gallery, Edinburgh.
Printed in China by 1010 Printing International Ltd

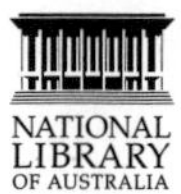

A catalogue record for this book is available from the National Library of Australia

9780522879520 (paperback)
9780522879537 (ebook)

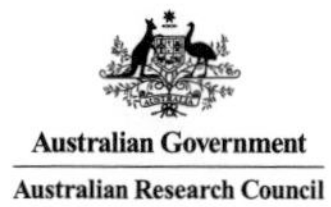

Contents

Acknowledgements

This book is dedicated to Helen Ennis, Jane Lydon and Brenda L. Croft, whose scholarship, curation and interrogation of photography is exemplary in excellence and integrity. I could not have undertaken this work without their gentle advice and support. I am humbled to have had their conversation and care at various stages of its development. Any omissions and errors are my own.

I am indebted to Ken Gelder and Rachael Weaver, who took on this project, and me, for their Colonial Culture series. They read and re-read this manuscript many times over. The book is better for their investment, perseverance and prompting to develop the argument in directions I had not considered. Thank you also to Foong Ling Kong, Duncan Fardon, Megan Ellis, Catherine McInnis, Sarina Rowell and the team at Melbourne University Press for their patience and care in shepherding this manuscript through to publication.

Craig Tuffin and James Tylor helped me think more deeply about (and, indeed, beyond) early photographic processes and practices. I am a much better art historian for having paused to make daguerreotypes with them both. The exceptional Justine Varga showed me, through her work and friendship, the importance of always looking right to the edges of photographs, and, back in 2015, Judy Annear taught me an important lesson about always flipping prints and frames over in archives, to take in the inscriptions on the verso and backing.

I am deeply grateful to the First Nations knowledge holders and Elders who spoke with me about historic photography and trusted me with preserving the integrity of those conversations in published form. Jilda Andrews, Brenda L. Croft and Julie Gough all helped me navigate my place as author in this work. I am thankful to Menang Noongar curator Shona Coyne, Menang Noongar Elder Lester Coyne and representatives of the seven Menang Noongar families who shared their reflections on the portraits Arthur Onslow took of their ancestors, discussed in Chapter 1. I look forward to a future where these images continue to be understood anew from the colonial archive. I would particularly like to thank Lester Coyne for taking me to the Wattierup/Oyster Harbour fish traps and prompting me to think differently about where photography sits in genealogies and knowledge of Country. Thanks to Garrick Hitchcock, Senior Anthropologist with the Wurundjeri Woi Wurrung Cultural Heritage Aboriginal Corporation, and Wurundjeri Elder Colin Hunter, for sharing their thoughts about the ambrotype of south-eastern First Nations people on the pastoral station discussed at the end of Chapter 3. I would also like to acknowledge the generosity of Wurundjeri cultural artefacts specialist Jack Norris, who helped me understand the possibilities and limitations in locating this portrait within Kin and Country networks. Stephen Gilchrist was tremendously gracious and generous in sharing his thoughts on the shield in this ambrotype and, consequently, directing my research to the Wurundjeri Woi Wurrung. Heartfelt thanks to Brenda L. Croft, Danie Mellor and James Tylor, who trusted me to discuss their practice and reproduce their important work in the Preface.

This book is one of the major outcomes of my Australian Research Council (ARC) Discovery Early Career Research Award (DE200101322), which I completed in the Centre for Art History and Art Theory at the Australian National University during 2020–23. I thank the three anonymous peer assessors who, back in 2019, saw the merit in this project, and I extend this thanks to the ARC for funding it. The ability to work across collections at international, national, state and regional levels has been invaluable. Within discrete collections, I am grateful to the following curators, conservators, archivists and librarians working with photography and colonial Australian art who have facilitated my access to relevant material: Bruce Adams (Forbes and District Historical Society); Jan Brazier and Jude Philp (Chau Chak Wing Museum, University of Sydney); Patrick Bugeja (formerly, Ayers House / National Trust South Australia); Alisa Bunbury and Christine Elias (Ian Potter Museum of Art / University of Melbourne Museums); Lesley Burnett (Royal Western Australian Historical Society); Nerida

Campbell (Justice and Police Museum / Museums of History New South Wales); Danielle Castronovo (Harvard University Herbaria and Libraries); Vicki Farmery (formerly, Tasmanian Museum and Gallery); Vanessa Finney (Australian Museum); Joanna Gilmour (formerly, National Portrait Gallery, Canberra); Graham Hogg (National Library of Scotland); Nicole Ioffredi (British Library); Magda Keaney (formerly, National Portrait Gallery, London—now National Gallery of Australia); Shaune Lakin and Anne O'Hehir (National Gallery of Australia); Shane Le Plastrier (independent collector); Susan Long (State Library of Victoria); Nicki Mackay-Sim and all the very patient Special Collections staff (National Library of Australia); Richard Neville and Damien Webb (State Library of New South Wales); Louise Pearson (National Galleries Scotland); Kay Peterson (National Museum of American History, Washington); Michael Pritchard (Royal Photographic Society, Bristol/ independent researcher); Ruth Quinn (National Science and Media Museum, Bradford); Chris Read (State Library of South Australia); Julie Robinson and Ken Orchard (Art Gallery of South Australia); Caitlin Sutton (Allport Library and Museum of Fine Arts); Antares Wells (formerly, Powerhouse Museum); Brigid Whitbread (Queanbeyan-Palerang Regional Library); Susan van Wyk and Maggie Finch (National Gallery of Victoria); Toni Young (State Library of Western Australia) and Stephen Zagala (South Australian Museum).

I was fortunate to present earlier iterations of some of the chapters at important international workshops, symposia and conferences. I thank Geoffrey Batchen, who invited me to speak at his Bodleian Libraries, University of Oxford symposium, 'A New Power: Photography in Britain 1800–1850', in March 2023. He did this knowing I would talk about the rich and complex histories of photography that emerged once the technologies *left* Britain. Thanks to him for that accommodation, and the platform to present my research to an audience of leading international historians and curators of photography. I would like to acknowledge all the other presenters at this occasion, but particularly Fionn Montell-Boyd, David Campany, Steve Edwards, Chitra Ramalingam and, of course, Geoff, whose scholarship, as referenced in the following chapters, made me think more panoramically about my own work as part of an international conversation. At the end of March 2023, I was a fellow at the Bibliotheca Hertziana–Max Planck Institute for Art History in Rome, at the biennial photography workshop run by Steffen Seigel and Elizabeth Otto. Thank you to Steffen and Libby for selecting me and my work to be part of this week-long conversation, and to Yazan Alloujami, Max Böhner, Madison Brown, Olena Chervonik, Angela Cheung, Samantha King-Shaw, Marie Meyerding, Oleksandra Osadcha, Juanita Solano Roa, Francesca Strobino and Tracy Stuber for sharing your rigorous insights and inspiring research. In July 2023, I had the privilege of convening the symposium 'Nineteenth-Century Worlds of Vision' in Kamberri/Canberra, which brought together the incredible, layered work of our community of curators and art historians working on Oceanic visual culture. I thank Julie Gough, Geoffrey Batchen, Emily Eastgate Brink, Alisa Bunbury, Jane E. Brown, Kathleen Davidson, Molly Duggins, Helen Ennis, Yvette Hamilton, the late David Hansen, Helen Hughes, Martyn Jolly, Julia Lum and Rebecca Rice for making this conversation so memorable—my citations illuminate how much you have all influenced my own thinking.

Many friends and colleagues have read and commented on draft chapters, none more so than Helen Ennis. Helen not only inspired this research with her indefatigable and peerless work on Australian photography, but also read some of these chapters many times over (while completing her own book, no less). Her calm intellectual camaraderie and conversation through the past few years has supported me in ways I cannot begin to describe and, no doubt, will ever be able to repay. I extend my thanks to Geoffrey Batchen, Isobel Crombie, Jarrod Hore, Martyn Jolly, Jane Lydon and Maria Nugent for their suggestions and corrections regarding various chapters and excerpts. Monika Bakke, Alisa Bunbury, Roger Butler, Rebecca Edwards, Ursula K. Frederick, Julian Laffan, Gael Newton, Chaitanya Sambrani, Sarah Scott and Kate Warren all listened patiently and astutely to my ideas as I worked out what I was trying to say. Konrad calmly endured the pure neurosis of sharing a house with an academic writing a book. I cannot imagine a more loyal listener. I am astounded that he never once faltered in the belief that I would finish, and because of that, I could. Anna, Saskia, Elise, Lily and Sita all kept me reading other things, cocooned me in their friendship when things got tough and prompted me to celebrate even the smallest of successes. And thanks, lastly, to my parents for their continued support.

Ngambri and Ngunnawal Country, 2025

Note on Naming

I use Aboriginal names for locations, landforms, waterways and cultural objects preceding colonial European dual naming, recognising and honouring an Indigenous connection to Country that dates to over 60,000 years. I pay my deep respect to Elders, past, present and emerging, who preserve this knowledge, and the First Nations artists, Elders, knowledge holders and curators who have shared their knowledge with me. I adopt the spelling and naming that First Nations people who I have spoken to or corresponded with have used. More generally, I have consulted sources such as the AIATSIS Map of Indigenous Australia. The spelling and capitalisation of Aboriginal names is shifting terrain as language moves through a process of restitution. Inevitably, I will have made errors, for which I apologise.

I acknowledge the Cammeraygal people on whose unceded Country I was born, the Ngambri and Ngunnawal people on whose unceded Country I currently live and work, and the unceded Country of all First Nations people where this book was researched.

List of Figures

NB: The dimensions of all illustrations are listed in centimetres in the captions except for daguerreotypes and ambrotypes, which are referenced through their standardised plate sizes. The below graphic is an annotated, comparison of these plate dimensions.

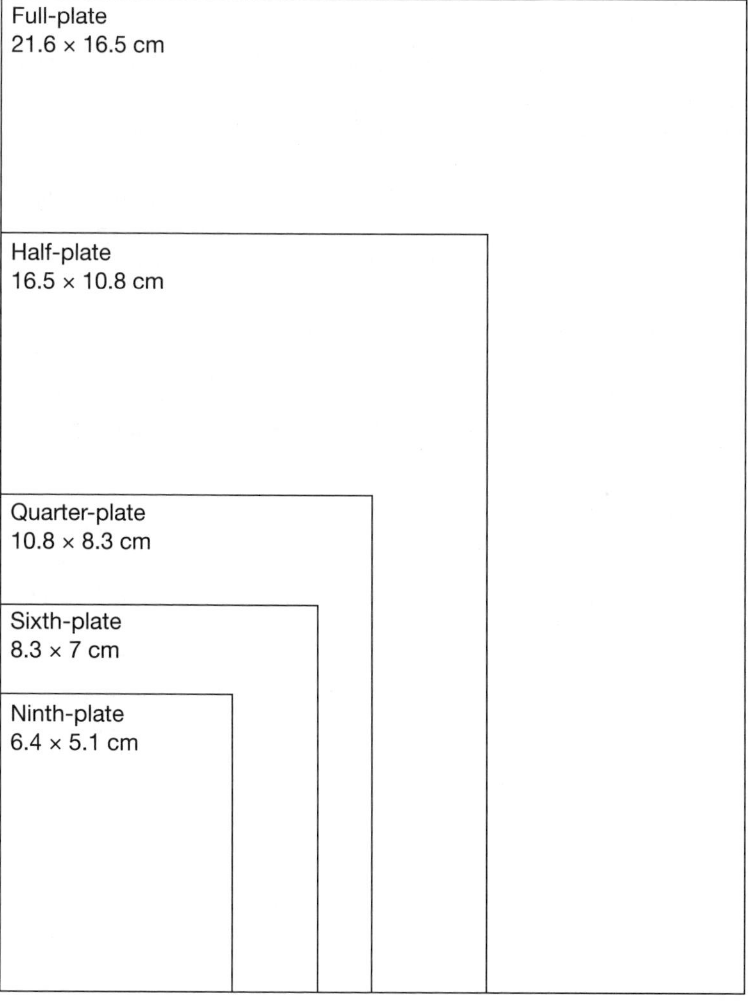

Preface

Photography's European inventors and earliest proponents almost immediately considered applications for the new technology in foreign geographies. In June 1839, the celebrated French physicist and astronomer Dominique François Jean Arago stood before a meeting of the Chambre des députés, the lower house of the French parliament, and proclaimed that the new invention of photography would be indispensable to the traveller, the archaeologist and the naturalist: 'Enfin, pour le voyageur, pour l'archéologue, aussi bien que pour le naturaliste, l'appareil de M. Daguerre deviendra d'un usage continuel et indispensable'.[1] These professions were intimately linked to the cultural and intellectual production of imperial knowledge. And, in following, Arago predicted that, after some time away, these individuals would return to France with their photographs. In the year of its commercial launch, Arago considered photography to be the most precise image-making technology—one that preserved features down to their smallest details with a delicacy hitherto unknown: 'formes jusque dans leurs plus petits détails ... avec une délicatesse inconnue jusqu'ici'.[2] He championed photography's unprecedented clarity and exactitude in representing the world, which he expected would stimulate new knowledge. But Arago anticipated the audience for these perfect renderings to be Europeans, in Europe.

This book picks up on a blind spot in Arago's predictions for photography, interrogating what happened when photographic technologies were taken out into the world, and used in the service of colonial customers and audiences. The five chapters that follow are guided by the question of *when* and *how* photography became colonial in an Australian context. I argue that this 'acclimatisation' was enacted shortly after knowledge of photographic processes and cameras arrived from overseas. Photography was used to create knowledge about people and place anew. But, contrary to Arago's declared aspirations for the medium, this knowledge was neither more comprehensive nor more exacting than understandings of the Country and its people that had a long and deep history here. Photography became colonial as it was wielded by colonists as a visual annotation or document in the broader project of colonisation: its ambitions, its 'achievements' or advancements, and its attempted erasures.

Presented here is a history of photography weighted towards its foundational colonial practice between the 1840s and 1860s. I argue that a colonial practice of photography coalesced in these early decades, influencing how the technology was used and understood for the remainder of the century and beyond. In *Photography and Australia* (2007), Helen Ennis noted that '[t]he most glaring shortcomings in Australian photographic history are in the area of colonial photography, especially those crucial first decades'.[3] Since Ennis's important survey, there have been a selection of publications on or including mid-nineteenth-century colonial photographs and photographers. As Ennis has since written, the resurgence of work on colonial photography has largely been undertaken within collecting institutions.[4] Recent writing on colonial photography has typically been tied to exhibitions, focused on the holdings of specific collections, or looked at discrete genres of practice: for example, Julie Robinson's *A Century in Focus: South Australian Photography 1840s-1940s* (2007–08) and Vanessa Finney's *Capturing Nature: Early Scientific Photography at the Australian Museum 1857-1893* (2019). There have also been a number of institutionally commissioned biographies of individual colonial photographers, such as the National Library of Australia's *A Modern Vision: Charles Bayliss, Photographer, 1850-1897* (2008), the National Gallery of Victoria's *Fred Kruger: Intimate Landscapes* (2012) and the Tasmanian Museum and Art Gallery's *Thomas Bock* (2018). My own book is indebted to and informed by curatorial publications such as these, with their succinct articulation of the significance of this material. Here, though, I aim to move across collection holdings, genres of practice and photographers' biographies in a less contained manner, to produce a wide-ranging study of the beginnings of colonial photography.

Beyond works from gallery and museum presses, there has been only one anthology dedicated to colonial photography published in the past few decades. Anne Maxwell and Josephine Croci's *Shifting Focus: Colonial Photography in Australia 1850-1920* (2015) brought together twenty-two authors to investigate the diverse avenues for colonial photographic production. These ranged from the illustrated news and the commodification and retail of colonial landscape photography, to the projection of colonial photographs in lantern shows and early cinematic productions. The bulk of chapters cover the period of the late 1860s to the 1880s. The editors regard the first decades of colonial photographic practice as 'unambiguously European', with a direct 'migration not just of photographers and images, but also styles and techniques'.[5] Yet, Jane Lydon's contribution, one of only two chapters to cover mid-century material, speaks to a more complex reality. Examining a photograph of the Wurundjeri Elder Simon Wonga, among other early examples of Kulin Nation portraits, Lydon argues that Aboriginal people encountered 'photography within a decade of white settlement of the colony of Port Phillip '.[6] She demonstrates that many early colonial photographs 'reveal and embody [Kin] and social networks' as colonisation impacted their lives and experiences.[7] We see from Lydon's study here and her scholarship more broadly that early photography is a barometer of the invasiveness of colonisation, but also one that registers stories of survival and self-expression among Aboriginal portrait subjects.[8] Marking out its differences from European styles and templates, photography was caught up in the violence of colonisation as it played out in and around photographic production.

We only have to look to recent survey exhibitions to see that the early practice of photography is unretractable from the broader story of settler-colonial art. Examples of early photographs featured prominently in Judy Annear's *The Photograph and Australia* at the Art Gallery of New South Wales in 2015–16. A sizeable room was given over to mid-nineteenth-century photography in both Cathy Leahy and Judith Ryan et al.'s NGV exhibition *Colony: Australia 1770-1861 / Frontier Wars* (2018) and Susan van Wyk's NGV exhibition *Photography: Real and Imagined* (2023–24). Annear wrote in the catalogue accompanying her exhibition: 'Given that the medium came into existence outside Australia it joins all art forms, except the Indigenous, as being something photographers in Australia have both adapted to and adapted for their own purposes'.[9] She conceived *The Photograph and Australia* as building on the survey exhibitions and survey publications of the country's first dedicated curators of photography, including Gael Newton's *Shades of Light: Photography and Australia 1839-1988* at the Australian National Gallery (now the National Gallery of Australia) in 1988 and Alan Davies' photographic history *The Mechanical Eye in Australia* (1985). Curating a narrative for photography around themes rather than a linear technological chronology, Annear highlighted resonances and evolutions in relationships between photographers and their subjects across time and situations.

Nevertheless, the necessary installation architecture that facilitates the display of early photographs in exhibition contexts operates to diminish our comprehension of these images' historic power and currency. We encounter examples of the earliest paper prints and cased photographs in temperature-controlled cases behind thick glass, with dim or cool lighting, and cushioned on bespoke armatures or supports. This treatment—what Rhiannon Mason and others have termed the construction of the 'autonomous artefact'[10]—drives the public's perception of mid-nineteenth-century photographs as delicate and vulnerable on account of their present-day materiality. Chitra Ramalingam has suggested that the priority of maintaining a 'stable work of art', irrespective of various levels of 'discolouration and image degradation, from fading and foxing',[11] has defined the way some of the best-known early photographs have been exhibited internationally.[12] In an Australian context, these necessary installation and collection access practices are equally fundamental to the preservation of such old images, but they can also divorce colonial photographs from an understanding of the volatile contexts of their creation. Such photographs may appear diminutive and fragile today, but this is not commensurate with their affective and ideological power in the colonial past, nor reflective of the legacy of colonial knowledge to which they contribute.

In contemporary art, we glimpse the potency and unresolved consequences connected with the beginnings of photographic practice in Australia. Early photographic processes have been redeployed and appropriated by contemporary First Nations artists as tools through which to reclaim agency over the representation of Country, Community and self. Brenda L. Croft— Gurindji/Malngin/Mudburra artist, with Anglo-Australian, Chinese, German, Irish and Scottish ancestry—weaves historic processes into her contemporary practice. Her ongoing series of large-scale portraits of First Nations women and girls, *Naabámi (thou will/shall see): Barangaroo (army of me)* (2019–present), were made with the assistance of photographic technician Prue Hazelgrove, using mid-nineteenth-century wet-plate collodion processing (**Figure 0.1**). Each small photographic plate is scanned and digitally enlarged, with the portraits printed far larger than life-size. Croft notes that the original wet-plate collodion process is a studio format 'we are very familiar with as First Nations Peoples: we were photographed [historically through this process] as ethnographic objects and eugenicist representations'.[13]

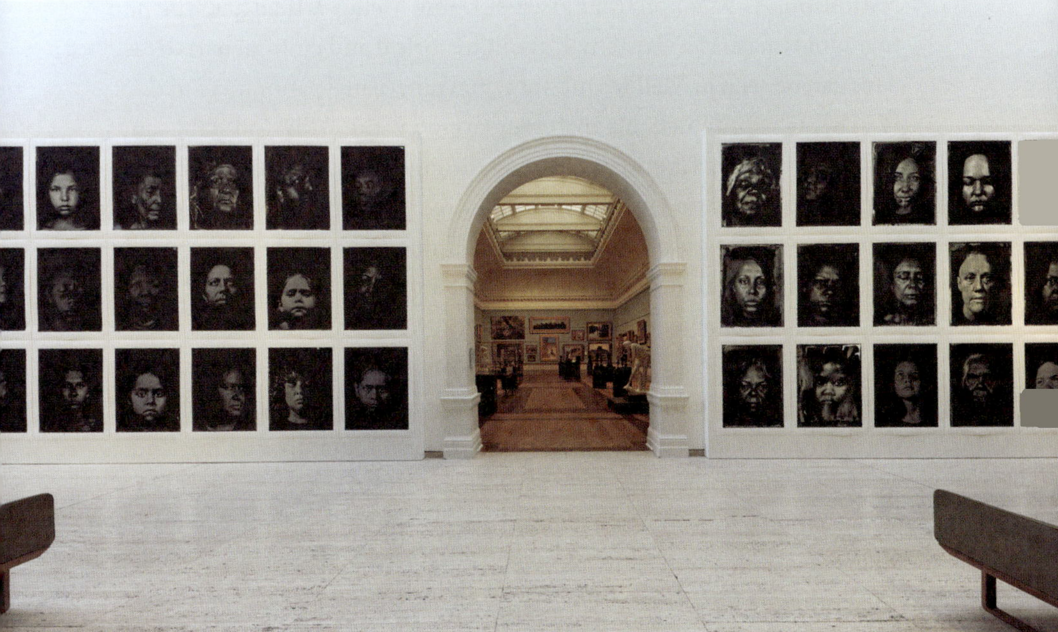

Figure 0.1: [Installation view] Brenda L. Croft, 'Naabámi (thou shall/will see): Barangaroo (army of me)', 2019–present, inkjet prints from original tintypes made with assistance from Prue Hazelgrove, each print 143 × 112 cm, on display as part of *The National 4: Australian Art Now* at the Art Gallery of New South Wales, 24 March–23 July 2023. © Brenda L. Croft; photo © Art Gallery of New South Wales, Mim Stirling.

She draws on the mid-nineteenth-century collodion process to tell a story that both critiques a period of colonial photographic representation and transcends it. The unflinching beauty and strength in the faces of each of *Naabámi*'s First Nations women and girls map an inherited staunchness from Cammeraygal warrior woman Barangaroo (c. 1750–91) and her (pre-photographic) engagement with colonisers on her Country.[14] Croft notes Barangaroo's role as steadfast sovereign leader 'at the time of first contact makes her as relevant today, as in the late eighteenth century'.[15] Croft shows that Barangaroo's strong female resolve endures through a period of colonisation (and colonial photography) into the present colonial nation-state. Installed side by side, in layers two or three high, *Naabámi*'s matriarchal community stand as defiant sentinels meeting their audience as a monolithic united front.

Consequently, in contemporary First Nations' practice, the representational violence of colonial photography is met by acts of repair and restitution. As Ngadjon/Mamu artist Danie Mellor articulates, 'the photographic image is a way to talk about historical and cultural narratives'.[16] This can be seen in Mellor's monumental nine-panel panorama *Landstory* (2018), which depicts his maternal Country, the Atherton Tablelands, and neighbouring Country extending through North Queensland's dense rainforest. It is crafted with modern infrared photography which registers light on a spectrum otherwise imperceptible to the human eye. Mellor then sensitively digitally layers historic Aboriginal portraits and photographed cultural objects onto his rainforest vista. These are removed from the colonial studio architecture of their original exposure and repatriated to show a softly rendered ancestral presence on Country (**Figure 0.2**). *Landstory* is an indictment of how colonial photography cast the land as 'available' and 'empty', themes that have been dissected in Jarrod Hore's recent monograph *Visions of Nature* (2022). Mellor works with opposing forces of visibility and invisibility to highlight how an Aboriginal occupation and knowledge of Country was compositionally erased by colonial contributors to the genre of landscape photography. His combination of different photographic mediums, historic and contemporary, conjures a landspace that has a 'past, present and future … a timeless dreaming and landstory'.[17]

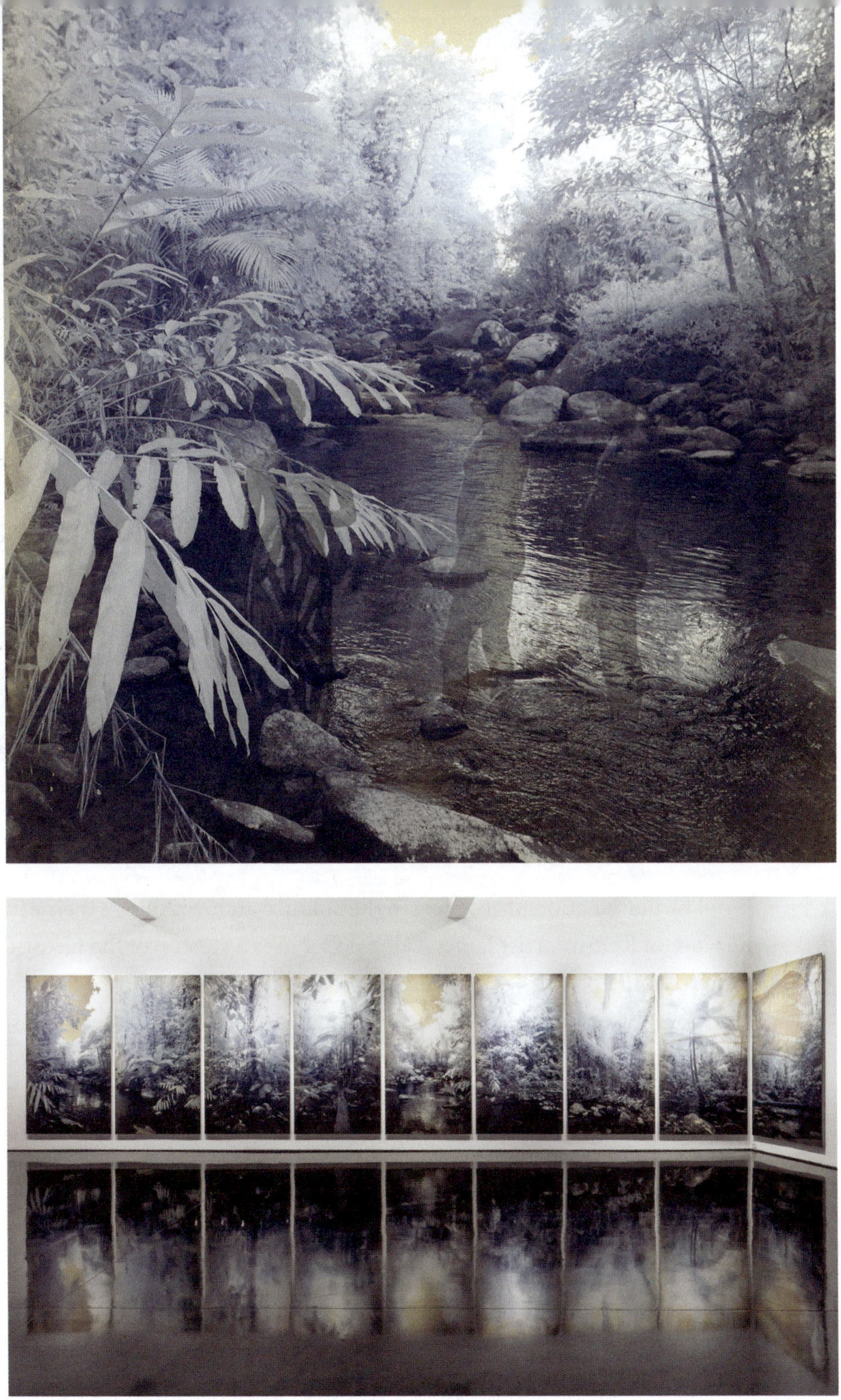

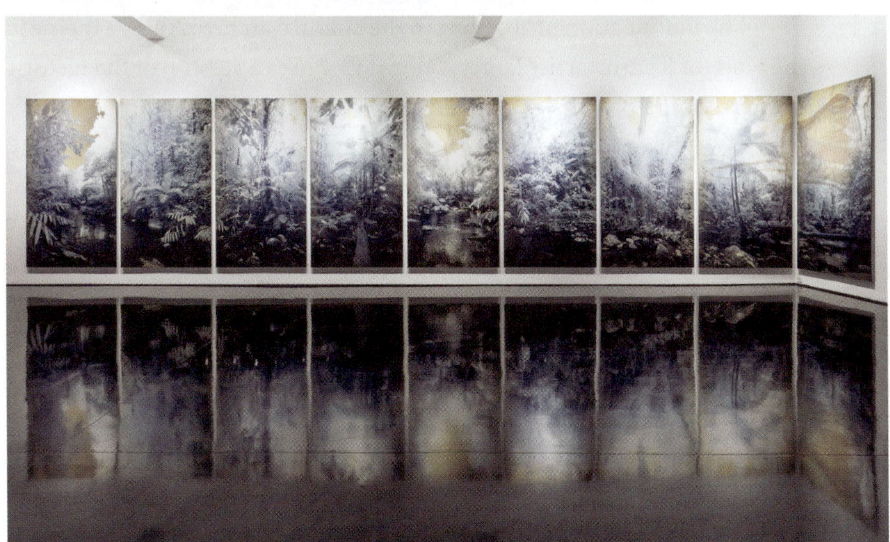

Figure 0.2: [Section, panel 1 of 9], Danie Mellor, 'Landstory', 2018, chromogenic prints, nine panels each 224 × 124 cm, overall: 224 × 1276 cm. Collections: National Gallery of Australia, Kamberri/Canberra, Australia and Fondation Opale, Lens, Switzerland. Installation view, Tolarno Galleries, Naarm/Melbourne, 2018. Images courtesy of Andrew Curtis and the artist.

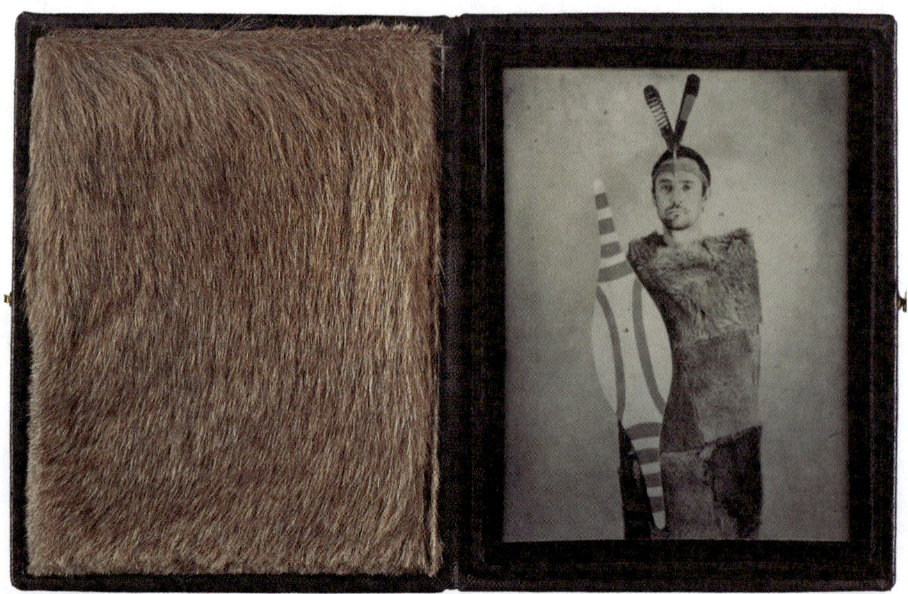

Figure 0.3: James Tylor with Elisa deCourcy, 'Self Portrait', 2022, half-plate, cased becquerel daguerreotype. National Portrait Gallery, London. Image courtesy of the artist and N.Smith Gallery.

The illumination of absences in the colonial archive is also a theme in the work of Kaurna artist James Tylor. Tylor uses a version of the historic daguerreotype process, widely employed in the 1840s, to provocatively 'transport' his audience back to the nineteenth century. Nevertheless, Tylor is quick to qualify that his work gestures to a past that was not photographed. Kaurna people appear in historic daguerreotypes as domestic servants or missionary subjects, dressed in European clothing and captured according to colonial roles.[18] In his *Self Portrait* (2022), Tylor stands in front of the camera as both the subject and architect of his image's production (**Figure 0.3**). He appears dressed in culturally significant items, wrapped in a Wadla watpa wallaby cloak, holding a murlapaka shield and wearing a manga headband with Tiwu red-tailed black cockatoo feathers. The portrait's case echoes the design of mid-nineteenth-century photographic cases but is lined with Wadla watpa wallaby fur, reiterating Tylor's agency over the image's presentation. He remarks that 'rather than living in a space of loss or deficit, I create the imagery that should exist'.[19] This is a form of creative recovery that

Narungga artist and academic Natalie Harkin has identified in her own practice as 'embodied reckoning'.[20]

❂

This book aims to capture the power and propulsion of a foundational period of colonial photography, which set in motion a practice of photography still deeply consequential in Australia. It is a study that is self-consciously written from the vantage of the present day. It offers new or expanded readings of a selection of colonial photographs by bringing them into conversation with diaries, letters, shipping manifests, journalism, pamphlets, and sketched, engraved and painted art, as well as court records and patent documents, to demonstrate their colonial uses and influence. Even so, this process of knitting together physically dispersed materials from local, national and international archives and gallery holdings can reveal gaps or silences in our understanding of certain photographs and photographic experiences. The perspectives of some sitters and photographers were not recorded in this adjacent material. We can also learn from this archival material of photographs that no longer survive. This is particularly the case with the photography of Aboriginal people, who were rarely the custodians of their portraits, and with the work of early women photographers, as documentation of their practice was infrequently preserved. Consequently, as Tiffany Shellam and Joanna Cruickshank emphasise, colonial archives are 'never neutral spaces'; they are instead inflected with the patriarchal politics at play at the time of their materials' creation and aggregation.[21]

Rather than collapse the story of colonial photography around these archival absences, this book operates to illuminate their presence. I evaluate how gaps in knowledge and understanding of certain photographs and photographic experiences reflect historic collecting practices. Where appropriate and possible, I work with Aboriginal Communities and knowledge holders to identify and offer possible interpretations of self-definition and self-expression in colonial photographic portraits, while also looking at how these photographs were potentially used or thought about at the time of their exposure. The aim here is to situate this material in the context of the history of colonisation it both reflected and progressed. My approach also recognises, in keeping with Tony Ballantyne's argument, that colonial archives have 'complex and shifting relationships' to cultural authority.[22] A significant portion of colonial photographic practice saw colonists turning the lens on themselves to create stories of dynasty and 'progress' on Aboriginal land. When it arrived in the colonies, photography was still in the early stages of its development. But, as this book will show, it quickly became a handmaid for the expression of colonial prosperity, central to colonial communications (e.g. in the form of journalism or private correspondence), and pivotal to construing the land as a terra nullius that was replete with resources—a means of validating the colonial project for both domestic and international audiences.

The chapters are organised thematically while following a loose chronology. Chapter 1 argues against a singular moment of photography's colonial arrival. In lieu of a definitive beginning, I canvass some of the avenues through which photographic knowledge and equipment travelled to the colonies, and the various places and publications in which people encountered photographic thinking and photographic images. This chapter reveals how photography's colonial beginnings were diverse, with cameras demonstrated on busy thoroughfares and used to mediate cross-cultural encounters. Photographic processes were experimented with by established artists, and the potential of photography was discussed in colonial philosophical and scientific societies. Chapter 2 follows the development of colonial photographic commercial enterprises. I take three different but complementary mid-nineteenth-century photographers—George Barron Goodman, J. W. (James William) Newland and (Elizabeth) Louisa How—as indicative of a developing colonial photographic scene. This chapter documents how colonial photography was first established in bustling port cities with maritime circuits delivering photographers, their supplies and photographic literature to studio addresses. It is in this foundational phase of commercial and—in the case of How—skilful amateur practices that photographers are compelled to recalibrate European photographic equipment and knowledge for the colonial atmosphere and conditions.

Chapter 3 and Chapter 4 offer different views of the spread of photography inland, with the emergence of itinerant studio businesses, and as an outdoor practice of photography increasingly turned towards the regional and remote geographies. The expansion of photography inland followed the encroachment of colonists on Aboriginal land as manifest in the pastoral and mining industries. Chapter 3 observes how colonial capital generated by mining and pastoralism was directly represented by the patrons of photography studios and the stories their portraits tell. This chapter presents studio portraiture as a dynamic and collaborative undertaking where the investment of the sitter, along with the personal items and props they brought to the studio, was crucial to defining the resulting image. The corollary of colonial expansion inland was the forced dispossession of Aboriginal people and the dislocation of Kin. These were experiences further articulated in the photography studio, where, as Croft and Tylor noted earlier, Aboriginal people were portrayed as domestic servants, missionary subjects and through a juggernaut of racist philosophies.[23] I discuss these uses for photography, but do not reproduce examples as illustrations, in order to avoid further perpetuating colonial visual stereotypes. Rather, and in collaboration with present-day Wurundjeri knowledge holders, I unpack an ambrotype taken by an itinerant studio photographer. This ambrotype complicates the reading of photography solely through metanarratives of colonisation and Aboriginal objectification and, in consultation, I observe where Aboriginal self-expression is recoverable.

Chapter 4 considers photography beyond portraiture, beginning with outdoor images taken from the windowsills and doorsteps of colonial studios. From these liminal locations, I chart the progression of photography into Country. This progression is in part facilitated by advancements in photographic technologies during the late 1850s and in part reflective of the inland development of colonial industries, as noted earlier. The chapter chronicles how colonists ignored Aboriginal sovereignty over Country to tell stories of colonial productivity and possibilities. It keeps in play the photography of both urban and rural landscapes, arguing that the construction of each relied on the counterweight of the other.

The final chapter completes the story of how photography became colonial, by tracing the medium's connections to a range of other colonial visual art practices, such as lithography, early printing, draughtsmanship and engraving. Photography's place within a broader mixed-media landscape—and particular photographs' relationships to paintings, sketches and prints—is a topic that recurs throughout this book. The final chapter, however, takes photographic translation and reproduction as its central theme. It looks at the affective and ideological power of colonial photographs as they were reproduced in journalism, commercialised as collectables, or copied to consolidate and update colonial family collections.

This book works to address the gap in our understanding of the beginnings of colonial photography that Ennis first identified two decades ago. It is not an exhaustive history of the foundational period of colonial photography but an indicative study highlighting, as contemporary First Nations practice equally shows us, that these first decades of colonial photography were deeply consequential to setting the course for Australian photography into the present day.

1

Arrivals

How do we identify the arrival of photography in the Australian colonies? Any survey exhibition, anthology, monograph, catalogue or lecture about photography's history on the continent has been compelled to address this question. Can we claim photography began in this part of the world with the physical arrival of the first camera? Did a practice commence with the first instance of a photograph being attempted or, rather, is a beginning more concretely represented by the certainty of the oldest surviving colonial photograph? The act of photographing requires a photographer and a subject. Is the point of arrival then contingent on a location and an identity? Perhaps the arrival of photography can be marked by the earliest documented instance of someone receiving a photograph in the mail, rather than by the work of an artist at a particular colonial site. Defining an arrival, or arrivals, is both necessary and futile. Possibilities abound and identifying a single definitive answer may not be possible. This chapter will look at several potential points of photographic arrival in the colonies, taking them (as it were) as a point of departure for the chapters that follow.

Most histories of Australian photography acknowledge the medium's European invention but commence when the first photographer, photograph, camera, or initial knowledge of the chemical configuration for a photographic process, had already arrived in the colonies.[1] We know from these accounts that news of the first commercialised photographic processes appeared in the colonial Australian press in 1839, the same year they were officially unveiled and promoted in Britain and France.[2] Within two years, colonial artists and amateurs had received instructions, paper and chemistry for executing early camera-less photographic impressions.[3] By May 1841—as I shall discuss below—the first camera had arrived in the colonies and was set up on Gadigal Country at Macquarie Place.[4] Here, without ceremony, the first camera-based photograph was reportedly exposed, although it has since been lost. The oldest *surviving* photograph produced in the colonies, a portrait now held at the State Library of New South Wales, dates from a few years later: early 1845.[5] As Chapter 2 will note, this portrait traces back to when the first dedicated colonial photographic studio was established. These markers all point to different facets of arrival. In this chapter, I aim to unpack some of these events to illuminate their conditions and contingencies. Only then can we resituate colonial photography in the global conversation about the medium to which it belonged and comprehend how a diversity of pre-photographic knowledges in the colonies framed markedly different first encounters with the technology.

The history of photography's arrival in the Australian colonies necessarily begins elsewhere, following the invention and commercialisation of photographic technologies in Europe. But the trail of export does not simply lead directly back to the Royal Institution in London, where, on 25 January 1839, Michael Faraday publicly presented several examples of polymath and inventor William Henry Fox Talbot's photogenic drawings.[6] Nor does it trace directly to the lectures Dominique François Jean Arago gave to explain artist and inventor Louis-Jacques-Mandé Daguerre's rival process, the daguerreotype. The first of these was at a closed meeting of the Académie des sciences in January 1839, followed by Arago's address to French parliament in June—described in the Preface—and, finally, his lecture at a joint meeting of the Académie des sciences and the Académie des Beaux-Arts in Paris in August.[7] These orations are cited as the public beginnings for a culture and practice of photography globally, in Helmut and Alison Gernsheim's *The History of Photography* (1955) or, more recently, in Mary Warner Marien's *Photography: A Cultural History* (2016) and Geoffrey Batchen's *Inventing Photography* (2023).[8] Yet, they tell us very little about the conditions of photographic technologies' reception beyond academic halls, public chambers and learned societies of Britain and France.

One important episode of colonial photographic arrival was catalysed by a shipwreck just beyond the harbour wall at Valparaíso, Chile, on 23 June 1840. Despite unfavourable weather conditions, French captain Augustin Lucas committed to the scheduled afternoon departure of his vessel, the *L'Oriental*—an *école flottante*, a floating school. Originally a commercial vessel, it had been refitted during 1838–39 to accommodate youthful pupils drawn from influential merchant families across Belgium and France.[9] By Valparaíso, *L'Oriental* was partway through a global journey. Its expedition had been devised by Lucas himself and its benefit was advertised as transporting students far away from the drudgery of the orthodox urban classroom. However, capital for and endorsement of Lucas's venture did not come from the families of pupils alone. La Société d'Encouragement pour l'Industrie Nationale had committed funding to the endeavour, in exchange for knowledge of ports and port officials vital to French trading relationships around the Atlantic and Pacific.[10] The vessel was carrying munitions provided by the French navy, and its students' syllabi was formulated by La Société de Géographie and La Société Ethnologique in Paris.[11] In all, *L'Oriental*'s expedition was a thinly veiled late-Enlightenment exercise aimed at gathering maritime and trading intelligence. Importantly, it was the first expedition of any kind to leave mainland Europe carrying camera equipment.

In July 1839, two months before *L'Oriental* set sail from Paimbœuf, Lucas had visited Daguerre's Parisian studio. Here, along with Jean Baptiste Jobard, the director of the Brussels Industrial Museum, Lucas was given a demonstration of the daguerreotype process. A daguerreotype is taken on a silver-coated copper plate, polished, and sensitised with a solution of silver iodide and bromine. The plate is then placed in a box camera with a simple lens, where it is exposed to light. The light sensitivity of the plate is stopped, and the photograph fixed, when the plate is fumed with mercury vapour and washed with sodium thiosulphate. The same plate placed in the camera is the one developed to reveal the final photograph. Consequently, there is no negative and positive, or negative and print, in this daguerreotype process. Due to the silvered surface of the plate, the resulting photograph takes on a mirror-like quality. As documented in Jobard's diary, this visit to Daguerre's studio enabled Lucas to acquire for his forthcoming expedition a daguerreotype camera, plate holders, buffeting and sensitising equipment, photographic plates and chemical solutions from the inventor.[12]

Lucas took at least one daguerreotype camera aboard *L'Oriental.* After departing mainland France in September 1839, the ship travelled down the coast of West Africa as far as Senegal, before traversing the Atlantic and making land at Brazil.[13] Maria Inez Turazzi has identified that one of *L'Oriental*'s crew, possibly the ecclesiastical tutor Louis Comte, took the first photographs in Brazil at Rio de Janeiro.[14] These are two sixth-plate daguerreotypes shot looking over the central square at Rio de Janeiro towards the Royal Palace, from a structure near or on the coastline.[15] One plate is extant and the other survives as an engraving made after the daguerreotype. From Brazil, the expedition sailed to Uruguay, then ventured further south, passing through the Strait of Magellan before again setting a course north, towards Valparaíso. At Chile, *L'Oriental* was scheduled to proceed along the coast of the Americas as far as California, before heading west towards the Philippines.[16] This itinerary was thrown into disarray on the afternoon of 23 June 1840. Just beyond the harbour wall, strong winds threw the ship onto the rocky escarpment below the lighthouse. Its hull was crushed on impact and repeatedly pummelled against the rocks. While no lives were lost, the ship was irreparably wrecked.[17]

The shipwreck altered the course of Lucas's expedition and, by extension, that of his camera equipment. By all reports, most of *L'Oriental*'s scholastic passengers and their tutors made their own passage back to France.[18] However, Lucas remained in Valparaíso, along with a salvaged daguerreotype camera and kit. Here he waited for his brother's ship, the *Justine,* which had been shuttling across the Pacific as a trading vessel for many years. The *Justine* left Valparaíso in November 1840 with Augustin Lucas aboard, sailing on to Tahiti and Aotearoa/New Zealand before docking at Warrane/Sydney Cove on 29 March.[19] Lucas's arrival was announced in the local paper, but it had already been anticipated by news of the wreck of the floating school, which, unlike the ship itself, had travelled the globe.[20] *L'Oriental's* demise had not only come at a cost to Lucas's pride but to his pocket. He now had to fund his return passage to France from Gadigal Country, and to do so, he put the daguerreotype camera and equipment up for sale. An advertisement was placed in the *Australasian Chronicle* on 13 April 1841, and the sale was arranged through the shipping agents Joubert and Murphy, whose store was located on Bridge Street.[21] A few weeks later, when no buyer had been forthcoming, a demonstration of the camera was announced.

To start the story of the first camera's use in the Australian colonies on 14 May 1841, when a photograph was reportedly taken from Macquarie Place—looking up Bridge Street towards Macquarie Street—would be to downplay the extraordinary journey the first photographic apparatus took before arriving in the colonies. Certainly, Lucas's knowledge of photography and, most likely, the equipment he was demonstrating in Warrane/Sydney Cove arcs back to Daguerre's own studio. But the photograph itself didn't attract much attention at the time. Only one newspaper, the *Australian,* sent a journalist to attend the demonstration and all knowledge of this event comes from their account. In an article published the following day, the daguerreotype resulting from Lucas's camera was described as an 'astonishingly beautiful and minute sketch'; its effect was translated for readers into the terms of a more familiar art.[22] The journalist went on to outline daguerreotype photography's expansive potential, especially its ability to be 'copied for the purposes of engraving and lithography'.[23] These comments suggest that photography would be quickly integrated into a colonial visual art scene. Curiously, the journalist made no mention of the public display of this inaugural photograph, or the reaction of any onlookers present that day. Lucas's daguerreotype camera and materials remained unsold.[24] Although it marked the first use of photographic apparatus in the colonies, Lucas's camera's demonstration could, in some ways, be considered something of a false start for a *practice* of colonial photography: an arrival without design or, indeed, commercial ramifications.

The story of Lucas's travelling camera is not the only episode of photographic arrival that deserves our attention. For a year prior to the camera's demonstration, artists and amateurs were in receipt of instructions enabling them to experiment with early photographic processes. In Warrane/Sydney Cove, celebrated painter Conrad Martens copied the instructions for photogenic drawing from English magazine the *Visitor or Monthly Instructor* into his notebook, *Notes on Painting*, during the early 1840s.[25] This photographic process had been developed and refined through the 1830s by William Henry Fox Talbot, although it was the instructions of British medical doctor and scientist Golding Bird that Martens was reading in the *Visitor*. Talbot conceived two kinds of photogenic drawing. The first was undertaken through a simple camera where a sheet of writing paper, sensitised with silver nitrate and common salt, was exposed to light. However, Talbot also published a camera-less version of the process. In this iteration, an object such as a botanical specimen or common household item was placed directly onto a sensitised sheet of paper, and its imprint rendered photographic when light turned the exposed areas of the paper dark. The image was stabilised but not steadfastly fixed when the paper was washed in a salt solution. This application, made public by Talbot in January 1839, spawned a global cohort of amateur photographers.[26]

Martens had arrived in the Australian colonies in 1835, travelling a not dissimilar route to Lucas and his camera. Having trained in England with preeminent watercolourist Anthony Vandyke Copley Fielding, Martens spent the first phase of his career painting the landscape around his Devonshire family home.[27] In 1832, he left England to join the crew of HMS *Hyacinth* as the topographical artist. In 1833, Martens joined Charles Darwin on the *Beagle* in Montevideo. He stayed on the *Beagle* as it made its way around South America and up to Valparaíso. From here, again much like Lucas (although without an intervening maritime disaster), Martens took a trading vessel across the Pacific onto Warrane/Sydney Cove.[28]

Martens was dedicated to the art of painting and never practised photography professionally. He may have been interested in photogenic drawing as an extension of his investigations into capturing the gradient of light in a two-dimensional rendering. Significantly, the entry preceding the 1840 instructions on photogenic drawing was transcribed from notes Sir Joshua Reynolds made 'during his stay in Rome' a century earlier.[29] Martens selected entries from Reynolds' published journals that pertained to recipes for different combinations of pigment used to render shadows in various atmospheres and settings. Much later, on 21 July 1856, he gave a public lecture on landscape painting at the Australian Library and Literary Institution (now the State Library of New South Wales), in which he advocated the use of daguerreotype photography as an aid to painters.[30] Clearly, photography was a tool for Martens to use, rather than an artform on its own terms.

No examples of Martens' photogenic drawing experiments have survived. Nevertheless, the entry in his *Notes on Painting* journal conveys a comprehensive understanding of the photogenic drawing process. It annotates the various chemical components needed to create a solution for sensitising paper and the ratios at which they should be mixed. Martens also noted various accommodations and allowances, such as for exposing multiple impressions on different areas of the same sheet of paper: 'should it be required to make a more sensitive description on the paper, after the first, the solution of salt should be applied, and the paper dried first …'.[31] Martens' notebook entry represents an arrival of photographic knowledge conveyed in granular-enough detail to facilitate, in theory, the execution of a photograph. But, much like Lucas's unsold camera, his photographic knowledge did not lead to a sustained colonial photographic practice.

Across the other side of the continent, on Menang Noongar Country in the south-western Australia, the personal correspondence of an aspirational pastoralist reveals the broad cross-section of colonial society that was engaged with the emerging international culture of photography. George Egerton Warburton had travelled to the colonies as an ensign in the 51st regiment before turning to a career in farming.[32] He attempted photogenic drawing during April 1841 with a pre-formulated kit, that was

ACKERMANN'S PHOTOGENIC DRAWING-BOX.

FOR copying objects by means of the Sun, containing the various requisites and instructions for carrying out this most important and useful discovery; particularly recommended to Botanists, Entomologists, and the Scientific, sufficiently clear to enable Ladies to practise this pleasing Art. —Price per Box, 21*s*.

N.B. The prepared Paper may be had separately, 2*s*. per packet.

London: published by Ackermann & Co. 96, Strand.

Figure 1.1: 'Ackermann's Photogenic Drawing-box', the *Athenaeum*, London, 10 April 1839, p. 1.

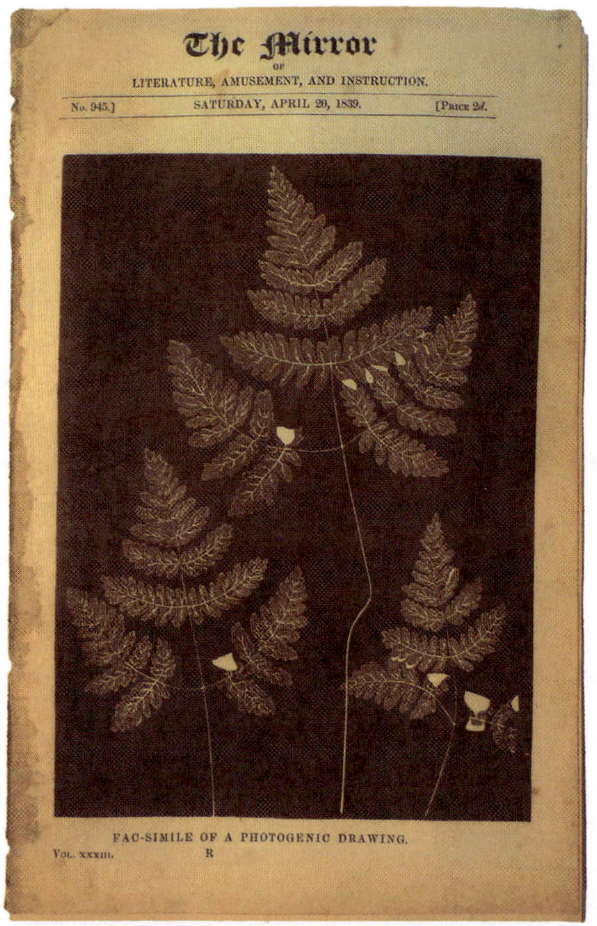

The Mirror
OF
LITERATURE, AMUSEMENT, AND INSTRUCTION.

No. 945.] SATURDAY, APRIL 20, 1839. [Price 2*d*.

FAC-SIMILE OF A PHOTOGENIC DRAWING.

Vol. xxxiii. R

Figure 1.2: 'Fac-simile of a photogenic drawing', *Mirror of Literature, Amusement, and Instruction*, London, 20 April 1839, p. 1.

a gift from his sister in Cheshire, England. It probably resembled those being advertised on the front page of the *Athenaeum* by stationers such as Ackermann's in London, boxed up for easy transportation (**Figure 1.1**).

Warburton's colonial photographic experiments did not spring from any prior artistic training. His regiment had been stationed in nipaluna/Hobart during September and October 1839, when the Van Diemen's Land newspapers were relaying from London and Edinburgh discussions about photogenic drawing.[33] It is possible that he was also reading firsthand English newspapers, which were belatedly circulating to the colony. In April 1839, the *Mirror* illustrated its front page with a wood-engraved reproduction of a photogenic drawing made, in this instance, by Golding Bird (**Figure 1.2**). Warburton may have been introduced to photogenic drawing by these reports but, unlike Martens, his experiments were not only the result of reading published instructions. He wrote to his father on 17 April 1841 with a message for his English sister: '... tell Soph that my Photogenic drawing failed from want of a proper preparation of nitrate of silver, if you can send me some more, I will try again.'[34] Warburton did not reveal in this letter the subject of his failed photogenic drawings, nor in later correspondence whether he received a second set of chemicals. But his letter highlights how photographic knowledge and materials travelled in familial epistolary exchange. Clearly, the profusion of popular interest in photogenic drawing in the British metropole was filtering through to the Australian colonies from various sources.

The earliest recorded discussion of a photograph in colonial Australia was, interestingly, the result of a photograph made elsewhere and sent as a copy. In early 1841, the governor of Van Diemen's Land, Sir John Franklin, received a letter from an English correspondent, Dr William Buckland. Long active in senior positions in the British Association for the Advancement of Science, Buckland was keen to share some images he thought were of the 'greatest importance to science and art'.[35] Among them was a lithographic print of silicified starfish from Devon. The lithograph was based on a daguerreotype photograph. The fossilised starfish was engraved directly on (and from) the photographic plate at the Polytechnic Institution in London. An ink tracing of the engraved outline of the specimen was made by Levett Landon Boscawen

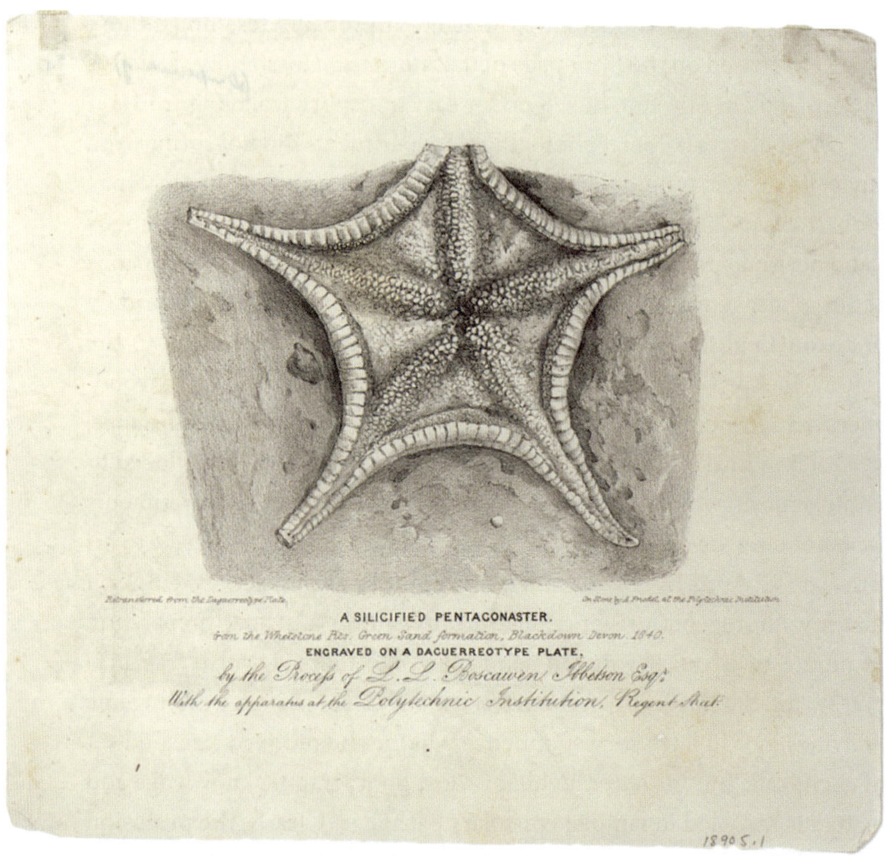

Figure 1.3: 'A Silicified Pentagonaster from Whetstone Pts. Green Sand formation, Blackdown, Devon 1840/ Engraved on a daguerreotype plate/ by the Process of L.L. Boscawen Ibbetson Esq. the apparatus at the Polytechnic Institute, Regent Street / Transferred from daguerreotype plate … on stone by A. Friedel at the Polytechnic Institute', 25 × 34.2 cm. Lithograph print. National Museum of American History, Smithsonian Institution, Washington.

Ibbetson. This tracing was then transferred to a lithographic stone by Adam Friedel. The image's artistic lineage is chronicled in the extended caption of the print (**Figure 1.3**). The process itself was outlined in an 1840 edition of the *Westminster Review*: 'When the impression was fixed upon the [daguerreotype] plate an outline of the image was traced upon it by an engraver in a dotting style: a print was taken from the plate and transferred to stone, [where] the shading required was filled in by a lithographic artist'.[36]

This protracted procedure enabled multiple copies, albeit in translated lithographic form, to be generated from the otherwise 'unique' daguerreotype. As Buckland wrote: 'There is no calculating the importance of this invention for multiplying figures in Natural History'.[37] The implication of Buckland's letter to Franklin is that he thought the accuracy of the original photograph of the starfish was retained in its lithographic copy. And, in reproducing the daguerreotype in multiple facsimiles, the potential audience for the scientific illustration could grow exponentially. The specific print sent to Franklin no longer survives but an identical print is held in the National Museum of American History in Washington, pointing to the far-flung transmission of the starfish's likeness, either at the time of its production, or later in collection. Buckland's rationale for writing to Franklin in 1840 was to present him with pertinent images for discussion among the colony's Philosophical Society. We know about the starfish's lithographed daguerreotype (and others sent in this same dispatch[38]) from the inaugural edition of the *Tasmanian Journal*, where an extract from Buckland's letter was reprinted, along with a footnote outlining its enclosed pictorial content.[39] Unfortunately, no other documentation of the Philosophical Society's meeting exists. The publication of Buckland's letter demonstrates that conversations initiated overseas about photography's role and its possibilities for the field of scientific illustration found their way into meetings of colonial intellectual societies.

We see from these episodes how photographic knowledge, materials, technologies and photographically based images were transmitted to the colonies through multiple channels: trading vessels, literary and press publications, personal correspondence and as lithographed facsimiles. We see, too, how colonists engaged with the new technology within a very short time of its invention. These engagements were framed by different ambitions for photography. The demonstration of Lucas's camera shows photography's envisaged use in documenting urban colonial geography, rendering its reproduction to scale and at a transportable size. Martens was curious about photography but ultimately regarded the medium as a draughtman's or painter's aid. Warburton understood photogenic drawing as a pastime to be shared with his otherwise distant family. And in reciting Buckland's letter at the Philosophical Society meeting, and having it published in the *Tasmanian Journal*, Franklin reaffirmed the new technology's anticipated scientific value. The journalist's account of the daguerreotype from Lucas's camera ('a beautiful and minute sketch'), much like Martens' entry on photogenic drawing in his *Notes on Painting* journal and the lithographed daguerreotype sent to Franklin, highlights how photography was not yet seen as a discrete or exceptional medium. It was embedded in relationships with other forms of visual art, which influenced how it was understood and practised. But colonial art and illustrated literature informed only colonists' encounters with the new technology.

To begin to understand photography's arrival in this part of the world, though, we need to step outside the insular colonial frame. Seventeen years after Warburton attempted photogenic drawing on Menang Noongar Country in the confines of his residence in Kinjarling/Albany, another photographic arrival took place. In February 1858, British survey ship the *Herald* docked in Mamang Koort/King Georges Sound. The ship was on a hydrographic expedition around Pacific, Torres Strait and Australian ports.[40] On board were two photographers: Arthur Onslow (who would later marry into the Macarthur Family in Warrane/Sydney Cove) and James Glen Wilson. Onslow and Wilson's remit was to photograph the shoreline while the remainder of the crew were charged with recording the depths and tides of the Sound as intelligence for colonial commerce and shipping. Onslow and Wilson were using simple box cameras and working with the new wet-plate collodion process. This is where a glass-plate negative is sensitised with a solution of sticky collodion, silver nitrate and silver iodide. Unlike the daguerreotype, the glass plate did not require polishing and, once developed, the negative could be used to make multiple photographic salted paper prints. At the behest of a local shipping agent, John MacKail, Onslow agreed to take portraits on the shoreline on 3 February 1858.[41] This opportunity to commission a photographic portrait caught the attention of Warburton, and his wife and young family. Warburton had maintained a relationship with photography in the seventeen years since his first attempts at photogenic drawing. This involved receiving cased daguerreotypes from his family in Cheshire, and commissioning from studios in Boorloo/Perth daguerreotypes of his own immediate family that he sent to Cheshire in return.[42] These familial and intimate transactions increased Warburton's own understanding of, and taste for, photography. He evaluated Onslow's salted paper print portrait of his wife and children as 'poor' and 'decidedly faux'.[43] Onslow, after all, was a survey photographer and not a studio portraitist. Warbuton's criticisms were presumably based on a comparison with superior photographs, in the sharper daguerreotype format produced by studio photographers, he had received and sent.

Colonists were not Onslow's only portrait subjects on 3 February 1858. A group of Menang Noongar men, women and children also came to the shoreline. Onslow notes in his diary that the Menang were initially fearful of the unfamiliar camera and photographic process. Yet, after they watched colonists have their portraits taken, and were encouraged with payments of 6d, Onslow was permitted to 'bring the lens to bear on them'.[44] This was almost certainly the Menang's first experience of photography. Onslow photographed a senior Menang man; a group of Menang women; and a group of Menang men, women and older Menang children together (**Figure 1.4–1.6**). These portraits were taken outside MacKail's shoreline storehouse, with slatted planks and drums appearing as backdrops. They show the Menang in traditional dress, except for one adolescent man in the group portrait, who wears trousers, a shirt and broad-brimmed hat. All Menang stare steadfastly into the camera. These portraits were almost immediately taken off Country and kept in Onslow's possession, after the *Herald* departed later that month. Once Onslow landed and settled in Warrane/Sydney Cove, he pasted the photographic prints into a scrapbook-cum-album full of diffuse content. This ranged from photographs from his time in the naval service, to images he had exchanged with artists in the eastern colony, to cuttings of ecclesiastic ephemera.

Onslow's photographic portraits hold a seasonal and cultural legibility to the Menang that went unrecorded in colonial sources. When I discussed these photographs with Menang Noongar curator Shona Coyne, at the National Museum of Australia, she drew my attention to the bookas (cloaks) the Menang were wearing. Coyne recalled how she had seen references to Menang people stretching animal skins, by pegging them to the ground after scraping away the bulk of the flesh and leaving ants to eat away the residue tissue.[45] The trails made by the ants remain perceptible until the skins have had some wear. It is Menang practice to wear the side with the fur against the skin in blustery conditions, leaving the underside of the skin facing the elements.[46] The latticed ant trails are perceptible in the dried and stretched skin of the bookas worn in the portrait of the senior male and the portrait of three Menang women (**Figures 1.4** and **1.5**). When I went with historian Jane Lydon to discuss these photographs with representatives of the seven Menang families in Kinjarling/Albany during June 2022, more significant details emerged. Many of the stories these photographs inspired during this meeting are not mine to tell. Conversation canvassed the practices of stretching and drying animal sinew, which is possibly what can be seen around the women's necks in **Figure 1.5**. The conversation also brought new context to the portraits, revealing how, at the time of their exposure, the Menang traded with Communities as distant as lutruwita/Tasmania. Historically situated on the cusp of a period of intensified colonial displacement, these portraits were a touchstone for Community, through which to contemplate a much longer Menang Noongar history. They function as a legible reference to an inheritance of Culture surviving today, despite colonisation.

As Isobel Crombie, Julie Gough and Jane Lydon's work has shown—and as will be discussed further in Chapter 3—the photography of Aboriginal people in the eastern and southern Australian colonies began in commercial studios during the late 1840s.[47] These portraits of Menang men and women are not the oldest or first photographs of Aboriginal people. But they do represent an arrival of photography for the Menang. This arrival can be understood in terms of a longer history of cross-cultural contact. Mamang Koort/King Georges Sound was a resting port for European and American sealers and whalers from the seventeenth to the mid-nineteenth century. European colonists, including George Vancouver in 1791, Nicolas Baudin in 1803 and Phillip Parker King in 1821, paused at Mamang Koort/King Georges Sound. They were carrying the indexical instruments of the Enlightenment, scaling and

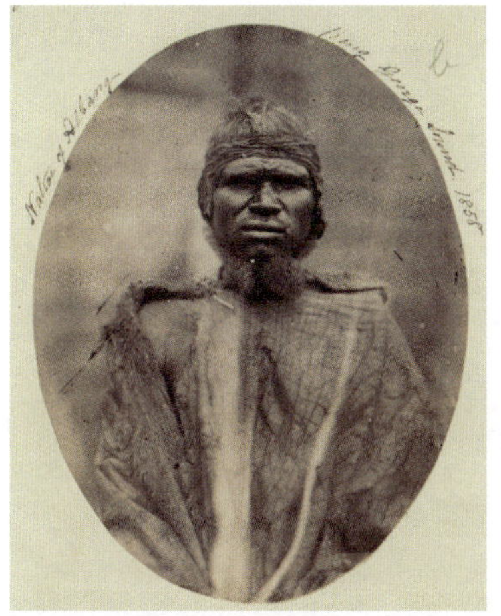

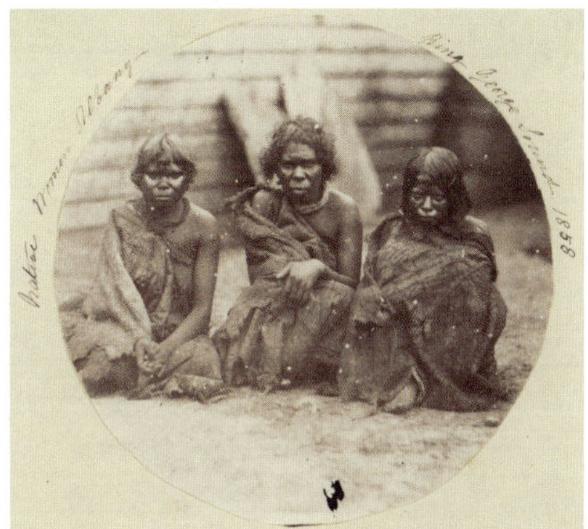

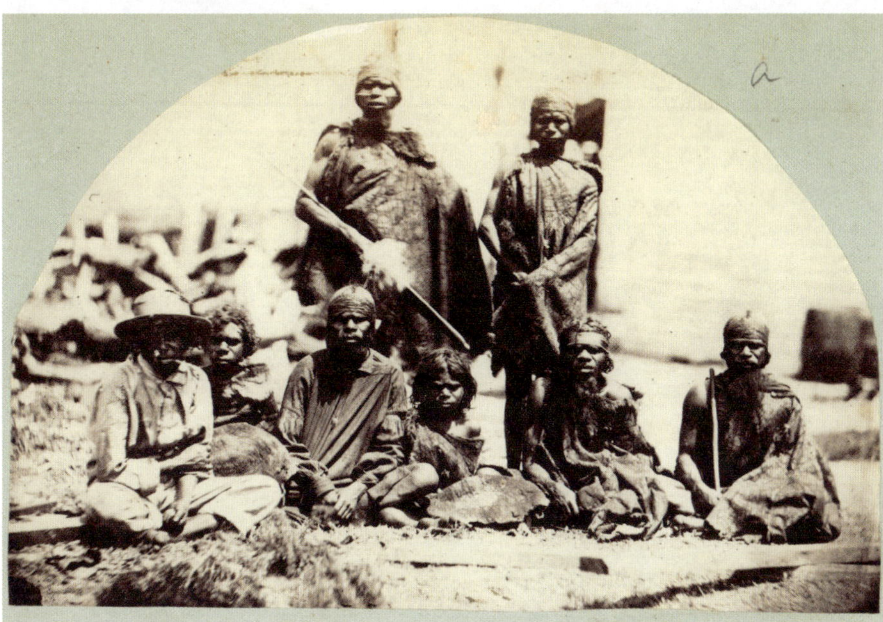

Figure 1.4: Arthur Onslow, salted paper print from collodion negative, 3 February 1858, Mamang Koort (printed 1859–60s, Warrane/Sydney Cove), from 'Album of views, illustrations and Macarthur family photographs', 1857–66 and 1879, p. 79. State Library of New South Wales.

Figure 1.5: Arthur Onslow, salted paper print from collodion negative, 3 February 1858, Mamang Koort (printed 1859–60s, Warrane/Sydney Cove), from 'Album of views, illustrations and Macarthur family photographs', 1857–66 and 1879, p. 136. State Library of New South Wales.

Figure 1.6: Arthur Onslow, salted paper print from collodion negative, 3 February 1858, Mamang Koort (printed 1859– 60s, Warrane/Sydney Cove), from 'Album of views, illustrations and Macarthur family photographs', 1857–66 and 1879, p. 148. State Library of New South Wales.

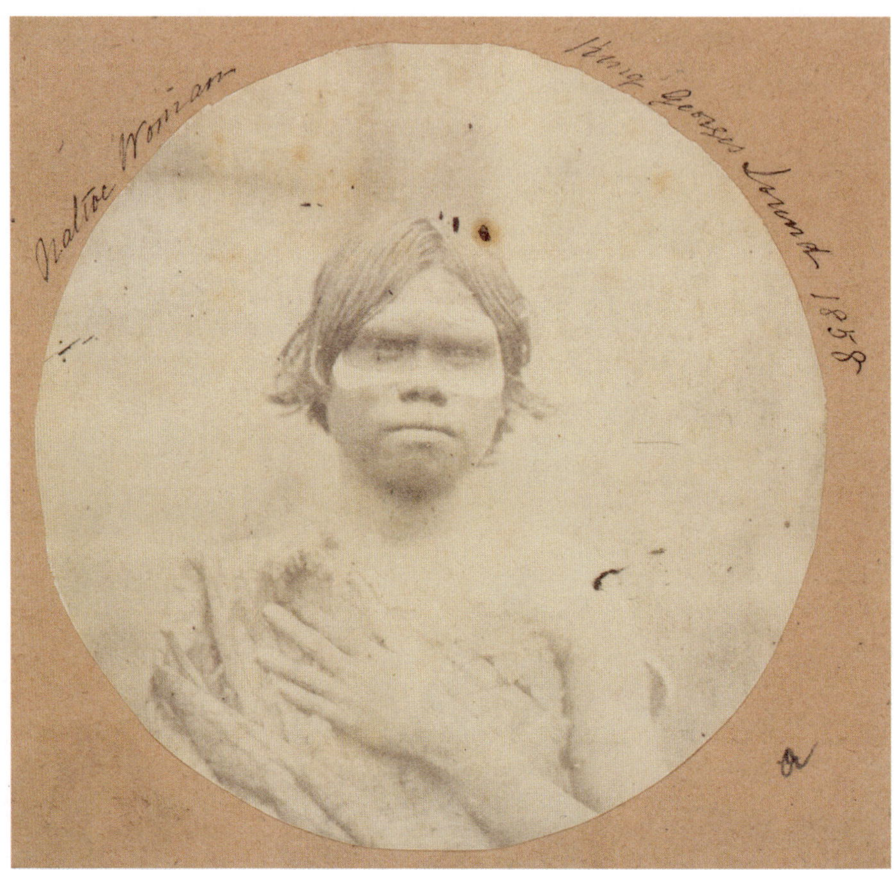

Figure 1.7: Arthur Onslow, salted paper print from collodion negative, 3 February 1858, Mamang Koort (printed 1859–60s, Warrane/Sydney Cove), from 'Album of views, illustrations and Macarthur family photographs', 1857–66 and 1879, p. 85. State Library of New South Wales.

translating data about place into hydrographic and cartographic maps, as the *Herald*'s expedition would also do in 1858. These men and their crews laid anchor at Mamang Koort/King Georges Sound to replenish their stores of fresh water and food. They were all taken by the Menang to where Kalganup/the Kalgan River drains into the sea.[48] Here, each of these parties was shown Wattierup/Oyster Harbour tidal fish traps, built around 6500–7000 years ago. This nutrient-rich environment attracts fish from across the Sound, with the largest getting trapped in the Menang's rocky infrastructure as the tide recedes. The fish traps testify that the hydrographic data each of these expeditions was compiling was already intimately known to the Menang, and deployed in accordance with the ecologies and rhythms of Country.

Tiffany Shellam's scholarship has revealed—in relation to Phillip Parker King's 1821 expedition—that, as a part of these shoreline meetings, the Menang 'smeared their faces with red ochre … replaced their old kangaroo skin cloaks … and carried lighted fire sticks' as a means of cultural introduction.[49] In the portraits taken by Onslow over three decades later, we see the senior Menang man in the group portrait holding a lit and smoking fire stick, while other men hold unlit fire sticks against their bodies (**Figure 1.6**). A young Menang woman was photographed with ochre (of an unidentifiable pigment in the sepia image) encircling her eyes (**Figure 1.7**). In all the portraits, the perceptible ant trails may indicate that these bookas have been recently stretched and dried. It is possible, then, that what was occurring in front of Onslow's lens was an exhibition of Culture and a display of cultural identity. This presentation was not influenced by the new conventions of holding a pose for the camera, or reports and experiences of European visual culture that informed other episodes outlined in this chapter. Rather, the Menang's conception of standing or sitting for a portrait by Onslow could be considered a continuation of a much longer tradition of visually articulating identity to unknown and uninvited visitors.

Onslow's portraits of Menang challenge our understanding and conception of colonial photographic arrivals, in two directions. First, they elongate the period of photographic arrival outwards from those early demonstrations and the receipt of the 'first' photographic news and 'first' photographically derived images in the 1840s. Pockets of the population were encountering photography and photographic technologies for the first time into the 1850s and beyond. In south-western regions official missionary activity and inland dispossession began in the 1850s and accelerated in the 1860s.[50] These portraits sit at a precipice of increasing intrusion into Menang Noongar sovereignty and at the commencement of a wilful colonial dislocation of Kin networks. The Menang portraits also move the chronology of photographic arrival in the other direction. If we read the Menang's participation in Onslow's portrait 'sitting' as part of a longer lineage of performing identity, as Shellam's work illuminates, the Menang's phenomenological *experience* of photography was informed by pre-photographic practices of visualising identity that cohered much earlier than the medium's invention.

These episodes establish that it was not a simple narrative of photography's unprecedented verisimilitude that characterised its arrival and reception in the colonies. The first colonial photographic experiences were woven into existing visual practices (of sketching, painting, lithography and embodied Cultural presentation) and described through established visual vocabularies. To write a history of colonial photography, it is necessary not to confine photography to a space of media isolation but instead to re-embed it in an expanding visual landscape. Certainly, the same can be argued for the way early photographic technologies were used and understood elsewhere, particularly throughout the British imperial world. Geoffrey Batchen's study *Apparitions* (2018) has shown this in relation to the reproduction of daguerreotypes issuing from the early London studios of Richard Beard and Antoine Claudet.[51]

What makes photography colonial in an Australian context is the convergence of its arrival and interactions with various political and social transformations in colonial governance. Conrad Martens was copying instructions for photogenic drawing into his painting notebook during the same year convict transportation to New South Wales came to an end. Photography was immediately tied to the task of representing the region's transition from penal outpost(s) to prosperous colonies and then nascent nation. Although transportation to Van Diemen's Land ended in 1853, Franklin's Philosophical Society, where Buckland's starfish image was discussed, and the *Tasmanian Journal,* where Buckland's letter was published, were initiatives aimed at building a 'civil' colonial society separate from its convict roots. Photographs offer, then, ways of looking back into a colonial society in flux and transition. Presented here is a story of colonial photography as shaped by and shaping a range of technological and communication developments. Warburton's letters and parcels gesture to the colonies' place in an expanding international postage system, which carried various kinds of literary magazines and publications, and would come to transmit both to and from the colonies illustrated news filled with photographically derived illustrations. Perhaps most importantly, photographs and photography offer us ways of seeing this tumultuous colonial period beyond a succession of historical events, and statistics of displacement, dispossession and genocide—but, instead, as the Menang Noongar portraits illuminate, as complex individualised experiences of colonisation mediated through camera technologies and photographic processes.

2

The Mobile Photographer

The first colonial photography studios were established to attract the patronage of aspirational colonists. They were run by photographers who were all born overseas: men and women whose migration south was motivated by their desire to consolidate wealth and elevate their social standing. Their studios opened at a time in the mid-nineteenth century when inbound migration to the colonies was radically changing, from shiploads of convict passengers to vessels of assisted and unassisted migrants. The identities of the practitioners, as well as the profile of their customers, was a sign of the increasing fortunes and social mobility of new generations of settler-colonists.

To attract a steady stream of customers, many of these first studio photographers were compelled to travel. During the 1840s, settler colonial populations remained clustered around the most inhabited ports, Warrane/Sydney Cove and nipaluna/Hobart—and by the 1850s, Naarm/Melbourne.[1] Whalers, fishers and merchant ships continued to transit through these ports, helping to sustain colonial populations that were, as Ross Gibson has argued, as much outward looking and maritime focused as they were terrane and committed to inland pastoralist expansion.[2] Port cities held an increasing density of colonial wealth, hosted a fluctuating traffic of goods and people, while receiving news, art and illustrations transacted along busy shipping routes. This chapter uses the biographies of three very different photographers—George Barron Goodman, J. W. (James William) Newland and (Elizabeth) Louisa How—to demonstrate how a practice of colonial photography was first developed in these liminal spaces, where the ocean meets the land. Colonial photographers adapted European photographic technologies to the atmospheres and climates of the Southern Hemisphere. Alongside these technical recalibrations, their photographs told stories particular to their location, giving expression to various aspects of colonial ambition and aesthetics.

Goodman arrived at Warrane/Sydney Cove from London aboard the *Eden* on 4 November 1842.[3] He was in possession of a licence to commercially practise photography in the colonies, as well as the component parts needed to build a photography studio (of English design). Goodman came from a middle-class Jewish family who resided in Regent's Park, London.[4] As the third son, he may have felt his prospects were limited at home. Goodman's colonial studio was the first to bear his name and was probably his foray into the business of photography, as there is no record of him working as an apprentice in an English establishment. J. W. Newland was also born in England but came from much humbler origins. The illegitimate son of a Suffolk woman, Eliza Newland, he left England when he was a young adult to work as a merchant in North America.[5] Newland's subsequent photographic career was shaped by his training in the American south. In 1845–47, he operated an itinerate studio business that transacted through Central and South America and across the Pacific, before arriving at Warrane/Sydney Cove in late 1847.[6] A photographic practice born from class ascent is most notable in the biography of this chapter's third photographer, Elizabeth Louisa How (née Richardson). The daughter of a publican, she began her working life as a milliner in St Peters, Cambridgeshire, before marrying James How, a farm labourer.[7] The couple travelled with their two young children, William and Edward, as assisted migrants to Naarm/Melbourne in 1849.[8] Unlike Goodman and Newland, How set out on her journey without photographic aspirations. How's photographic study was a product of her family's expanding colonial fortunes, which afforded her the time and financial support to stage a significant amateur studio at her harbourside home on Cammeraygal Country, North Sydney.

These three individuals represent a spectrum of early photographic practices in the colonies. Goodman's was authorised and franchised from Britain; Newland's was a product of his own peripatetic trans-Pacific career; and How's was formulated sometime after her arrival, through her reading of various periodicals, and as a way of reflecting on the commercial and industrial developments at Warrane/Sydney Cove. The patrons who visited their studios, and the photographs and photographic experiences that issued from them, demonstrate how photography was understood in conversation with an expanding colonial visual art scene being transacted in port cities.

Light

Goodman emigrated to the colonies on a merchant ship, the *Eden*, which coincidentally bore the same name as the last vessel to transport convicts to the colony of New South Wales two years earlier, during 1840. It was packed with produce, which took over half a newspaper column to list, and included fifty cases of cheese, nineteen barrels of pork, 960 kegs of paint, a package of Ottoman scarves and a piano.[9] Nestled among this disparate collection of cargo were Goodman's three cases of daguerreotype supplies and twenty-seven boxes of sheet glass. With this equipment, he would begin in Gadigal Country what the demonstration of Lucas's camera one-and-a-half years earlier had failed to ignite: a colonial practice of photography.

In both architecture and intention, the first iteration of Goodman's photography studio in Warrane/Sydney Cove was a structure that gave the appearance of elaborate immobility. Goodman commenced construction of the studio on the roof of the Royal Hotel on George Street within a week of his arrival.[10] Before leaving England, he had purchased a licence to practise daguerreotype photography from the English patentee, Richard Beard. Beard was an industrialist and railway entrepreneur, who had bought the patent right (from Daguerre's agent, Miles Berry) to control the commercial practice of daguerreotype photography throughout the

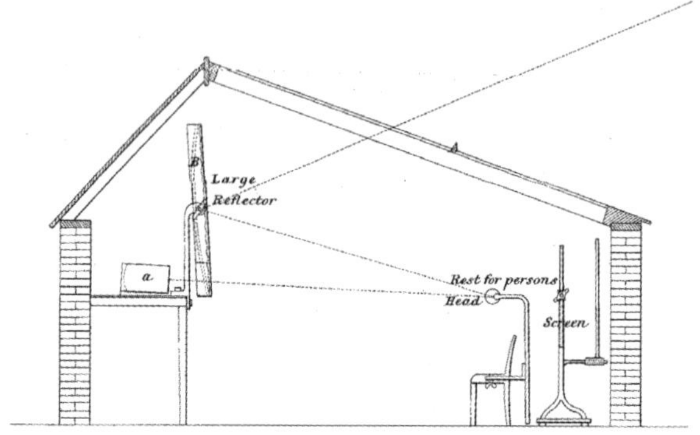

Figure 2.1: [Section] instructive drawing from' Patent No. 8546 'Apparatus for Obtaining Likenesses', 1840 (lodged by Richard Beard), George Edward Eyre and William Spottiswoode, London, p. 7. British Library.

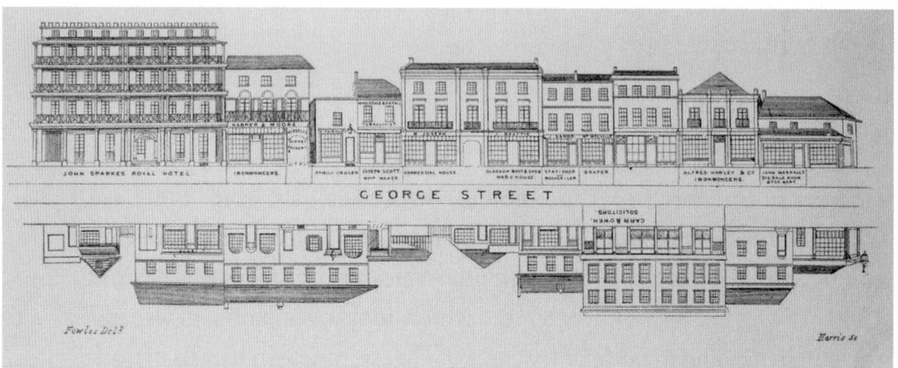

Figure 2.2: 'George Street' [Royal Hotel top left] from Joseph Fowles, *Sydney in 1848: A Facsimile of the Original Text and Copper-Plate Engravings of its Principal* [sic] *Streets, Public Buildings, Churches, Chapels, etc. from Drawings by Joseph Fowles*, 4th edn?, Ure Smith, Sydney, 1962, p. 55.

British imperial world.[11] Beard provided all his licensees with cameras, daguerreotype plates, and cases to hold and present the plates, as well as materials to construct and furnish a studio and, eventually, backdrops to use in these spaces. Although the jurisdiction of his patent extended to the Australian colonies—indeed, to 'all Britain's colonies and plantations'—Beard himself had never travelled south of the equator.[12] His blueprint for the daguerreotype studio was conceived in the smoggy, soot-filled atmospheres of industrial English cities (**Figure 2.1**). In such locations, the prismatic glass structure allowed for maximum light to enter the space, accelerating the otherwise protracted exposure of the daguerreotype photographic plate.

In his first colonial advertisements, Goodman presented himself as an ambassador for the new technology of photography, tracing his business's pedigree back to 'Mr Beard who holds the patent'.[13] The location of his first studio on top of the Royal Hotel was no doubt selected for its centrality in the city, but its elevation also added a sense of spectacle to the photographic occasion (**Figure 2.2**). Joseph Fowles, artist and author of the illustrated book *Sydney in 1848* (1849), later noted that 'few buildings strike new arrivals with more surprise than the external appearance and internal appointments of this huge structure'.[14] Fowles described how the hotel dwarfed surrounding architecture to such an extent that the balconies at the front were the only buffer, 'in hot and sultry weather, giving shade and shelter to adjoining rooms'[15]. No images or drawings of Goodman's rooftop studio survive. However, newspaper descriptions of this structure as 'a glass laboratory; built on the leads [the lead roof and parapets] of the Royal Hotel'—as well as Goodman's self-identification as a licensee of Beard—strongly suggest he was working with the English design for the daguerreotype studio.[16] In **Figure 2.3**, we see the principles of the glass studio, possibly that of London-based daguerreotypist Jabez Hogg or one of his London-based associates, modelled for the camera. The daguerreotypist stands outside the studio, timing the exposure of the plate on his pocket watch. This placement makes the photographer more prominent in the pictured scene but, impractically, divorces him from his camera and from overseeing the exposure supposedly taking place.

Goodman was very much an empresario in his studio. The structure took almost a month to build, and when it opened in December 1842, it was said to have attracted more than sixty paying clients in its first weekend of trade. He charged £1 1s for bust portraits, £1 10s for three-quarter length portraits and £2 2s for full-length portraits.[17] To put this into context, the average weekly wage for a baker in Warrane/Sydney Cove in 1842 was £1 10s; a bricklayer or a carpenter, £2 8s; a general labourer, £1 4s; a stone mason, £2 14s; and a saddler, £1 5s.[18] Goodman's daguerreotypes were therefore well outside the means of the urban working classes, but affordable for an elite and moneyed colonial middle-class

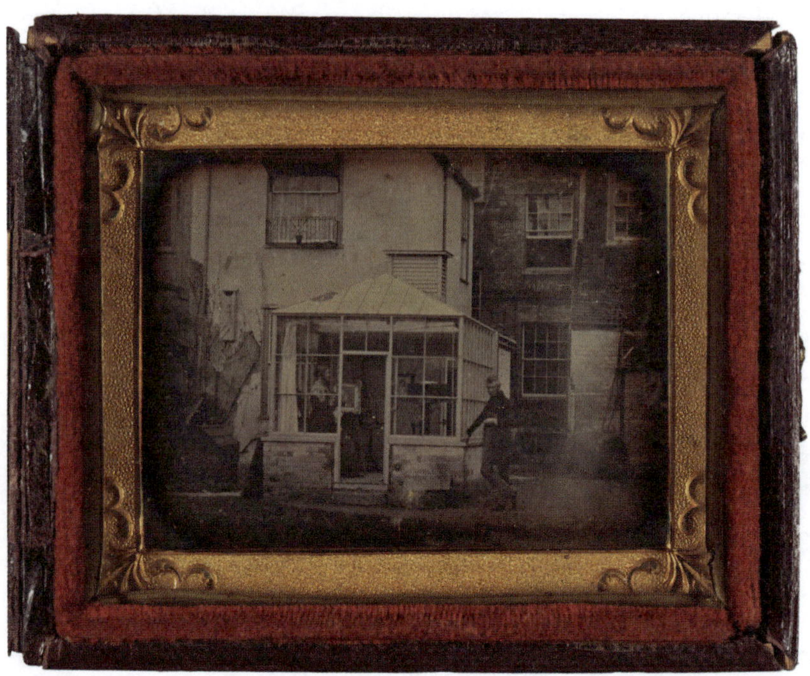

Figure 2.3: Unattributed (possibly by Jabez Hogg or an associate), 'An Early Photographic Studio in London', c. 1843, ninth-plate, uncoloured, cased daguerreotype. National Portrait Gallery, London.

keen to consolidate mobile likenesses of themselves and their families. In January 1843, George Gipps, the governor of New South Wales, visited Goodman's studio and commissioned six daguerreotypes of himself and his son but, curiously, none of his wife, who had accompanied him for the occasion.[19]

Goodman encouraged all his colonial clients to imagine they were sitting in 'Beard's own [English] atelier'.[20] Had he been following Beard's studio set-up and exposure-time calculations as closely as his advertisements suggest, the warm summer sunshine on top of the Royal Hotel would have rendered his daguerreotype portraits overly saturated with light. A mere four months after the studio's opening, however, and still without competition in the commercial photographic marketplace, Goodman's customers began to dwindle. Perhaps he had exhausted his client base in the city, which, in the early 1840s, was going through a period of economic depression. Later reports point to other factors, though. After the initial flurry of enthusiasm, journalists came to describe posing in Goodman's glass studio as 'a trial of [the] nerves' for any sitter who dared commission a portrait on the 'burning lead roof'; 'a trial that was too great for many'.[21] Additionally, the resulting daguerreotype portraits were criticised by the press as 'lacking in life' and, at worst, having a 'cadaverous, unearthly appearance … The ladies appearing the worst served, the sun no flatterer'.[22] There are no attributed daguerreotypes from this first iteration of Goodman's studio surviving in public collections, even though (despite later negative reflections on his work) the output must have numbered in the many hundreds. The unflattering effects that these newspaper commentators describe all point to the glass studio's strong sunlight as excessive to the execution of the daguerreotype process.

Goodman began to comprehend how the climate of the Australian continent made it necessary to modify the English daguerreotype template, as he set out on a period of travel between colonial ports. By mid-1843, he had packed down his elaborate glass architecture and transported it to nipaluna/Hobart, where he re-assembled the studio on Patrick Street in the city centre.[23] A month into Goodman's nipaluna residency, ex-convict and colonial portraitist Thomas Bock began offering daguerreotypes alongside oil-on-canvas and charcoal and China White portraits, but without a licence from Beard or a glasshouse within which to expose them. According to his son's later recollections, Bock had bought the daguerreotype camera from an 'impecunious Frenchman' transiting through the city.[24] During the 1840s, rather like Conrad Martens, Bock received published English lectures and manuals on early photographic processes, which he judiciously copied into his own notebook.[25] As a part of this transcription, he tested processes including those for daguerreotype photography, and recalculated exposure times for the southern atmosphere and various weather conditions (**Figure 2.4**). Goodman immediately took issue with Bock's unlicensed commercial offering of daguerreotype photography. He suggested in a letter to the editor of the Hobart *Courier* on 6 October that it was impossible Bock could have mastered the technical skill to execute daguerreotype photography without proper [English] instruction and suggested, rather threateningly, that his practice broke the law.[26]

The Bock–Goodman contestation did little to upset Bock's practice, as I've argued elsewhere,[27] but it did spell the end of the glass structure for Goodman. In March 1844, he sold the glass panels, along with his first camera, to his studio assistant, John Flavelle, who continued to photograph with the architecture for less than two months in Launceston.[28] Discarding the glasshouse resulted in improvements in the quality of Goodman's daguerreotypes. After his return to Warrane/Sydney Cove in 1844, it was reported that his more recent daguerreotype portraits 'entirely obviated the deathlike appearance which was characteristic of earlier productions'.[29] On the roof of the Royal Hotel, Goodman's business had been an English satellite of photography and spectacularly exclusive, perched above the

for 1/6 Plates.
opening of 30 millimetres

State of the atmosphere	Seconds	Seconds
The sky cloudless, the Model being sheltered by veils	— 2 – 5	10 – 15
The sky with White Clouds (the Model being without shelter	— 2. 5	10 - 15
with shelter	— 5 - 10	15 - 30
Sky covered with deep Clouds / not sheltered by veils.	— 10 – 15	30 – 45

Remarks.

When the business is, to take views, all the above mentioned precautions are dispensed with, and with the employment of Bromine; indispensible in obtaining a good effect in the nearly instantaneous production of Portraits: But then, the duration in the Camera is from 2 to 3 minutes.

Figure 2.4: [Section, p. 21] Thomas Bock, 'Notes on Photography, including Talbot's calotype process and daguerreotype manipulations', 17 July 1841–31 December 1850, stitched into a 17 July 1841 edition of the *Athenaeum*. Allport Library and Museum of Fine Arts.

pedestrian and commercial traffic of the colonial city. The second iteration of his Warrane/Sydney Cove studio was, by contrast, in ground-floor rooms on Hunter Street. By moving down to street level, Goodman established a more proportional relationship with southern light.

The oldest extant photographic portrait made in the Australian colonies is a ninth-plate daguerreotype of convict surgeon William Bland, made in Goodman's Hunter Street rooms sometime in late 1844 or early 1845. Light entered this studio on one side, with the window's rectangular structure reflected in Bland's eyes (**Figure 2.5**). The new studio's configuration allowed for adequate but not excessive sunlight, with window light perhaps being controlled and trained towards the portrait subject through the aid of a reflector. Bland sat for Goodman with his elbow resting on the side table, steadying his upright pose. The posture would have been further secured by means of a head brace for the duration of the exposure, which would have lasted around twenty seconds. Bland wears a double-breasted, collared coat, which strains at the buttons around his middle. As a medical practitioner, it is his hands that are the central feature of this portrait. They are cast in strong relief, pale against his dark-clad torso. An announcement was made in the *Sydney Morning Herald* in January 1845, inviting prospective patrons to come and view the surgeon's daguerreotype in Goodman's studio before commissioning their own.[30]

Bland's portrait is indicative of Goodman's refashioning as a colonial photographer; it also suggests the surgeon's attempts to present himself as a respectable leader in colonial society. Bland had begun his medical career as a naval surgeon, but he arrived in the Australian colonies as a convict, having mortally wounded a colleague in a duel while stationed in Bombay. He was transported to New South Wales in 1814, aboard the *Frederick*.[31] Despite the severity of the offence, Bland's profession and first posting on Bidjigal Country as surgeon at Castle Hill Lunatic Asylum helped him to secure a pardon just one year into his sentence.[32] This pardon did not, however, come with the reinstatement of his naval rank. In lieu of a military post, Bland opened a private practice on Gadigal Country, where he did not retire quietly into civic life. He was an irascible man, regularly in and out of court, suing parties who allegedly defamed his reputation.[33] Importantly, though, Bland also championed

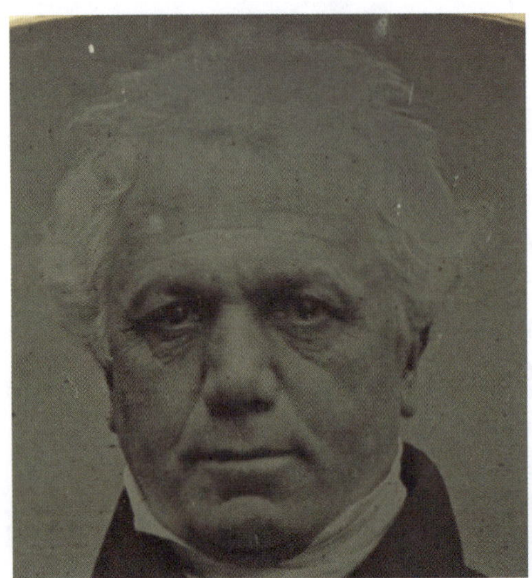

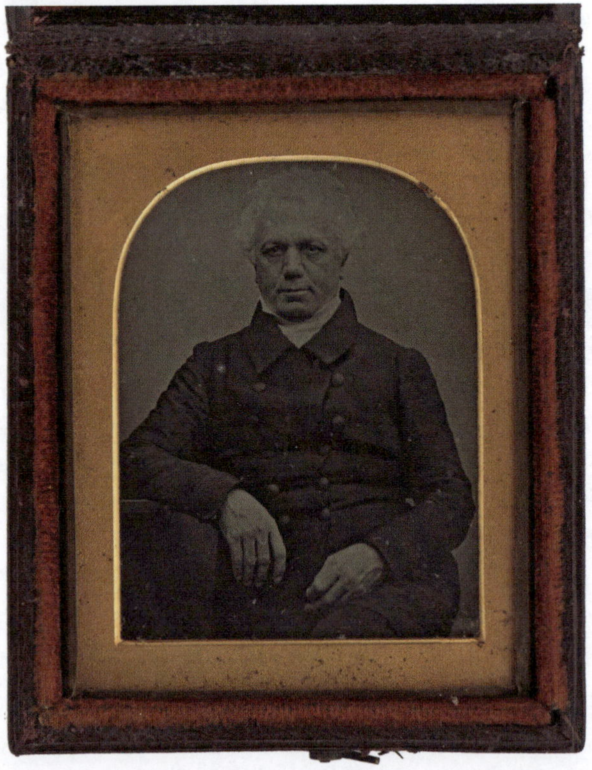

Figure 2.5: George Baron Goodman, 'Dr William Bland', 1844–45, ninth-plate, uncoloured, Wharton-cased daguerreotype + section detail. State Library of New South Wales.

the formation of the Sydney Mechanics School of Art in 1833, which, by the time of his own daguerreotype, was a common meeting ground for colonial portraitists.[34] In 1843, he was elected to the Legislative Council as a representative for Sydney, on a platform that (perhaps surprisingly) advocated for the reintroduction of transportation and opposed the Crown's control of large land grants.[35] Bland benefited from the sale of large tracts of stolen Aboriginal land that he would then sell for a profit rather than work himself.[36] His daguerreotype was thus captured at a time when he was profiting from the economy of land theft and at the peak of his professional life, both holding public office and practising medicine.

The portrait connects Goodman to a colonial art scene where artists' earnings were amassed, as Richard Neville has noted, through the steady and significant patronage of vainglorious figures such as Bland.[37] This tiny daguerreotype, 5.1 × 6.4 cm in size, was used as reference for a later, much larger watercolour of Bland attributed to society portraitist Richard Read. In the watercolour, we see Bland not in the pared-back photography studio but ensconced among lavish drapery and occupied with anatomical study (**Figure 2.6**). The daguerreotype was also used to inform William Nicholas's sketch of Bland, which was lithographed for the 18 December 1847 edition of the popular Sydney periodical *Heads of the People* (**Figure 2.7**). Nicholas provided 'typical' colonial figures for the frontispiece of each weekly issue, which together represented a scaffold for colonial society, as Tim Bonyhady has suggested.[38] In *Heads of the People*, Bland is portrayed under a new guise: 'The Philanthropist'. Despite this change to his persona, the centrality of the daguerreotype as a reference for these portraits is revealed by the exact replication of the positioning of Bland's hands. Notice also how the highlights in Bland's hair, accented by light in his daguerreotype, have been reinscribed with China White in the watercolour and a thickened line in the lithographed sketch. The relationship between the portraits is verified in how the top two buttons of Bland's coat escape their loopholes in his daguerreotype, a sartorial anomaly echoed in the portraits by Read and Nicholas. The watercolour and the sketch were both shown at the June 1849 exhibition held by the Society for the Promotion of Fine Arts in Australia. On this occasion, the *Sydney Morning Herald*'s reviewer reaffirmed their

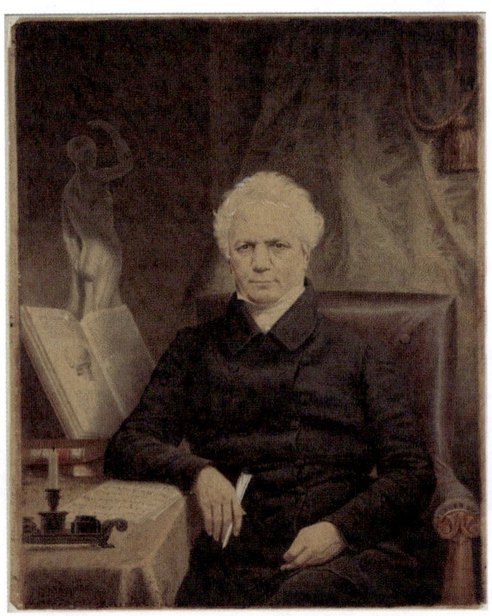

Figure 2.6: Richard Read (attributed), 'Dr William Bland', 1845–49, ink and watercolour on paper, 33 × 27 cm. State Library of New South Wales.

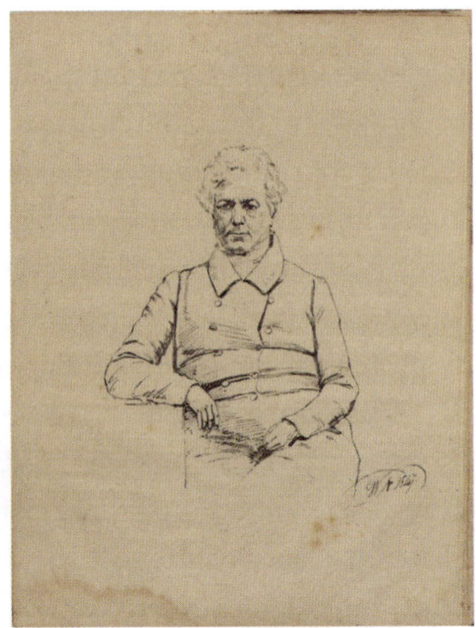

Figure 2.7: William Nicholas, 'The Philanthropist' [Dr William Bland], lithograph, 27.5 × 21 cm, frontispiece to *Heads of the People*, 18 December 1847. State Library of New South Wales.

relationship to the original photograph, describing Read's watercolour as 'evidently daguerreotypish' and Nicholas's lithograph as 'produced the same way … but several shades inferior'.[39]

Once Goodman did away with his glass-panelled studio, the dexterity of his practice gained a new vigour. From the second iteration of his Warrane/Sydney Cove studio, he made excursions inland to connect with new customers. In 1845, he travelled to Wiradjuri Country, Bathurst, and Dharug Country, Windsor, to take the portraits of 'the first [settler-colonial] families in the district'.[40] Nevertheless, Goodman's colonial trade continued to focus mainly on port cities.[41] From August to December 1845, he ran a studio on Little Flinders Street in Naarm/Melbourne, which generated a profit of over £870.[42] And, in January and February 1846, he worked in Rundle Street, Tarntanya/Adelaide, before returning to Warrane/Sydney Cove.[43] Pastoralist John Cotton travelled to Naarm/Melbourne in late 1845 to commission a Goodman daguerreotype, which

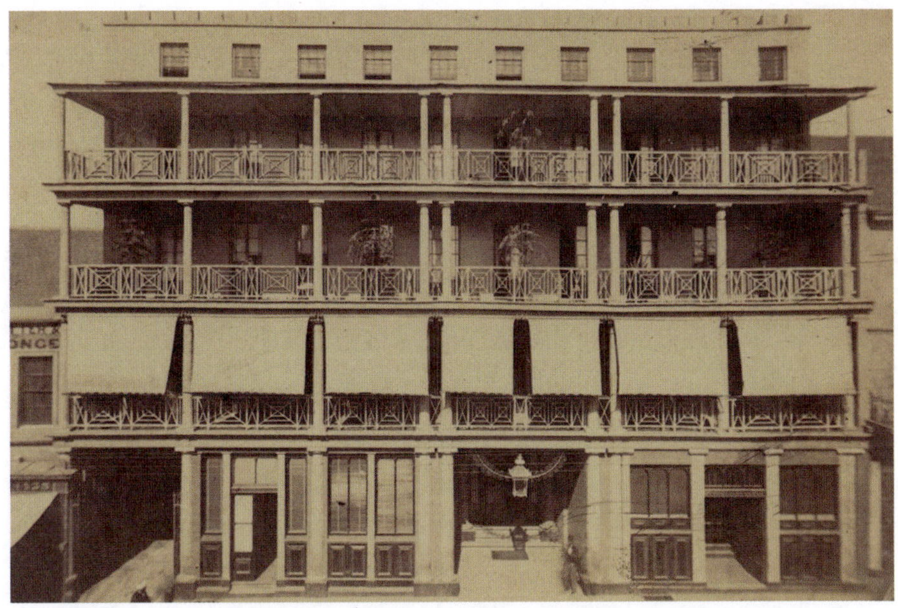

Figure 2.8: American and Australasian Photographic Company (attributed), 'The Royal Hotel, George Street, Sydney', 1870s, carte de visite, 6.4 × 10.2 cm. State Library of New South Wales.

no longer survives. In a letter to his brother, Cotton assessed his portrait as 'generally well managed and more forcible in light and shade than those I saw done in England, owing probably to the stronger and clearer light here'.[44] Goodman's photography business was, by this time, no longer measured against his ability to replicate the English photography studio experience for his colonial customers but against the daguerreotypes being issued from English studios themselves.

Warm, bright sunlight would come to typify a proto-nationalist practice of photography in the Australian colonies in the late nineteenth century. As Melissa Miles has outlined, light was an essential ingredient for and a definitive subject of photography from the 'sunny south', both in freer-form portraiture and, more generally, in the photography of natural and built environments.[45] However, the story of Goodman's colonial practice emphasises that light was an element to be reckoned with by colonial photographers right from the establishment of the earliest commercial studios. The location of his first business, the sunlight-steeped Royal Hotel, was the subject of an 1870s carte de visite by the highly mobile Henry Beaufoy Merlin and Charles Bayliss of the American and Australasian Photographic Company. The pair were itinerant photographers, working from a horse-drawn cart during the early 1870s to comprehensively photograph street views of the major cities and towns around Victoria and New South Wales.[46] In their photograph of the Royal Hotel we see the wilting potted plants on the upper balconies, the lowered blinds of the first floor, and the perfectly imprinted shadow of the awning lamp on the entranceway steps, and can only imagine the intensity of sitting in a glass studio on the building's roof (**Figure 2.8**).

Narratives of Place and Modernity

Goodman began his colonial career inciting prospective clients to imagine their studio experience as tethered to a culture of photography developed and refined in England. This vector between metropole and colony was an avenue of transaction where updated information and knowledge about photographic processes, and indeed photographers, shuttled. However, it was not the only channel through which photography moved. Colonial photography was impacted and informed as much by a trans-Pacific migration of photographers, which would intensify with the gold rushes of the 1850s. These individuals constructed narratives of place and brokered experiences of visual modernity that transcended the imperial–colonial relationship. Among them was J. W. Newland, who, in 1848, transported 'upwards of two hundred daguerreotypes' he had taken at ports through Central and South America across the Pacific: the largest cargo of photography to have traversed the ocean.[47]

Newland's photographic training had not been mediated by patented instructions nor undertaken in a British studio. As a young man, he left England to work as a merchant in Galveston, Texas. He opened his first photography rooms in May 1845, at the junction of Royal and Canal streets in New Orleans. He took commissions for daguerreotype portraits, which he housed in cases manufactured by famous New York photographer Mathew Brady. Newland blind-stamped the mat (a gold-coloured frame) with his own name, behind which each of his portraits were cased and presented.[48] Canal Street was the main thoroughfare up from the Mississippi docks. Three other daguerreotype businesses were also located at the crossroads: those of James Maguire, Hutchings & Whittemore and Jacobs & Johnson.[49] All Newland's rivals, and his east coast supplier, Brady, coupled their studio rooms with substantial galleries (**Figure 2.9**). These were places where prospective patrons could see a sizeable display of daguerreotypes before commissioning their own. Unable to compete with these more established rivals, Newland began a period of itinerancy from June 1845.

Over the next two years—before his arrival in the Australian colonies—Newland practised photography across the ex-Spanish colonial world, and the French and British empires. Stopping first at Honduras, he made his way to ports at Jamaica, Haiti, Grenada and Venezuela, before crossing Panama and heading south to Peru. In Peru during 1846, he

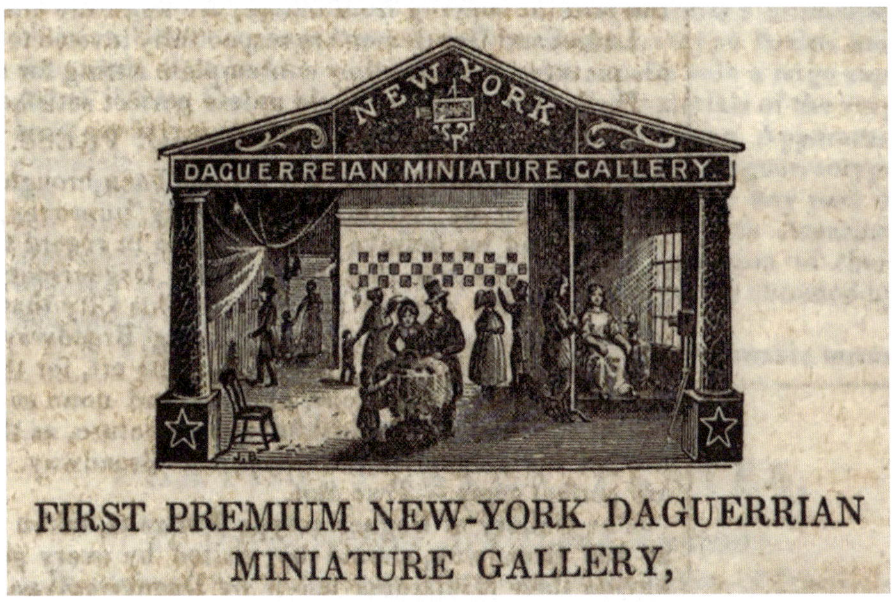

Figure 2.9: 'First Premium New-York Daguerreian Miniature Gallery (of Mathew Brady)', advertisement, wood engraving in Sheldon & Co.'s Business or Advertising Directory: Containing Cards, Circulars, and Advertisements of the Principal Firms of the Cities of New-York, Boston, Philadelphia, Baltimore, &c., &c., John F. Trow & Company, New York, 1845, p. 41.

toured inland briefly to Arequipa, before returning to Callao and sailing for Valparaíso. Experienced at working in the warmer climate of the American south, Newland was never constrained by elaborate studio infrastructure. He operated throughout the Americas from rooms in hotels and masonic halls, soliciting portrait commissions from the newly affluent middle classes.[50] Newland took two exposures for paying clients, casing one daguerreotype portrait for the customer while gradually amassing second exposures for his own collections. He also took his camera outdoors to photograph views of the port settlements through which he was passing. On 8 July 1847, Newland was at the American Hotel in Valparaíso, exhibiting a small selection of his Peruvian views and selling some of his superfluous camera equipment.[51] He never took his cache of Central and South American daguerreotypes back to North America for exhibition. Neither did Newland return to North America to relaunch his business in the context of the emerging landscape photography movement, which would prove a boon for other American photographers such as Charles and Jacob Ward, Robert H. Vance and Carleton E. Watkins.[52] Much like Augustin Lucas had almost a decade earlier, he chose instead to head west across the Pacific.

Newland's ship, the *Sarah Ann*, called at Papeete, Tahiti, its neighbouring islands, Moorea and Raiatea, Aitutaki in the Cook Islands, and the Bay of Islands, Aotearoa/New Zealand, before docking in Warrane/Sydney Cove on 19 February 1848.[53] In 1843, the French invasion of Tahiti had expelled British Protestant missionaries and left the indigenous monarch, Queen Pomare IV, a mere constitutional figurehead to an invading French power.[54] In Aotearoa/New Zealand, Māori attacks on British colonisers and their garrisons at Russell, near the Bay of Islands, had challenged the port's colonial security as a rest point for international shipping and whaling.[55] Both conflicts received global coverage in the press and were followed closely in Warrane/Sydney Cove on the Pacific's periphery.[56] Within weeks of arriving, Newland opened his first studio in rooms on the corner of George and King streets, just up from the docks. His only competitor was Goodman's brother-in-law Isaac Polack, who had taken over Goodman's studio. After seeing Newland's first advertisement, Polack closed his rooms, unable to compete with the newcomer's spectacular repertoire.[57] Newland informed his prospective clients that they could see: 'upwards of 200 daguerreotypes … amongst which may be seen the only correct picture taken of Queen Pomare … the King, the Royal Family, Chiefs … [portraits of] New Zealanders; Feejans [by which he meant Indigenous people of Aitutaki], Peruvians, Chileans, Grenadians & Co. Panoramic View of the City of Arequipa & co'.[58]

In its design, Newland's Daguerrean Gallery was much like those of his New Orleans competitors, or those of now much more famous names in early American and British photography, such as Brady, John Plumbe, Edward Anthony and Antoine Claudet. The gallery was set up in a room adjoining the studio, to allow clients to preview the daguerreotypist's work. However, as a suite of portraits, Newland's now-lost collection was unparalleled. It was drawn from his unique and far-ranging route through the Americas and the Pacific. The centrepiece was Tahitian Queen Pomare IV's 'correct picture'. Newland banked on colonial audiences' curiosity about Pomare's 'true' likeness, generated over the past decade by her multiple incarnations in the illustrated press and print culture, in the wake of the French invasion. These representations, in sketched, engraved and lithographed form, cast her as a pliant beauty, an embattled Madonna and a Christian mother (**Figure 2.10**). They speak to the malleability of the queen's non-photographic image in imperial printed literature, where it was imbued with a dizzying variety of devices: allegory, racialisation, sexualisation and satire.[59] Newland's studio–gallery offered the first chance any audience outside Tahiti had to see Pomare IV's likeness beyond caricature.

Significantly, Newland's gallery was configured around class identity as much as it reflected the racially diverse Pacific and Pacific rim communities with which his itinerant practice connected. It comprised the second plates, or second exposures, of paying clients. We can assume Newland was selective in who was included in his gallery, seeking out visually interesting or unfamiliar subjects, and rotating his display of portraits and port scenes. But there is no mention of Aboriginal people being photographed by Newland during his time in New South Wales or in lutruwita/Van Diemen's Land. This places his practice at odds with that of Goodman, who reportedly took portraits of Wurundjeri

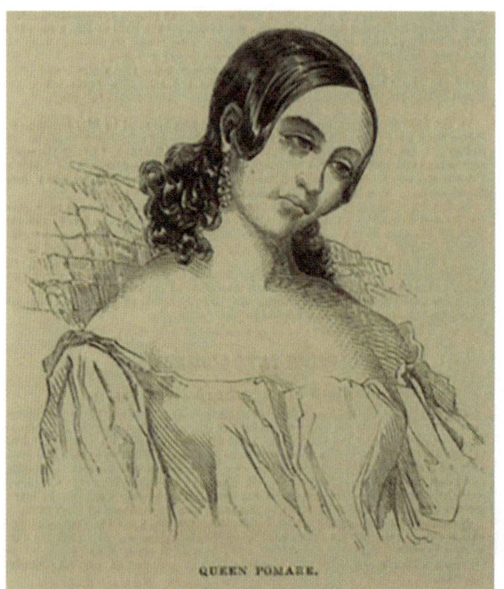

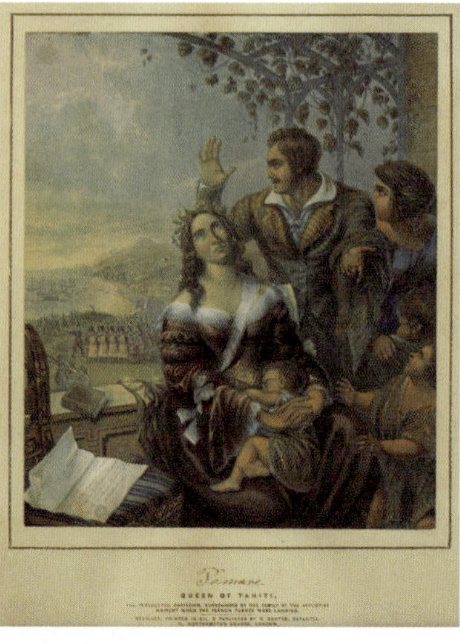

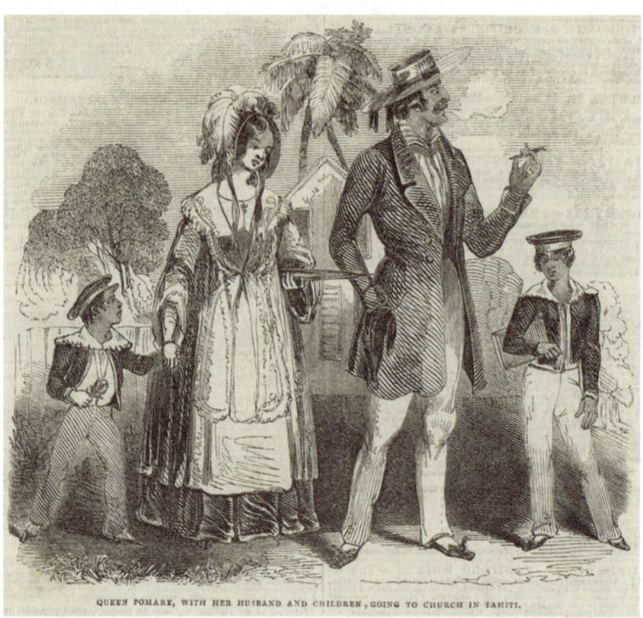

Figure 2.10: (L-R; T-B): 'Queen Pomare', wood engraving, the *Illustrated London News,* 24 February 1844, p.116; George Baxter, 'Pomare: Queen of Tahiti', 1845, Baxter print, 26.3 × 22.6 cm (print), mounted on card. National Library of Australia; 'Queen Pomare, with her husband and children, going to church in Tahiti', wood engraving, the *Pictorial Times*, London, 21 December 1845, p. 396.

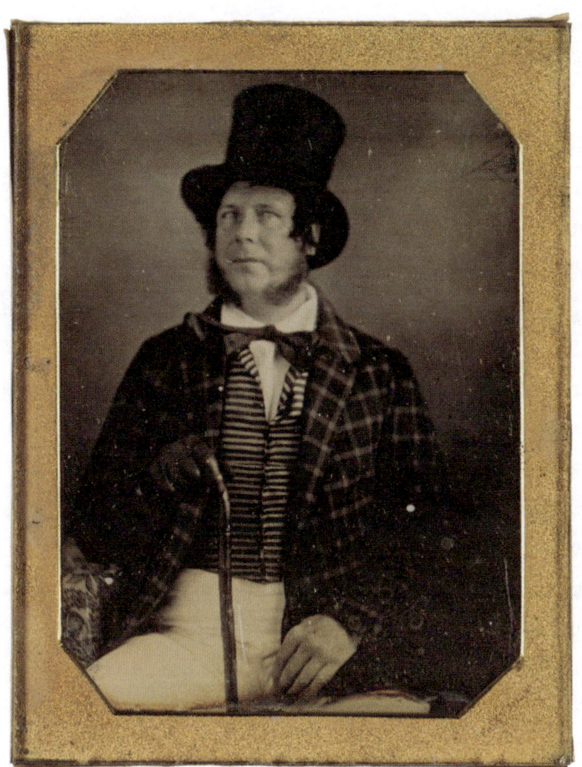

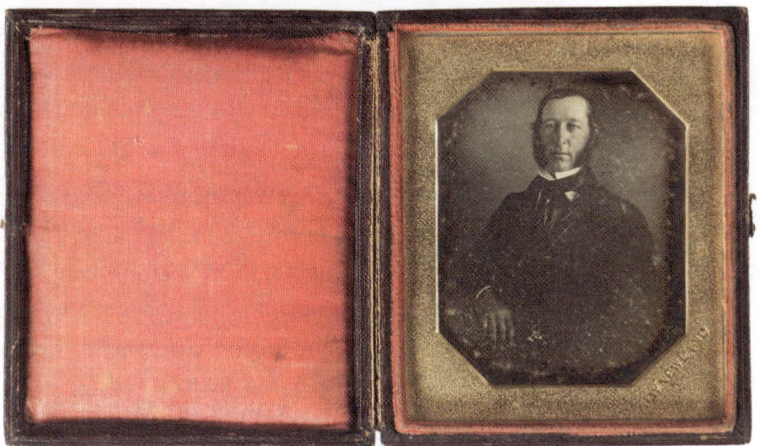

Figure 2.11: J. W. Newland, 'Edward T.Y.W. McDonald', 1848, quarter-plate, uncoloured, cased daguerreotype. Macleay Collection, Chau Chak Wing Museum, University of Sydney.

Figure 2.12: J. W. Newland, 'John Lord', 1848–49, sixth-plate, uncoloured, cased daguerreotype. Allport Library and Museum of Fine Arts.

Woi Wurrung during his stay in Naarm/Melbourne in 1845 (although these plates have not survived).[60] It also distinguishes him from Douglas Kilburn, who, as we shall see in Chapter 3, daguerreotyped Kulin men and women between 1846 and 1847 in his colonial studio, only to sell their images to multiple international print media publications for translation and reproduction as wood engravings.[61] Newland's photography business was reactive to imperial hostilities, which he leveraged to his commercial advantage. He was not an innocent actor within the colonial world. Yet his portraits were not simply racialising or ethnographic in the way photography was beginning to be used. Newland's clients belonged to Pan-Pacific indigenous and settler-colonial middle and upper classes, who had access to capital, and actively sought to commission a portrait and participate in the photographic marketplace. None of his photographs were reproduced as wood engravings for the press, where their appearance or meaning could be altered to service imperial journalism. Reportedly ill at ease with various sketched, etched and painted representations of herself, Queen Pomare IV would, in the wake of Newland's visit, come to embrace photography as a mode of influencing which image of herself went into circulation.[62]

It may have been this unique opportunity of placing one's own daguerreotype portrait among a sea of Pacific and American faces and views that enticed publican Edward McDonald, in Warrane/Sydney Cove, and pastoralist John Lord, in nipaluna/Hobart, to visit the photographer's celebrated rooms (**Figure 2.11 and 2.12**). McDonald was the owner of the Forth and Clyde Hotel, which, as Martyn Jolly has noted, was located at the rather 'louche area' of The Rocks.[63] This was not McDonald's first public house. He had made a career of licensing taverns all over the city for the preceding two decades.[64] Such businesses would have made him a familiar face among the city's colonial population, if a second exposure of his daguerreotype was included in the gallery's Sydney presentation. He appears to have been barely able to contain his enthusiasm at the prospect of a portrait. Dressed in a clashing arrangement of a lattice-patterned jacket and striped waistcoat, McDonald's tie is imperfectly fastened, and his sideburns sleeked with perspiration. His cloudy eyes betray his inability to hold his gaze for the duration of the exposure, while he sits with one gloved hand holding his cane and the other, ungloved, hand falling in his lap, demonstrating he made an effort to perform for the camera but ultimately affected a rather uncomposed attitude. By comparison, at Newland's next studio in Murray Street, nipaulna/Hobart, later in 1848, John Lord presents a demure and unexcitable demeanour. He sits stiffly, not just as a requirement of the portrait process but due to an assurance of his social class. Lord's extended family was one of the wealthiest in the southern colony at the time of his daguerreotype, occupying sizeable tracts of Aboriginal land around the port city, where they bred horses and cattle.[65] Newland's daguerrean studio and gallery emboldened his diverse colonial customers, from the expanding middle and elite classes, and shifted the pictorial narrative. He encouraged patrons to imagine themselves not simply stationed at a British colonial outpost but as swept up in the aspirational, volatile and political terrain of the Pacific world.

In the late 1840s, Newland carved out a Pacific arc for his various audiences at the ports of Warrane/Sydney and in lutruwita/Van Diemen's Land. He only momentarily diverted from this coastal circuit, travelling inland to Wonnarua Country, Maitland, in August 1848.[66] In Maitland, Sydney and Launceston, he entertained paying customers during the evenings, with lantern projections, showing hand-painted slides. These projections displayed classical European scenes and monuments, casting the imaginative lens not across the Pacific, as his gallery did, but in a different geographic direction, to a view of classical Europe.[67] Newland's passage to the Australian colonies also anticipated the trajectory of photographers caught up in the gold rush migration half a decade later. Some of them, such as T. S. Glaister and Townsend and Sanford Duryea, will be discussed in the following chapters. Most importantly, Newland's career challenges the exclusively British or European roots of colonial photography, demonstrating how the Pacific world offered experiences of photography that were formative in generating a colonial practice. As the nineteenth century progressed, this trans-Pacific relationship would strengthen, becoming reciprocal. We see, for example, that the colonies of Victoria, New South Wales, South Australia and Queensland all had pavilions at the Philadelphia International Exhibition of 1876.

Much like Newland's gallery, imperial and international exhibition spaces were locations that created middle-class narratives of Empire and industrialisation, while visually erasing Aboriginal and indigenous histories of custodianship and occupation.

Negotiating Peripheries

As noted earlier, Elizabeth Louisa How arrived in Naarm/Melbourne with her young family in November 1849, which was ten months after Newland left the colonies for Kolkata, India.[68] She may have heard whispers of Newland's daguerreian studio and gallery, but she was too late to see it firsthand. There is also no record of How practising or being trained in photography in England. The Hows' passage to the colonies in 1849 was aboard the *Royal George*, from Gravesend. They travelled as assisted immigrants through a scheme that subsidised the passage of free settlers at the end of transportation and especially encouraged the migration of labourers to populate an increasingly stretched colonial workforce. Elizabeth Louisa How is listed in the customs documentation at Port Phillip as a 'housekeeper', a common shorthand for married women.[69]

The How family's migration was likely inspired by the forward travel of James How's cousin Robert How.[70] From the late 1830s to the 1850s, Robert How was active in buying and selling unceded Gadigal and Dharug Land through various government land grant auctions.[71] During this time, he also traded in wharf licences on unceded Cammeraygal Country.[72] These ventures made Robert How a successful colonial businessman and the Hows later travelled north from Naarm/Melbourne to join him. Around this time, Elizabeth Louisa How dropped her Christian name and henceforth went by her middle name, Louisa, possibly as an exercise in colonial reinvention. Robert and James How partnered with Thomas Walker to form the shipping company How, Walker & Co., which operated from Campbell's Wharf. James, Louisa and their sons resided on the other side of the harbour, in Kiarabilli/Kirribilli, at a waterfront homestead called Woodlands.[73]

In the decade between Newland's departure and the Hows' mercantile success, around a dozen photographers had opened commercial studios

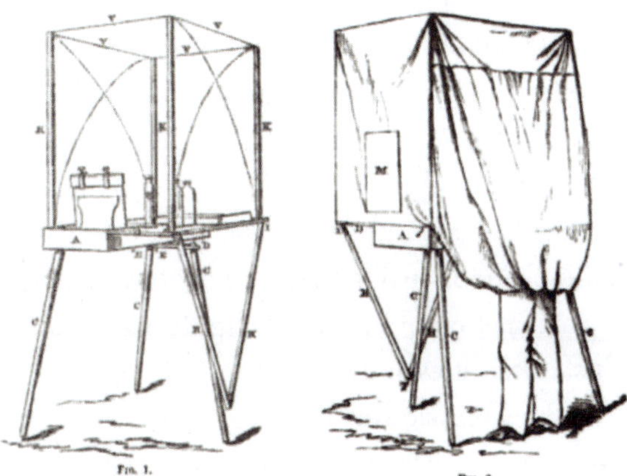

Figure 2.13: [Portable darkroom – two views], the *Photographic News* (London), 18 February 1859, p. 284.

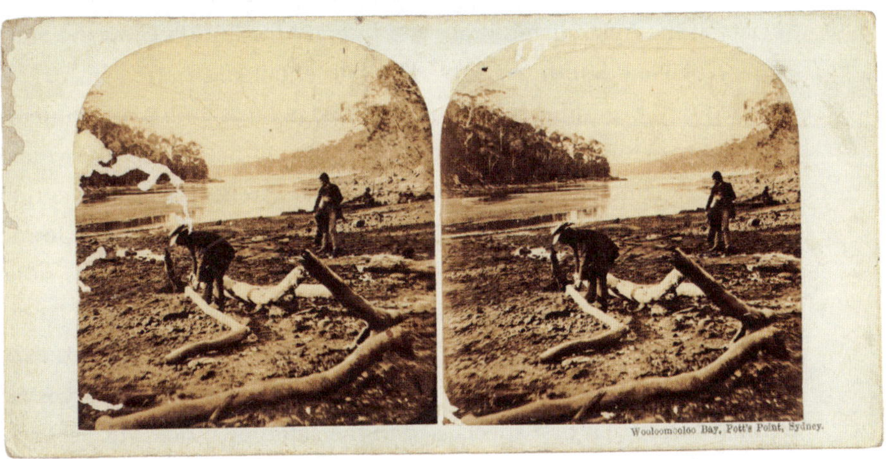

Figure 2.14: William Hetzer, 'Woolloomooloo Bay, Potts Point, Sydney', c. 1858–59, stereo-print mounted on card, 8.4 × 17.4 cm (mounted). State Library of New South Wales.

on Gadigal Country in Sydney. The second half of the 1850s coincided with the international commercialisation of the wet-plate collodion photographic process. Materially cheaper than creating a daguerreotype, it involved sensitising a glass plate with a solution of gum cotton ether, potassium iodide and silver nitrate. The plate needed to be exposed and developed, with a solution of pyrogallic acid, and then fixed with potassium cyanide, within roughly fifteen minutes of its initial preparation. This compelled the photographer to operate in proximity to a darkroom. However, the infrastructure of the darkroom began to take on more mobile qualities, as seen in the 'Portable Darkroom Tent' advertised in English periodical the *Photographic News* (**Figure 2.13**). From the glass negative, positive images could be made, initially through the salted paper contact printing process. Innovations such as this also further facilitated an expansion in amateur participation in the photographic market.

During the late 1850s, fraternities and learned societies in colonial Sydney became locations for the discussion of new photographic processes. On 9 September 1857, for example, visiting British photographer Frank Haes lectured to an audience of '40 gentlemen' of the Philosophical Society at the Australian Library and Literary Institution (now the State Library of New South Wales).[74] His talk entailed a potted history of the medium, beginning with Thomas Wedgwood's 1820s experiments with light, before moving on to the contributions of Daguerre and Talbot. He concluded with Frederick Scott Archer's latest invention of the collodion process in England, commenting on its application in making photographic positives from collodion negatives. At this same meeting, Edwin Dalton, who ran a large photography studio on George Street, formally joined the society. George Street was also the location of German-born William Hetzer's studio. Hetzer established a successful colonial career that first specialised in the calotype process in the early 1850s and then expanded into new collodion formats later in the decade.[75] In addition to his commercial photographic endeavours, Hetzer convened a camera club comprising professional men who set off on weekends to photograph the urban landscape around the port city (**Figure 2.14**). They used new mobile stereoview cameras. One of this party, possibly Hetzer himself, is the unnamed correspondent who submitted three successive columns titled 'Australian Nature and the Art of the Photographer' for publication in the *Photographic News* in July and August 1859.[76]

All this photographic activity culminated in an exhibition staged by the Philosophical Society at the Australian Library and Literary Institution on 22 December 1859. This was an occasion where hundreds of photographs were hung, many of which were made in new collodion formats. There were fourteen colonial contributors, all of whom were men. They included Hetzer, Dalton, the Freeman Brothers—whose studio was credited with introducing the wet-plate collodion process to the colony—and John Flavelle, who by this time had abandoned the glass studio he had inherited from Goodman. By December 1859, Arthur Onslow was living in Warrane/Sydney Cove. He used this opportunity to show stereoview prints from his time in Kinjarling/Albany (noted in Chapter 1).[77] The colonial content was interspersed with imported views from England and Europe, and installed alongside a selection of new lens-based technologies, including compound microscopes and stereo-viewers. Louisa How would have known of Hetzer and his camera club. However, on account of her gender, she was excluded from his photographic outings and the meetings of fraternities such as the Philosophical Society where conversations about photography were taking place. Nevertheless, possibly after a small amount of private instruction in a commercial studio,[78] and after reading about photographic processes in imported journals, Louisa How mastered collodion-based photography. While a boom in commercial studios and photographic excursions was unfolding in the surrounding areas, How was busy assembling an album of her photographic prints at her home, Woodlands, on the other side of the harbour.

In the late 1850s, the photographic album was only vaguely conceptualised and certainly there was no industry for manufacturing such compendiums. Louisa How may have been aware of commercial photographers, such as O. William Blackwood, discussed further in Chapter 4, who was selling standardised albums pre-populated with urban views of colonial Sydney. However, for her own project, she repurposed a leather-bound book made by the London stationery firm De La Rue & Co.[79] The firm's list was stocked in stores such as Chatto and Hughes Stationers on George Street, in the heart of this colonial photographic scene.[80] Roughly A4 in size, this was probably an item originally designed for scrapbooking. The book's blank paper pages were segmented with half a dozen brightly coloured inserts of thicker card. Louisa pasted photographic salted paper prints of her husband, their friends and the immediate surroundings of her home in a uniform fashion throughout the volume, even on the

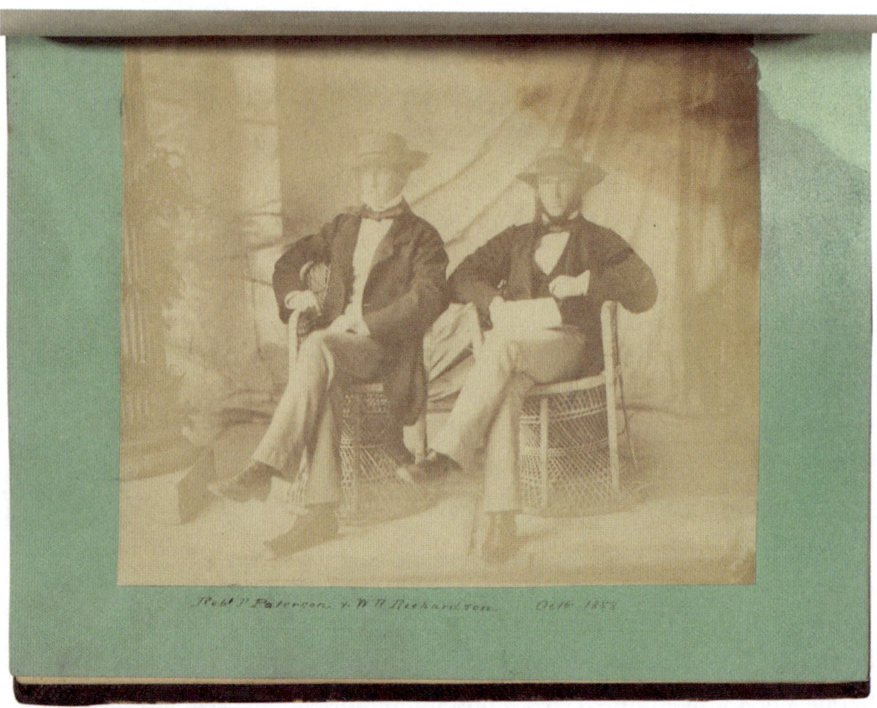

Figure 2.15: Louisa How, 'Rob Paterson + W. R. Richardson. Oct 1858', salted paper print, 15.8 × 18.6 cm (print), from Louisa How's untitled album. National Gallery of Australia.

coloured leaves, recalibrating the volume's intended use. As the century progressed, a mixed-media culture of scrapbooking would increasingly absorb and integrate photography.[81] Louisa How's album is at the forefront of this popular tradition.

How's friends and acquaintances posed for portraits in a mock studio she assembled on her home's sandstone balcony. She affixed a large piece of light-coloured cloth to fall from the overhanging roof at one end of the balcony, occasionally allowing the veranda's vine-ringed colonnade to remain within the photographic frame (**Figure 2.15**). The inclusion of the colonnade ingeniously evoked a feature of classical portraiture and anticipated (albeit in dimensional form) what would become a motif on the faux backdrops of commercial photographic studios.[82] How's portraits are predominantly of merchants and colonial administrators. These men

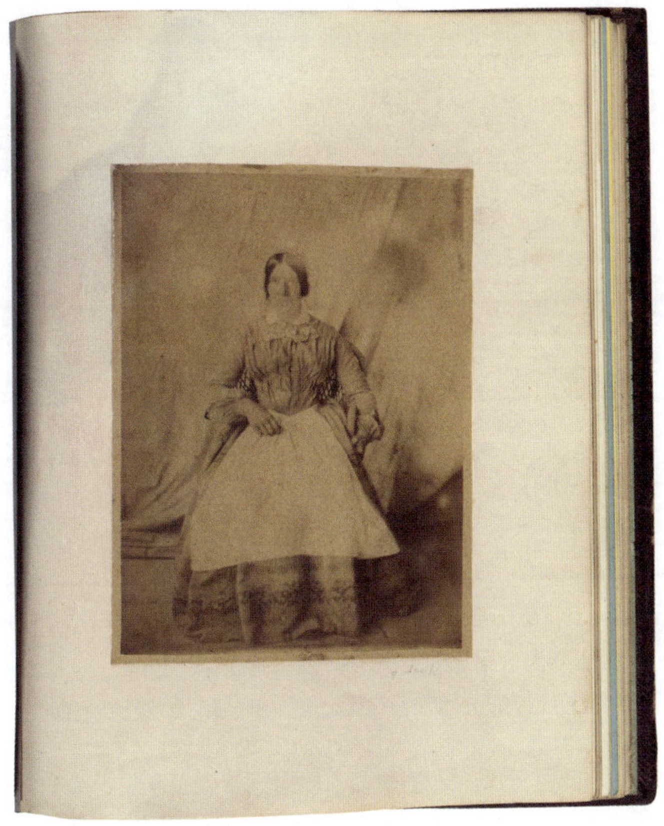

Figure 2.16: Louisa How [uncaptioned but identified as 'Mrs Lamont' on the album's contents page], 9 January 1859, salted paper print, 15 × 11 cm (print), from Louisa How's untitled album. National Gallery of Australia.

were photographed holding books and unfurled letters: signifiers of correspondence and learning over distance. Remarkably, though, there is an overwhelming representation of subjects with photographic stereo cards and stereoviewers, giving a sense that Woodlands was also a place for discussing new photographic techniques and technologies. How's portraits are captioned, and many are dated. The earliest, a single portrait of Robert Paterson, is inscribed with 'September 1858', which indicates that How's project was well underway before the December 1859 Philosophical Society exhibition was held on the other side of the harbour.

Louisa How's album is an important corrective to the masculine-steeped photography scene that has come to dominate histories of nineteenth-century colonial photography. Jan Brazier has recently shown that women, including Thekla Hetzer (married to William Hetzer),

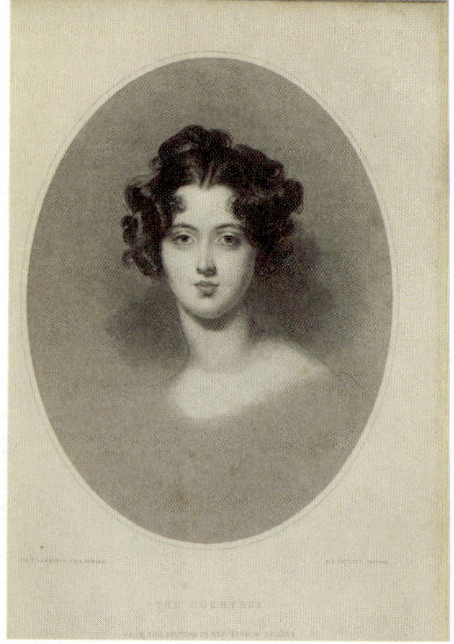

Figure 2.17: **(L)** Louisa How [uncaptioned but identified as 'A Lady' on the album's contents page], c. 1858–59, salted paper print, 11 × 8.6 cm (print), from Louisa How's untitled album. National Gallery of Australia. **(R)** Sir Thomas Lawrence (painter) and R. A. Artlett (engraver), 'The Countess: From the Picture in the Vernon Gallery', the *Art Journal*, London, 1850, opp. p. 296.

were active in the studios that carried only their husband's names. They prepared photographic plates, hand-coloured photographs and greeted customers, directly engaging with the technologies and the patrons of photography.[83] Isobel Crombie's foundational research on How's album in 1984 revealed that she was neither an adjunct nor auxiliary to a male photographer, but the architect of both the elaborate photographic setting and the ensemble of the associated images.[84] Her compendium of salted paper prints is the oldest extant photographic work by a woman living in the Australian colonies. This attribution is made more significant by the fact that her album additionally includes the oldest extant photograph taken by a woman *of* a woman in the Australian colonies. On 9 January 1859, How took a portrait of 'Mrs Lamont', who Crombie believes to be the family's servant, wearing a clean apron and an embroidered skirt (**Figure 2.16**).[85] An artistic communion between the two women, mediated by the camera, is supported by the fact that no other portraits included in the album are from this date. These factors make it hard to construe Lamont's portrait as a 'test' for a later sitting. Indeed, its placement in the album indicates How was happy with the photograph, and looked to include Lamont among her cast of friends and visitors.

There is only one other female subject in How's album of around fifty salted paper print photographs, the dowager countess of Darnley. She was not photographed from life but from a stipple engraving published in the 1850 edition of English magazine the *Art Journal* (**Figure 2.17**). The engraving itself was a copy of Sir Thomas Lawrence's oil-on-canvas portrait of the countess, first exhibited at Vernon Gallery in London in 1847.[86] In How's album, the photographic reproduction of the countess's portrait(s) is indexed on the contents page simply as 'A Lady'. The same edition of the *Art Journal* included an instructive essay on 'Photography on Glass Plates' by English pioneering photographer and scientist Robert Hunt.[87] It also included a column by a T. A. Malone on the relative merits of using glass-plate negatives over paper negatives, and several short columns on photographic news.[88] Clearly, the periodical would have been of interest to How for more than just its illustrations.

The album's contents, such as the photographically reproduced stipple engraving, allude to the international conversations on photography that were filtering through to Warrane/Sydney Cove and specifically to Woodlands. However, the importance of How's album also lies in the mobile traffic it documented from its stationary, domestic vantage point. From her home, How shot the view over to Government House, the view to Campbell's Wharf, and the waterway scene to Fort Denison, among other views of the harbour. Common to all these photographs is a concentration on commerce and connectivity: ships pulling into dock or lulling in the bay (**Figure 2.18**). The album positions Louisa How, as photographer, in the middle of a mercantile or maritime web of activity.

How's album also functioned as a visitors book of the people who circuited through her home. 'Landowner', surveyor and explorer William Landsborough visited Woodlands with his brother John and his Aboriginal guide. The occasion of their visit and its exact date are not noted, but their portraits appear towards the end of the album, alongside

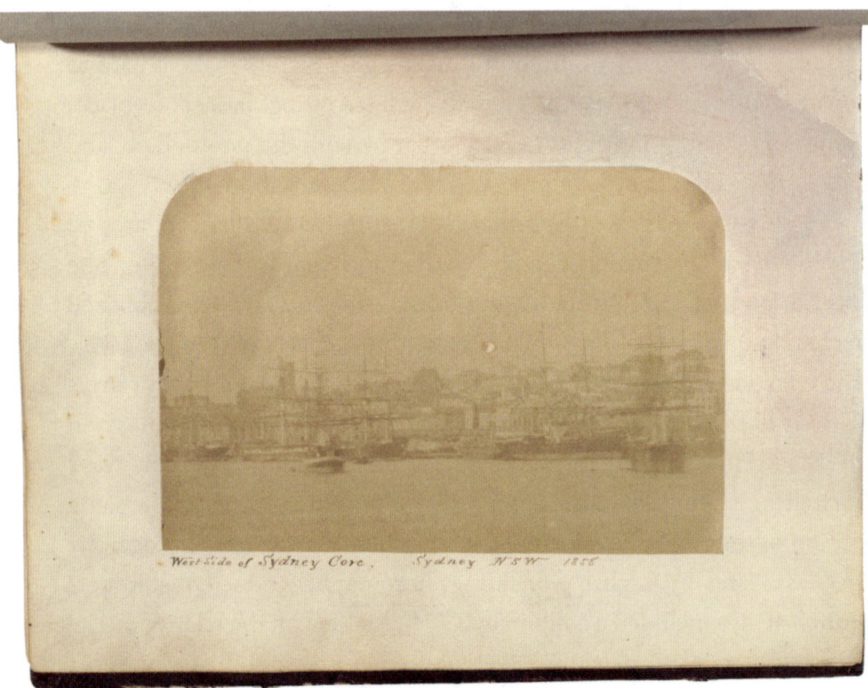

Figure 2.18: Louisa How, 'West Side of Sydney Cove. Sydney NSW 1858', salted paper print, 11.2 × 16.8 cm (print), from Louisa How's untitled album. National Gallery of Australia.

others from 1859. William Landsborough had spent time between 1857 and 1859 surveying Guwinmal and Gangulu Country north of Meeanjin/Brisbane.[89] In 1861, he would lead a search for Robert O'Hara Burke and William Wills, which, although unsuccessful, consolidated his own pioneering celebrity as the first European to cross the continent from north to south. This was a profile he actively cultivated through the publication of his expedition journal less than a year later.[90] William and John Landsborough both claimed tracts of unceded Gayiri Country in mid-north Queensland. In 1859, they had subdivided the land into stations, and were selling it off using How, Walker and Co. as brokers.[91] John Landsborough resided in Gadigal Country, Sydney, and his familiarity with the Hows is implied through the captioning of his portrait in Louisa's album with simply his initials 'J.L.'

The young Aboriginal man who accompanied the Landsboroughs to Woodlands is the only Aboriginal person Louisa How photographed. She took multiple portraits of the Landsborough brothers, and the young man referred to only as 'Tiger'. 'Tiger's' Country and Kin are not recorded in the colonial archive. He is not identified in Landsborough's notebooks as being among the guides and trackers who led Landsborough's surveying party through Country south-east of Mackay earlier in 1859.[92] Much older guides—Wamba-Wamba man Jemmy, and Jack Fisherman from the Meeanjin/Brisbane region[93] —accompanied Landsborough's search for Burke and Wills two years later, and they are depicted in the photographically derived frontispiece illustration to his published expedition journal.[94] There is very little information about where and under what circumstances Landsborough and 'Tiger' met.

The trio's visit to Woodlands may have been over several days, considering the changes in clothing across portraits. Two salted paper prints of 'Tiger' exist outside the album. In one, held at the Art Gallery of New South Wales, the Landsborough brothers sit cross-legged on wicker chairs on the balcony looking into the distance, with 'Tiger' seated cross-legged on the floor between them. Louisa has lowered the camera to 'Tiger's' eye level, and he stares directly back at her.[95] In this photograph, otherwise composed to suggest 'Tiger's' subservience to the colonial men, How has constructed a direct dialogue between herself and the young boy, mediated by the camera. In a second photograph at the National Gallery of Australia—which is also not in the album—William Landsborough sits on a cloth-covered chair and 'Tiger' stands by his side, cap in one hand, with his elbow resting against the back of the chair (**Figure 2.19**). Landsborough again gazes off into the distance, while 'Tiger' stares directly into the lens. Jane Lydon has argued that we cannot construe colonial photographs of Aboriginal people to be 'solely an expression of the white man's gaze'.[96] There is a notable power imbalance in the relationship between Landsborough and 'Tiger' but, as Lydon argues, this does not discount how Aboriginal people could 'actively participate in the picture-making process'.[97] 'Tiger's' engagement

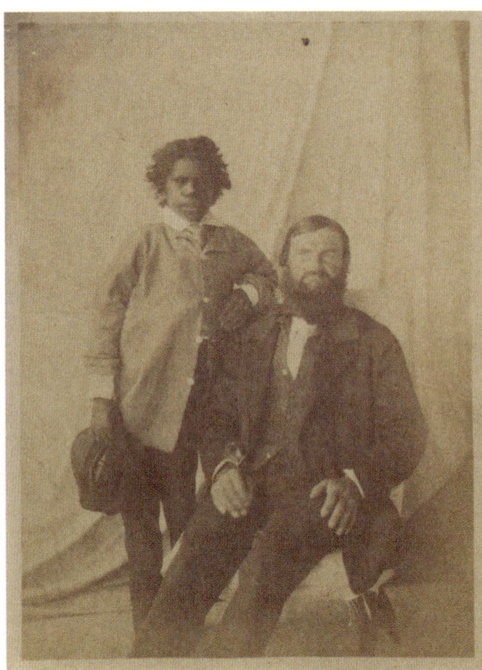

Figure 2.19: Louisa How, 'William Landsborough and his native guide "Tiger"', c. 1859, salted paper print, 15.5 × 11.5 cm. National Gallery of Australia.

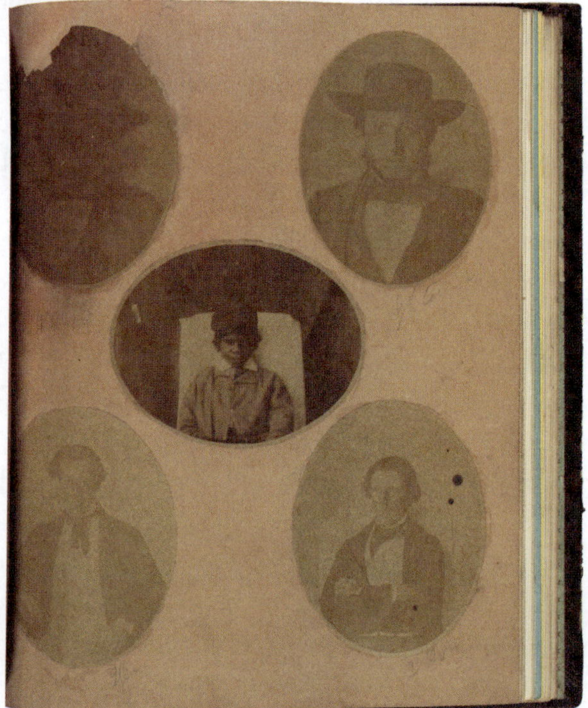

Figure 2.20: Louisa How, 'W.W.R., G.S.C., J.G., J.H. & Tiger', c. 1859, vignetted salted paper prints, various sizes, from Louisa How's untitled album. National Gallery of Australia.

with Louisa's camera renders him as more than a diminutive figure in her improvised photography studio. Although stripped of his correct name and Country in the captions—and dressed in oversized European clothes (which conceal any possible display of scarification) —he holds his own presence in front of the camera.

In the album, William Landsborough appears in portraits on his own, as does his brother Robert. 'Tiger' was photographed on his own as well, seated on the same cloth-covered chair as the other guests. 'Tiger's' portrait in How's album does not appear with those of either of the Landsborough brothers. Rather, it is vignetted on a page with the portraits of three other Woodlands visitors and Louisa How's husband (**Figure 2.20**). 'Tiger' again maintains a steadfast composure and a strong gaze. Through this arrangement, Louisa pictorially upsets the master–servant relationship, constellating a new order among her guests. She positions 'Tiger' at the centre of the page, somewhat fetishised but also with a prominence and agency of his own.

Excluded from the colonial (men's) camera clubs, Louisa How engaged with an increasingly globalised culture of photography transmitted through illustrated publications. She digested literature about photography imported from overseas while following, also at a distance, local photographic activity. How set out to construct her colonial world, picturing her own maid posing on her front porch, then photographing her husband, friends and visitors to Woodlands, before moving outwards to document the maritime commerce and waterways that delivered her photographic news. These shipping routes tracked right back to the dowager countess's portrait in London and metropolitan conversations about photographic innovation. Louisa's album of colonial salted paper photographs is full of contradictions and complexities. It is domestic in its perspective but expansive in the commercial and artistic worlds to which it gestures. The album reflects a particularly acute colonising moment of surveying and dispossession, intersecting with the lives of colonists involved in these activities. More than this, the album's very existence and Louisa How's photography practice were financed by the profits the extended How family made through their colonial land trade and maritime business ventures. Yet the volume is also sensitive: not compiled for publication, exhibition or a general audience, beyond that of the guests at Woodlands. In these ways, How's album is a provincial and peripheral piece of colonial photographic ephemera, while also being at the centre of a conversation about photography that *she* was hosting in the port city.

3

The Photography Studio

Colonial photography studios were dynamic places of overt self-fashioning, and sites for more subtle but steadfast articulations of identity. Studios could be provisional and temporary, erected in hotel rooms, or assembled from cloth and furnishings in outdoor locations, as the previous chapter demonstrated. They could also have lavishly decorated interiors, matched by various options for the presentation and packaging of portraits. The colonial photography studio was a transactional space and, in the case of commercial studios, directed towards making a profit. Photographers followed the extension of the colonial frontier, branching out by the late 1840s from the major cities and established photographic circuits. Mining and the expanding pastoral industry generated new customers for photography. These industries fuelled the dispossession of Aboriginal communities from Country, and propelled their forced relocation to missionary stations and indenture in colonial households. The photography studio was a place to (re-)stage these colonising narratives but also, on occasion, a venue to complicate them.

This chapter focuses on the photography studio and the human negotiations that fed the production of photographs. It can be tempting to infer from the stilted faces and rigid poses of mid-nineteenth-century colonial photographs that the portrait process was a passive and prescriptive undertaking, which only gradually loosened as the century progressed and technologies developed, reducing exposure times. Certainly, photographers coached their prospective clients on how to dress and pose for flattering effect. Nevertheless, from the outset it was the composure and investment of the sitter, as much as the technical skill of the photographer, that contributed to the success of the final image. Customers brought objects to the photography studio and came with intentions for what they wanted their photographs to communicate. Studios were sites of ceremony and purpose, but they were not purely contrived or insular spaces. As David Campany reminds us, every photograph represents a visual excess unable to be entirely controlled and ordered by its maker.[1] Portraits taken in these spaces gesture to the colonial project occurring just beyond their frame. The output of mid-century colonial studios positioned the camera not simply as a technology of benign visual record but as a device directly entangled in the history of colonisation being laid out before it.

Minerals in and of the Studio

This synchronicity between the business of photography and the industries of colonisation is visually distilled in the studio daguerreotype of South Australian mining administrator, and later colonial governor, Henry Ayers (**Figure 3.1**). Ayers sat for his portrait on Ngadjuri Country, Burra, sometime in 1847–48. For the occasion, he brought lumps of ore to be placed on the studio's side table. This action rehearsed a theme that would come to dominate the photographic portraiture of mining districts over the next three decades. Here, though, it was not gold nuggets that Ayers is seen to be clutching. He was appointed secretary of the South Australian Mining Association in 1845, the same year as prospectors from the company broke ground at Burra. Referred to as the 'monster mine', Burra concealed large reserves of copper.[2] By the end of the 1840s, copper mining in this region employed over 1000 men and, at the time of Ayers' portrait, South Australia was the third-largest copper-producing state or territory in the world.[3]

There were no established photography studios at Burra during the 1840s. Ayers' daguerreotype was taken by a 'travelling artist', as a note in its case, penned by his own hand, recalls. The artist might have been English-born watercolourist and draughtsman S. T. (Samuel Thomas) Gill, who arrived in South Australia in 1845. Aside from painting supplies, Gill was carrying daguerreotype equipment. He was adept at the daguerreotype process, although it was adjunct to his primary practice as a painter.[4] In 1847, Gill travelled to Ngadjuri Country, and completed several sketches and watercolours of the colonial township of Kooringa and the interiors of the Burra mine. These were sent back to England, translated into engravings and published as a full-page spread in the *Illustrated London News*, reflecting the growing imperial interest in colonial mineral deposits.[5] Years before his trip to Burra, Gill had sold some daguerreotype supplies and a camera to the Tarntanya/Adelaide-based ornithologist Robert Hall. Hall would become one of South Australia's longest-operating colonial photographers, practising for almost

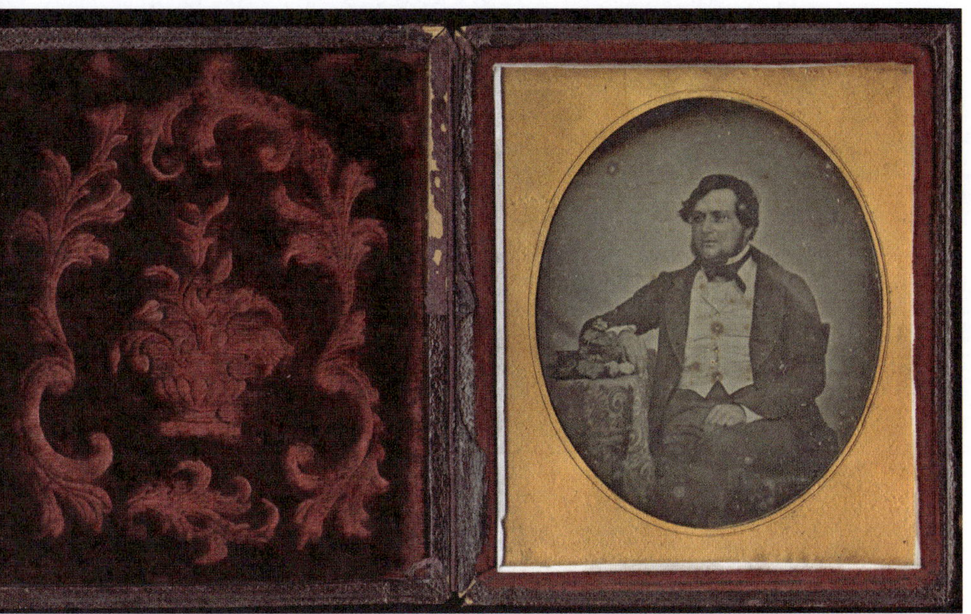

Figure 3.1: Unattributed, 'Henry Ayers', 1847–48, sixth-plate, gold-accented and lightly colour-tinted, cased daguerreotype. State Library of South Australia.

twenty years between 1847 until his death in 1866.[6] It is possible that Ayers' daguerreotype was instead taken by Hall, who ran a commercial studio on Hindley Street during 1847–48.[7] The one-day trip north from the colonial capital to Burra would have been a commercially safe and presumably lucrative way for Hall to expand his studio's custom.[8]

Ayers' portrait, like all daguerreotypes, is exposed on a silver-coated copper plate. The plate's primary mineral component was the same as the one he was mining. However, in the 1840s, there were no smelting facilities in Burra. Copper ore extracted from Ngadjuri Country was sent back to England to be refined in the Swansea smelters.[9] Some of this copper would have been further refined into silver-coated copper plates and exported to the Australian colonies, which at that time also had no local photographic plate manufacturing firms. Recent research has traced the silver used by pioneering British photographers back to mines in Central and South America. Fionn Montell-Boyd has demonstrated that photographers such as William Henry Fox Talbot were not simply the recipients of silver sourced from colonial and ex-colonial contexts. Talbot also held shares in mining companies, including the Anglo-Mexican Mining Association, which owned and managed substantial silver mines, such as 'Valenciana' in Guanajuato, Mexico.[10] This profiteering from photography's raw materials extended to colonials such as Ayers. It is tempting to imagine that he requested the ore's presence in his portrait as a means of narrating his tenure at Burra, which stretched right back to the beginning of the South Australia Mining Association's venture. During his first five years as secretary, between 1845–49, Ayers consolidated a sizeable personal fortune due to the fifteen dividends paid at 200 per cent on his original £5 shares in the association.[11] Copper both physically supports this photograph and was the mineral that paid for its commission.

The discovery of gold in the colonies on the east coast during the 1850s expanded the studio enterprise, particularly in nodal towns and cities en route to the mining fields. Many of the new class of professional photographers arrived as prospectors themselves or initially worked in professions adjacent to the mining economy. British-born American migrant T. S. (Thomas Skelton) Glaister disembarked the *Chalmers* in November 1852 at Boon Wurrung Country, Port Phillip, listed at customs as a 'stonemason'.[12] Glaister had spent the previous decade working across several eastern American states in a range of occupations, before finally joining the Meade Brothers photography firm in New York.[13] He left North America with photographic training and connections. By 1854, he was running one of the most lavish and successful colonial photography studios, initially under the name of his former American employer: Meade Brothers and Co.

Dressing for the Camera

Glaister understood how the photographic experience, and the photograph itself, was impacted by choices the patron made before entering his studio. Press advertisements targeted at his prospective Naarm/Melbourne clients included suggestions for clothing: 'Figure or dark dresses, of any material excepting velvet, are preferable for ladies … Dark vests and scarfs or handkerchiefs are preferable for men'.[14] Glaister boasted he could take pictures 'in any weather' but that the very young were best served in the middle of the day, when the sun was brightest and thus the exposure quickened. His studio was located on the second floor above Thompson and Co.'s tea exchange at 5 Great Collins Street. Sitters entered through a waiting room. Here, in a toilette-like arrangement, ladies were assisted by a 'young female attendant' prior to their sitting.[15] Glaister's studio was not marketed to the spontaneous customer passing by with ten shillings to spare, although this was the advertised price of his cheapest ninth-plate (5.1 × 6.4 cm) daguerreotype. Rather, he sought clients willing to invest financially and dress consciously for the occasion of their portrait.

One has a sense that the gentleman in **Figure 3.2** had read Glaister's sartorial directives ahead of his studio visit. He is dressed in a flat, dark colour. His suit is tailored perfectly to his willowy form, suggesting a bespoke fitting. As a full-plate daguerreotype (of 21.5 × 16.5 cm), this was a portrait of considerable expense. This plate size was far more common for portraits of wealthy families, outdoor views or even the photography of professional or civic groups—sittings where multiple subjects needed to be accommodated within a single frame.[16] The unutilised or unpopulated space around the unidentified man on this

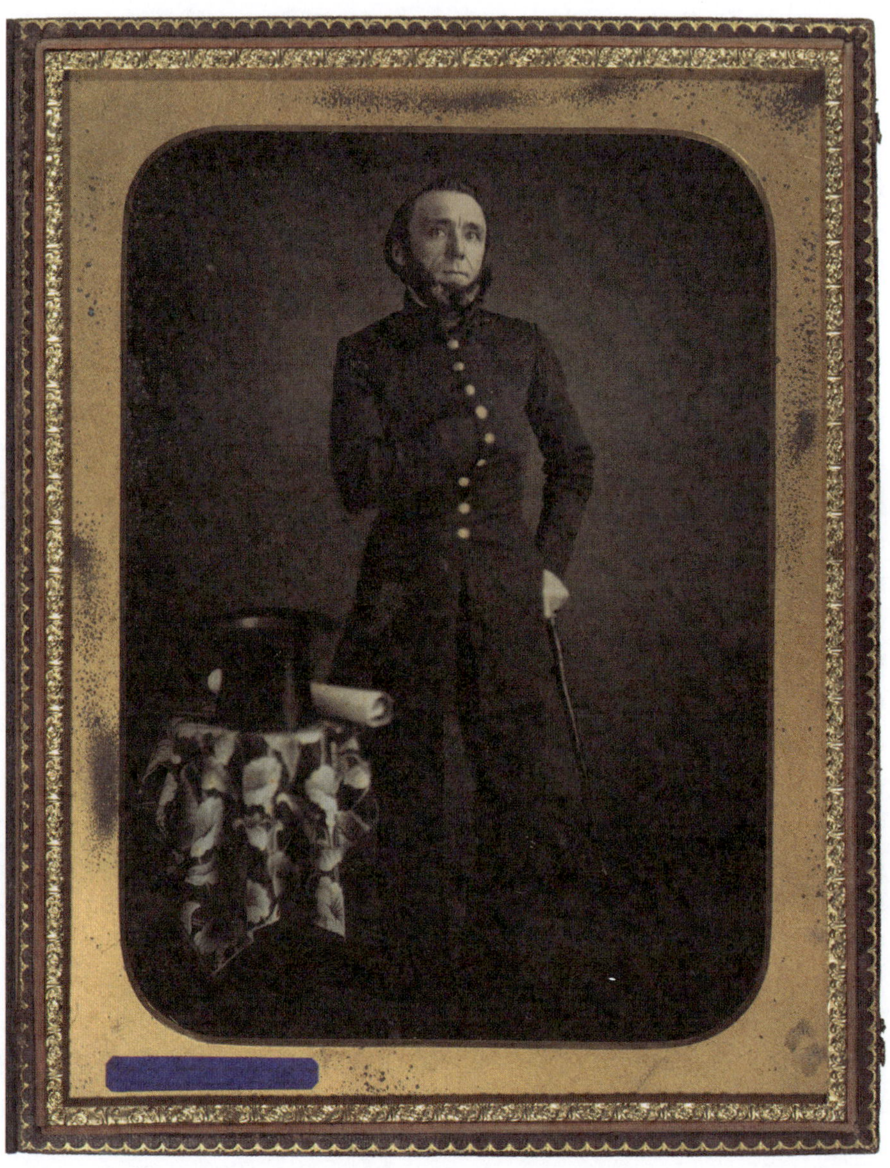

Figure 3.2: T.S. Glaister operating as Meade Brothers and Co., (Unidentified man), 1854, full-plate, gold-accented, cased daguerreotype. National Gallery of Victoria.

plate marks it out as a commission of excess. The gentleman's top hat has been removed for the exposure, so as not to shadow his face, but it remains in view on the side table to reinforce his upper-class status. The scrolled documents behind the hat might be title deeds or architectural plans. We can certainly assume they are significant for the subject, if not the reason behind the commission, due to the lack of other personal objects in the frame. The man steadies himself with a cane and tucks his other hand into a gap in the fastened buttons of his frock coat, which have been accented with gold paint. As Arline Meyer outlines, 'hand-in-waistcoat' was a gestural tradition established in eighteenth-century British portraiture to convey social decorum.[17] Glaister's subject may have struck this pose to graft his daguerreotype onto a longer lineage of elite portraiture; on the other hand, he might have been concealing an injury or disfigurement. Peeping out, at the height of his ankle, is one of the clawed feet of a head brace. This support, something like the one in the diagrammatic drawing **Figure 3.3**, would have extended the length of his body to cradle the back of his head for the approximately 25-second exposure, helping hold steady his whole figure.

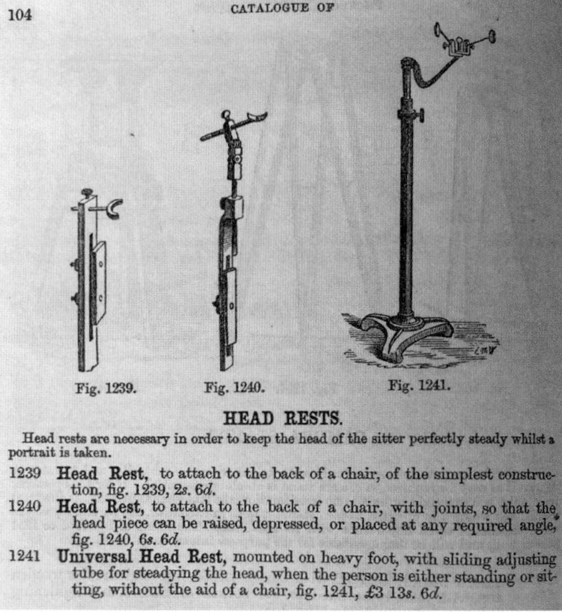
104 CATALOGUE OF

Fig. 1239. Fig. 1240. Fig. 1241.

HEAD RESTS.

Head rests are necessary in order to keep the head of the sitter perfectly steady whilst a portrait is taken.

1239 **Head Rest,** to attach to the back of a chair, of the simplest construction, fig. 1239, 2*s*. 6*d*.

1240 **Head Rest,** to attach to the back of a chair, with joints, so that the head piece can be raised, depressed, or placed at any required angle, fig. 1240, 6*s*. 6*d*.

1241 **Universal Head Rest,** mounted on heavy foot, with sliding adjusting tube for steadying the head, when the person is either standing or sitting, without the aid of a chair, fig. 1241, £3 13*s*. 6*d*.

Figure 3.3: [Section] 'Head Rests' from Horne and Thornthwaite's *A Guide to Photography* (trade catalogue), London, 1856, p.104.

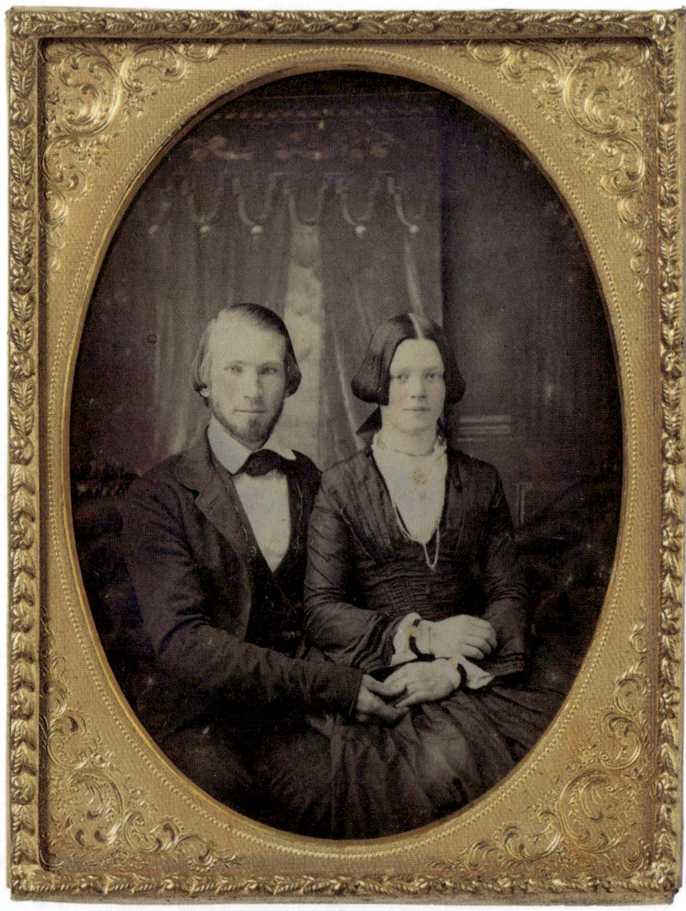

Figure 3.4: Unattributed, 'Portrait of gold miner John Dickson Love and his young bride, Sarah Purvis', 1854, sixth-plate, gold-accented, cased daguerreotype. National Gallery of Victoria.

Glaister's Meade Brothers and Co. studio sat at the forefront of the expansion of colonial Victorian studio culture, spurred by the migration and economic activity surrounding gold prospecting. In the 1840s, there were only four commercial photography studios in the greater Port Phillip region. Three of these belonged to travelling photographers: George Barron Goodman (discussed in Chapter 2), Launceston-based daguerreotypist Thomas Browne and New South Wales itinerant Lawson Insley.[18] Only Douglas Kilburn, brother of the London-based royal photographer William Edward Kilburn, operated a photography studio in

Naarm/Melbourne for a length of tenure beyond one year. By the 1850s, however, over seventeen businesses opened in the region in the first half of the decade alone.[19] Some of the new studios were close to the diggings. Others sent studio assistants—in Glaister's case, G. W. Perry—inland temporarily, to seek commissions from mining communities directly.[20]

We cannot determine whether Creswick miner and pastoralist John Dickson Love took his fiancée Sarah Purvis to Naarm/Melbourne for a matrimonial portrait, or if the couple waited for a photographer to visit their region (**Figure 3.4**). As an indicator of the occasion, Dickson Love holds Purvis's ring finger, as the couple pose on a chaise longue against a faux backdrop showing lavish drapery and a colonnade.[21] The portrait reflects a newly achieved level of social respectability for Dickson Love. His prospecting success, not overtly signalled in the daguerreotype, enabled his marriage and facilitated his purchase of land. This portrait sits not only at the threshold of Dickson Love's married life, but also his transition from miner to pastoralist and justice of the peace.[22]

The profit that photographers, such as Glaister, generated from mining-related patrons allowed them to expand their studio enterprises. Glaister chose to undertake this expansion while moving his business north to Gadigal Country, Sydney, in 1856. Here, he opened studio rooms on Pitt Street, this time under his own name. Glaister's Excelsior Photographic Galleries absorbed the new collodion-on-glass formats into his updated suite of portrait offerings but remained dedicated to capturing the elite and discerning end of the photographic portrait market. His instructions on dress for prospective clients became more and more elaborate. Not satisfied with simply signaling his place in the colonial studio scene through press advertisements, Glaister typeset his own four-page pamphlet in late 1856–57, sporting a wood engraving of Daguerre's own studio portrait on the front (**Figure 3.5**). Included alongside snippets of reviews laden with praise for his Pitt Street establishment were updated and more detailed directives on the fabrics, cut and colours of outfits that would take best in the monochrome format:

> Dark dresses of any material, save velvet, are preferrable for Ladies and Children; dark red, green and orange take black; dark blue takes drab; pink,

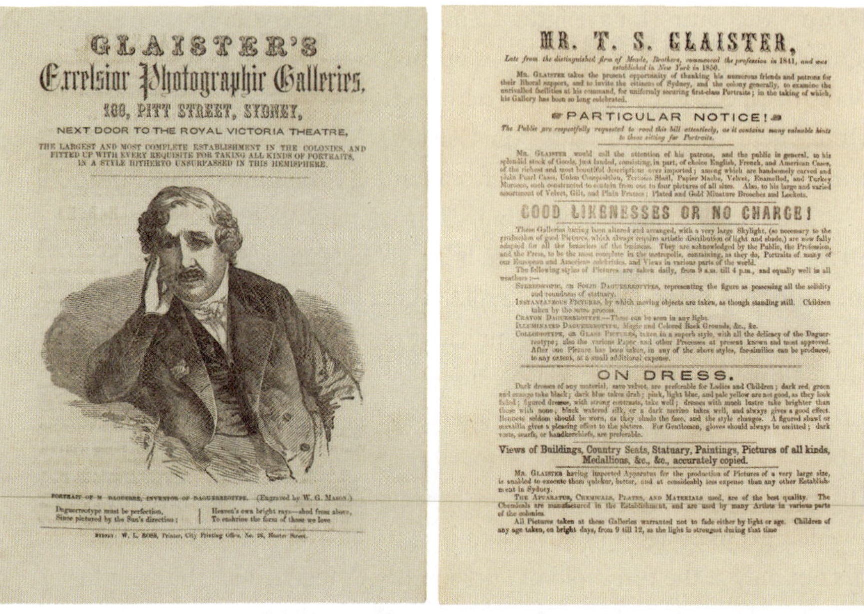

GLAISTER'S
Excelsior Photographic Galleries,
188, PITT STREET, SYDNEY,
NEXT DOOR TO THE ROYAL VICTORIA THEATRE,

THE LARGEST AND MOST COMPLETE ESTABLISHMENT IN THE COLONIES, AND FITTED UP WITH EVERY REQUISITE FOR TAKING ALL KINDS OF PORTRAITS, IN A STYLE HITHERTO UNSURPASSED IN THIS HEMISPHERE.

PORTRAIT OF M. DAGUERRE, INVENTOR OF DAGUERREOTYPE. (Engraved by W. G. MASON.)

Daguerreotype must be perfection,
Since pictured by the Sun's direction;
Heaven's own bright rays—shed from above,
To enshrine the form of those we love

SYDNEY: W. L. ROSS, Printer, City Printing Office, No. 26, Hunter Street.

MR. T. S. GLAISTER,

Late from the distinguished firm of Meade, Brothers, commenced the profession in 1841, and was established in New York in 1850.

MR. GLAISTER takes the present opportunity of thanking his numerous friends and patrons for their liberal support, and to invite the citizens of Sydney, and the colony generally, to examine the unrivalled facilities at his command, for uniformly securing first-class Portraits; in the taking of which, his Gallery has been so long celebrated.

PARTICULAR NOTICE!

The Public are respectfully requested to read this bill attentively, as it contains many valuable hints to those sitting for Portraits.

MR. GLAISTER would call the attention of his patrons, and the public in general, to his splendid stock of Goods, just landed, consisting, in part, of choice English, French, and American Cases, of the richest and most beautiful descriptions ever imported; among which are handsomely carved and plain Pearl Cases, Union Composition, Tortoise Shell, Papier Mache, Velvet, Enamelled, and Turkey Morocco, each constructed to contain from one to four pictures of all sizes. Also, to his large and varied assortment of Velvet, Gilt, and Plain Frames; Plated and Gold Miniature Brooches and Lockets.

GOOD LIKENESSES OR NO CHARGE!

These Galleries having been altered and arranged, with a very large Skylight, (so necessary to the production of good Pictures, which always require artistic distribution of light and shade,) are now fully adapted for all the branches of the business. They are acknowledged by the Public, the Profession, and the Press, to be the most complete in the metropolis, containing, as they do, Portraits of many of our European and American celebrities, and Views in various parts of the world.

The following styles of Pictures are taken daily, from 9 a.m. till 4 p.m., and equally well in all weathers:—

STEREOSCOPIC, or SOLID DAGUERREOTYPES, representing the figure as possessing all the solidity and roundness of statuary.

INSTANTANEOUS PICTURES, by which moving objects are taken, as though standing still. Children taken by the same process.

CRAYON DAGUERREOTYPE.—These can be seen in any light.

ILLUMINATED DAGUERREOTYPE, Magic and Colored Back Grounds, &c., &c.

COLLODIOTYPE, or GLASS PICTURES, taken in a superb style, with all the delicacy of the Daguerreotype; also the various Paper and other Processes at present known and most approved. After one Picture has been taken, in any of the above styles, fac-similies can be produced, to any extent, at a small additional expense.

ON DRESS.

Dark dresses of any material, save velvet, are preferable for Ladies and Children; dark red, green and orange take black; dark blue takes drab; pink, light blue, and pale yellow are not good, as they look faded; figured dresses, with strong contrasts, take well; dresses with much lustre take brighter than those with none; black watered silk, or a dark merino takes well, and always gives a good effect. Bonnets seldom should be worn, as they shade the face, and the style changes. A figured shawl or mantilla gives a pleasing effect to the picture. For Gentlemen, gloves should always be omitted; dark vests, scarfs, or handkerchiefs, are preferable.

Views of Buildings, Country Seats, Statuary, Paintings, Pictures of all kinds, Medallions, &c., &c., accurately copied.

MR. GLAISTER having imported Apparatus for the production of Pictures of a very large size, is enabled to execute them quicker, better, and at considerably less expense than any other Establishment in Sydney.

THE APPARATUS, CHEMICALS, PLATES, AND MATERIALS used, are of the best quality. The Chemicals are manufactured in the Establishment, and are used by many Artists in various parts of the colonies.

All Pictures taken at these Galleries warranted not to fade either by light or age. Children of any age taken, on bright days, from 9 till 12, as the light is strongest during that time

Figure 3.5: W. L. Ross (printer), *Glaister's Excelsior Photographic Galleries*, four-page pamphlet, 1856 or 1857. Cover and p. 2. State Library of New South Wales.

> light blue, and pale yellow are not good as they look faded; figured dresses, with strong contrasts, take well; dresses with much lustre take brighter than those with none; black watered silk, or a dark merino takes well, and always gives a good effect. Bonnets should seldom be worn, as they shade the face, and the style changes. A figure shawl or mantilla gives a pleasing effect to the picture. For gentlemen, gloves should always be omitted; dark vests, scarves or handkerchiefs, are preferable.[23]

Concluding this advice was a notice that his studio had imported a camera 'very large in size' for taking mammoth-plate photographs.

The chance to commission photographic portraits of such unusually large proportions must have been one of the factors that prompted Thomas and Jane Day's visit to Glaister's Excelsior Photographic Galleries in 1858. In December 1857, the *Sydney Magazine of Science and Art* had endorsed Glaister's mammoth-plate ambrotypes as 'being as nearly as possible life-size'.[24] The ambrotype is a direct positive: the glass plate, sensitised with a solution of iodised collodion and silver nitrate, was exposed in the camera, and this same plate was developed and fixed. The glass plate alone, though, produced only a cloudy, undefined photographic impression. To achieve the full tonal range, the reverse side of the exposed glass plate was painted with thick black lacquer, or the plate was cased against a piece of black felt, to fill in the definition of the dark areas of the image. It did not have the mirror-like surface of a daguerreotype, which made this format more conducive to the application of hand-colouring.

Curiously, the Days complied with some of Glaister's recommendations on dress while defying others. Thomas Day had lived in Gadigal Country since his birth on 8 February 1795.[25] He was the son of convict Thomas King, who had been transported to New South Wales aboard the *Scarborough* as part of the Second Fleet.[26] King was sentenced to seven years' imprisonment at London's Old Bailey on 29 October 1783. His offence was the theft of a bundle of haberdashery that included two muslin aprons, three handkerchiefs, two caps, three lace ribbons and five plain ribbons.[27] This term was increased to life and coupled with transportation to New South Wales when King absconded from his hulk.[28] Nevertheless, after making the passage, the subsequent colonial phase of King's sentence was quickly reduced, leading, ironically, to a career in policing, where he assumed the surname 'Day' as part of his self-reinvention.[29] His son, Glaister's portrait subject, made a considerable fortune in the boat building industry and owned a large house, Rose Cottage, on Gadigal Country at Pyrmont.[30] Seventy-five years after Thomas King's original sentence for haberdashery theft, his daughter-in-law sat in front of Glaister's mammoth-plate camera in an outfit variously trimmed and tailored with ribbon and lace (**Figure 3.6**). Both Thomas and Jane Day's garments are in fabrics of a notable lustre, and in colours that took well and preserved their definition photographically. However, Jane chose to retain her lace-trimmed cap for the portrait and Thomas removed only one of his gloves for the sitting (**Figure 3.7**), contrary to Glaister's published advice and indicating the specific preferences of his clients.

At the significant size of 53 × 47 cm framed, and overlayed heavily with paint, Thomas and Jane Day's portraits sit somewhere between the

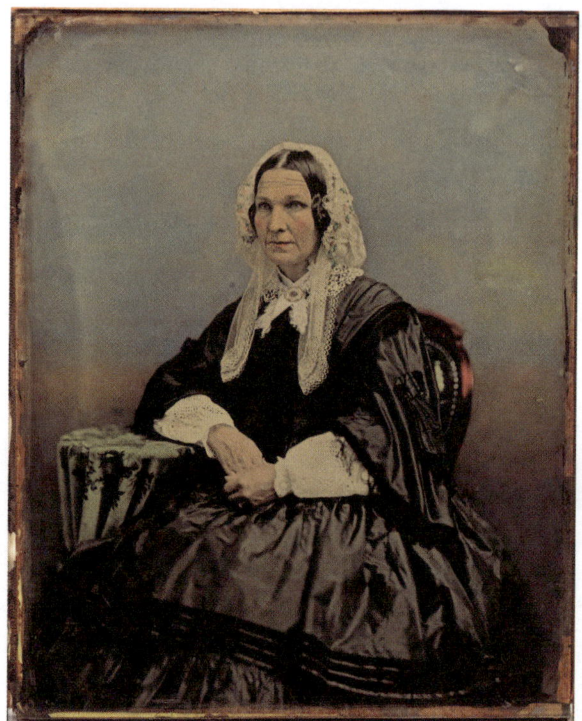

Figure 3.6: T.S. Glaister 'Jane Day (née Fairweather)', 1858, mammoth-plate, hand-painted, framed ambrotype (shown here unframed). 29 × 23.7 cm (image); 53 × 47 cm (framed). State Library of New South Wales.

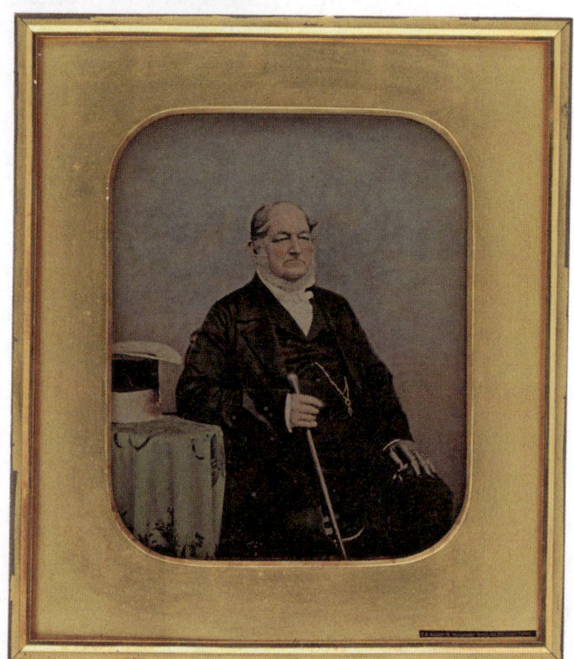

Figure 3.7: T.S. Glaister, 'Thomas Day', 1858, mammoth-plate, hand-painted, framed ambrotype. 29 × 23.7 cm (image); 53 × 47 cm (framed). State Library of New South Wales.

logic and materiality of a photograph and an oil-on-canvas. The expense of this commission would have been compounded substantially by the extensive hand-colouring. Glaister's studio produced daguerreotypes, ambrotypes, and salted paper and albumen prints, from sizes small enough to fit into lockets and up to this mammoth-plate format. The spectrum of dimensions was coupled with Glaister's guarantee that his portraits 'would not fade' and his boast that his was 'the only establishment where a Photograph Coloured in Oil could be obtained'.[31] Certainly, as we have seen, many artists were using gold paint to tint and accent aspects of their photographs by the late 1850s. Glaister's Warrane/Sydney competitors, such as the studio of Edwin Dalton, were also beginning to employ a colour palette to enrich their otherwise monochrome photographs.[32] Both Glaister and Dalton were part of a broader colonial tradition of idiosyncratic photographic colouring that had begun in the commercial studios of lutruwita/Van Diemen's Land during the 1840s, and was well established in the southern colony by the 1860s.[33]

The examples of Glaister's work in public collections today are distinctive for the extent of their hand- colouring and the subtlety of their palette. His distinguishing style is especially apparent in how colour is used to enliven skin tone, in the fine colour-tinting applied to the eyes, and in the way colour articulates tiny patterns and embellishments on the clothing.[34] This gravitation towards life-likeness in both colour and proportions positions Jane and Thomas Day's ambrotype portraits as objects of posterity.[35] Further celebrated with large gold frames, these images were not meant to be gifted for private contemplation, as was the envisaged use of cased photographs. Exacting in the manner of a photograph but with a vitality achieved through paint, the Days' portraits project an achieved colonial social status. We can imagine them hanging in a prominent position in the couple's property—the photographs themselves entangled in the story of colonial property—crafting a visual dynasty for their family.

Back on the Victorian goldfields, more modestly sized cased ambrotypes were being commissioned by men in the mining districts whose fortunes were changing. Most studio portraits from mining contexts, now housed in Australian collections, are of Anglo-American

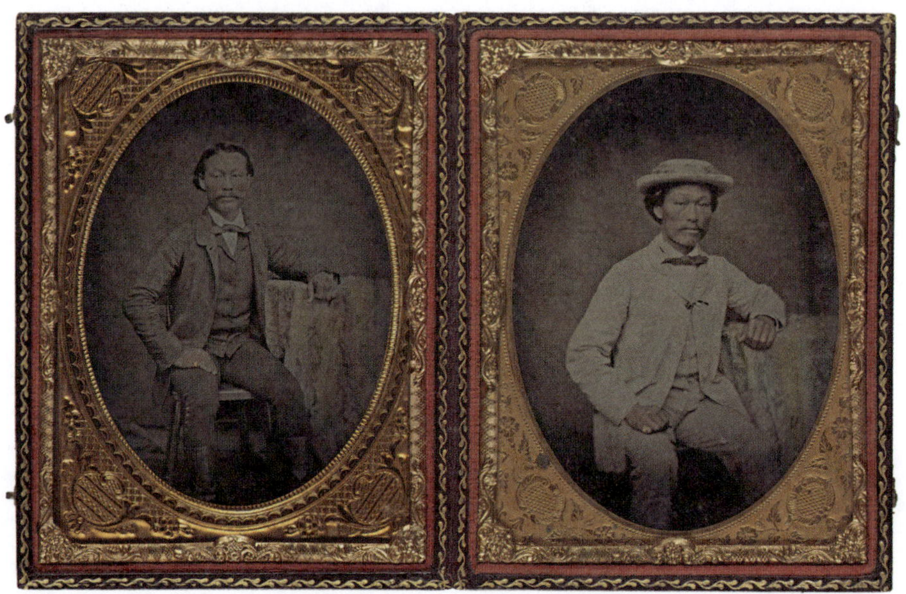

Figure 3.8: Unattributed, 'Henry Kay', 1860s, quarter-plate pair of colour-tinted, cased ambrotypes. State Library of Victoria.

miners—that is, 'white' settler colonists. Chinese miners appear in street photographs and documentary images of mining activities, as is the case in the Dunolly series discussed in Chapter 4. However, miners of Chinese heritage are virtually absent from mid-century colonial studio photography. This does not necessarily indicate the exclusively 'white' patronage of these businesses. More likely, the racially skewed sample reflects how these images were used. Itinerant and international miners would have sent their photographic portraits home or took them when they left the colonies.[36] Within local collections, only one mid-century cased photograph of a Chinese miner is known, that of Henry Kay. Kay was one of around 24,000 Chinese-born prospectors who travelled and worked in colonial Victoria during the middle decades of the nineteenth century. For Kay, this was a circuitous passage. He had first panned for gold in California before sailing across the Pacific in 1853. After landing in Warrane/Sydney Cove, he made his way south to the Stawell and Ararat fields on Dja Dja Wurrung Country.[37] By 1870, Kay had ascended to the position of manager for the Albion Gold Mining Company at Avoca.[38]

He sat in the studio of an unrecorded photographer around the time of his promotion (**Figure 3.8**).

Kay's portraits are exceptional for how they illuminate the ambrotype's contingency on the opposition between light and dark, and play with the studio as a site of self-fashioning. They are packaged side by side in a twin case. This presentation was almost universally used to signify a pairing or relationship across portraits: for instance, that of a husband and wife, or siblings.[39] Kay, however, commissioned two photographs of himself to make up the couplet. In one, he appears dressed in a light-coloured linen suit, accessorised with a miner's flat straw hat. In the other, he is outfitted in a dark three-piece suit with riding boots and his hair is sleeked back. Although the angle of the camera has been slightly altered between the exposures, we can assume that these ambrotypes were taken in successive sittings on the same day, due to how colour (some of which is now dissipated) was applied identically to his cheeks and the side table in each frame. Kay also sports the same starched white shirt, flat bow tie and gold-accented signet ring in both portraits. These portraits show Henry Kay in black and in white, in an ambrotype format that itself required these same initially separate, but ultimately combined, tonalities to make the photograph visible. This commission's curious presentation completes the performance of the subject's ascent in occupation and class. Kay flaunts for the studio photographer's camera his navigation across labouring and administrative professions, which ultimately enabled his portrait commission.

At the Threshold of Photography and the Studio

The studio would continue to be the site for orchestrated performances of identity as the nineteenth century progressed. However, its interior spaces were increasingly unable to contain the practice of portrait photography. We see this in how the business of the studio evolved, particularly in mining districts. English-born entertainer Henry Beaufoy Merlin had cultivated an itinerant studio business, alongside occupations as a puppeteer and panorama painter, in the Australian colonies since 1848. In 1866, he employed 16-year-old Charles Bayliss as his photography studio assistant in Naarm/Melbourne.[40] The pair toured widely in regional Victoria and New South Wales, photographing street and outdoor scenes. In 1872, they paused to open a dedicated studio, the American and Australasian Photographic Company, having followed the gold rushes to Wiradjuri Country, Hill End. Merlin and Bayliss's business was on Tambaroora Street, in the town centre, where they took portraits while also offering their services in photographically documenting mining claims.[41] The year of the American and Australasian Photographic Company's establishment in Hill End coincided with the extraction of one of the largest gold nuggets to be unearthed in the Australian colonies. This was achieved by a mining syndicate, Star of Hope, headed by German immigrant Bernhardt Otto Holtermann. Bayliss and Merlin went on to photograph Holtermann with the nugget.

Holtermann's syndicate of eight miners located a 286-kilogram lump of ore, consisting of a mixture of slate, quartz and gold, in the early hours of 19 October 1872.[42] When day broke, Merlin and Bayliss were summoned to document both the specimen and the party of ecstatic miners. In **Figure 3.9**, we see the nugget supported by a trestle, or perhaps a repurposed studio brace. It was photographed outside, against a white wall, in the strong morning light. A piece of card outlining the nugget's dimensions and weight was placed against the collodion glass negative during the printing process, giving an extra sense of legibility to the nugget in the albumen print. The print was additionally hand-coloured to emphasise and differentiate the mineral consistency of the rock. Holtermann was also photographed with the nugget by Merlin and Bayliss at Hill End. In **Figure 3.10**, he stands next to the rocky mass for the camera. In the sparse, intensely lit setting, his body functions as a further index to the scale of the specimen, while his hand rests on the nugget's penultimate jagged peak as an articulation of claim of ownership for the camera.

Holtermann attempted to buy out the other syndicate members' shares in the nugget, but an agreement could not be reached and, as a result, the specimen was crushed and its component parts separated within a month of its extraction.[43] Perhaps as a reflection of his disappointment with these events, Holtermann set out to further memorialise

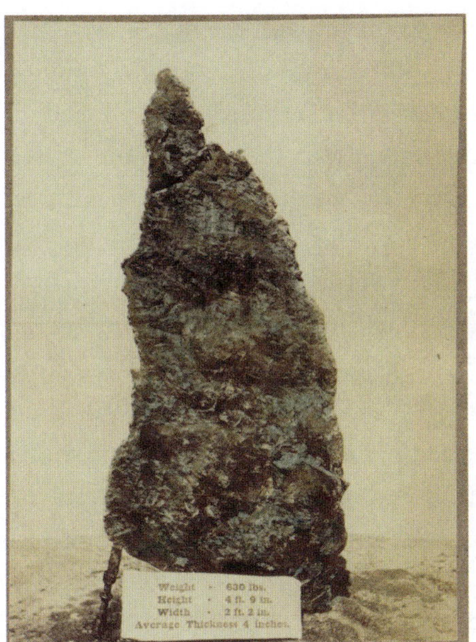

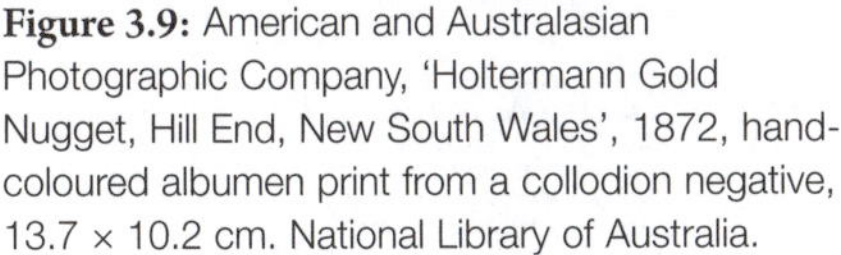
Figure 3.9: American and Australasian Photographic Company, 'Holtermann Gold Nugget, Hill End, New South Wales', 1872, hand-coloured albumen print from a collodion negative, 13.7 × 10.2 cm. National Library of Australia.

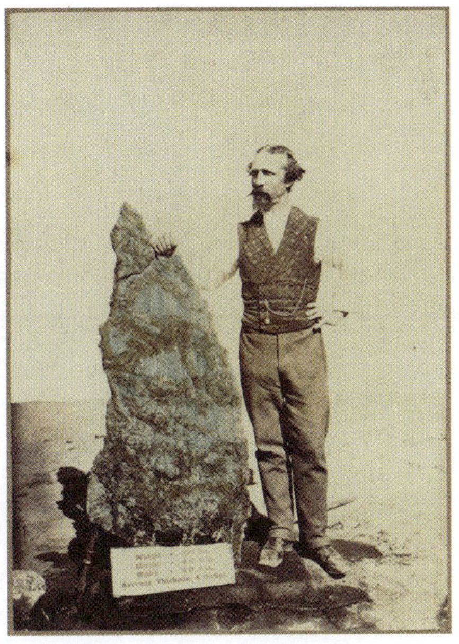
Figure 3.10: American and Australasian Photographic Company, 'B.O. Holtermann with the Holtermann gold nugget, Hill End, New South Wales', 1872, hand-coloured albumen print from a collodion negative, 16.3 × 11.7 cm. National Library of Australia.

photographically the trophy nugget and his association with its discovery. An additional portrait exists of Holtermann posing in the American and Australasian Photographic Company studio, perhaps in Wiradjuri Country, Hill End, or maybe in Cammeraygal Country, Sydney, where both Holtermann and Bayliss subsequently settled. This version, which survives as a collodion negative, shows Holtermann posing without the specimen, against a dark studio backdrop in a rather dusty space (**Figure 3.11**). He appears in the same outfit he originally wore in **Figure 3.10**, although it is neater and more well defined in this context of less intense light. Holtermann stands supported by a full-length studio brace, which can be seen behind his lower legs. But a second studio brace, upon which Holtermann rests one hand, is present in the portrait, fully revealed to the camera. This indiscreet use of studio props suggests that this version was never intended to be a 'complete' portrait in and of itself.

Later iterations of Holtermann's portrait with the nugget were not straightforward studio productions but composite images, compiled from several photographic experiences. For example, the portrait in **Figure 3.12** appears to show Holtermann with the nugget, much later, between 1875 and 1876, at the doorway of the mansion he built on Cammeraygal Country in North Sydney. This residence was completed in 1875, long after the specimen had been crushed. Indeed, Holtermann's share in the nugget's value contributed to funding the completion of the mansion. Consequently, the portrait in **Figure 3.12** is contrived from multiple negatives: one of the nugget, as it was captured in Wiradjuri Country, Hill End; one of Holtermann, most likely in the same studio session that issued the staged portrait in **Figure 3.11**, since he wears the same outfit; and one simply of the entranceway to his new home, against which sections of the two former images were collaged. After Merlin died in 1873, Bayliss was commissioned to undertake additional photographic

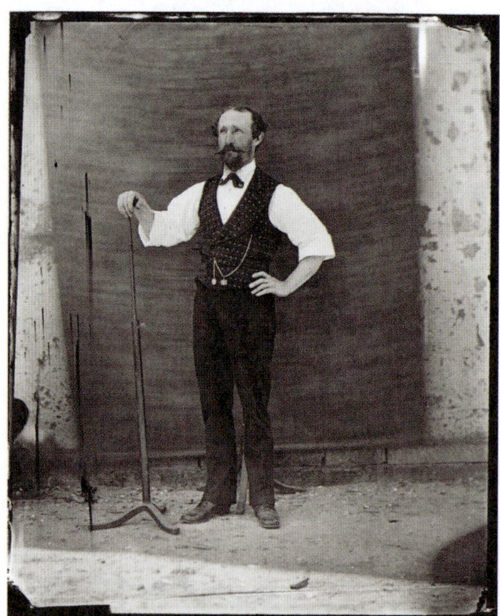

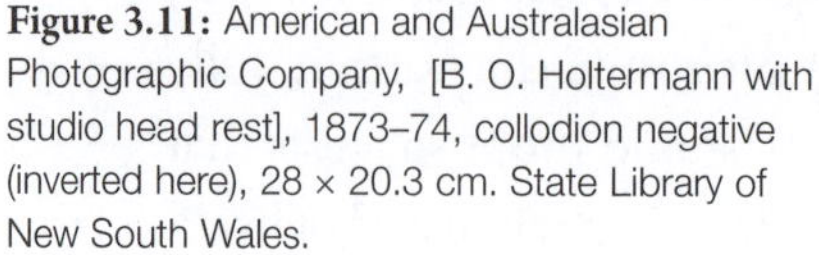

Figure 3.11: American and Australasian Photographic Company, [B. O. Holtermann with studio head rest], 1873–74, collodion negative (inverted here), 28 × 20.3 cm. State Library of New South Wales.

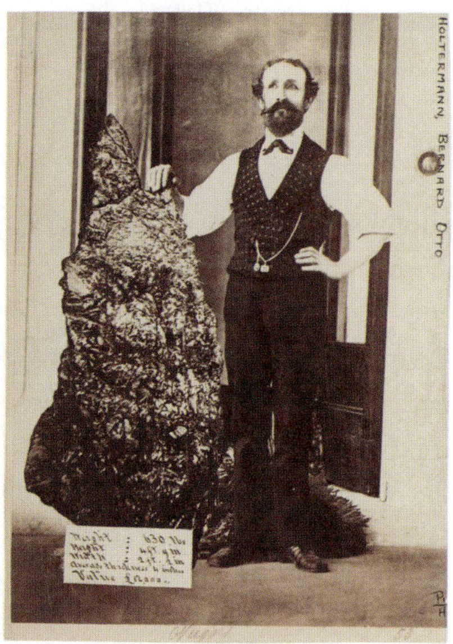

Figure 3.12: American and Australasian Photographic Company, 'B. O. Holtermann with the Holtermann Nugget', 1874–76, 28 × 20.3 cm, albumen print from multiple collodion negatives. State Library of New South Wales.

productions for Holtermann, which famously included a 23-frame panorama of Warrane/Sydney Cove, shot from the turret of Holtermann's mansion, discussed further in Chapter 4.[44]

Other versions of Holtermann's trophy portrait were made later in the 1870s. One recontextualises Holtermann with the photographed nugget in a fictitious romanticised rural scene rendered in watercolour and ink.[45] We see, then, how a tradition of hand-colouring photography, begun in the 1840s and mastered by studios such as Glaister's in the 1850s, was not necessarily improved as the century progressed but built upon to construct new 'truths' photographically. The photographic production surrounding the nugget shows how photography itself was employed as an elaborate trophy of mining success. But Holtermann and the American and Australasian Photographic Company did not engineer this use of the medium. Rather, they were part of a succession of vainglorious colonial men who brought valuable ore to the photography studio.

Family, Photography and the Studio Enterprise

Other migrant photographers made brief forays into the goldfield economies before pursuing studio businesses that connected to pastoral wealth. Much like Thomas Glaister, American-born, New York-trained photographer Townsend Duryea arrived in colonial Victoria with a high degree of technical skill in the daguerreotype process, on account of his design of photographic equipment. Duryea had probably worked in an American east coast studio, but it was not one whose name he evoked in the colonies.[46] In June 1852, he had lodged a patent from Williamsburg, New York, for a wheel and rotor-based apparatus constructed to evenly apply pressure in a circular motion when polishing silver-coated copper daguerreotype plates (**Figure 3.13**).[47] This device was meant to be a substitute for the hand-held polishing bow that often left lined scratches on the daguerreotype's silver-plated surface. However, the customs records do not suggest that Duryea intended to practise photography in the colonies. Indeed, he was in possession of a miner's gold-washing trough after disembarking the *Canton*, at Boon Wurrung Country, Port Phillip, on 25 August 1853.[48] His prospecting ambitions proved short-lived,

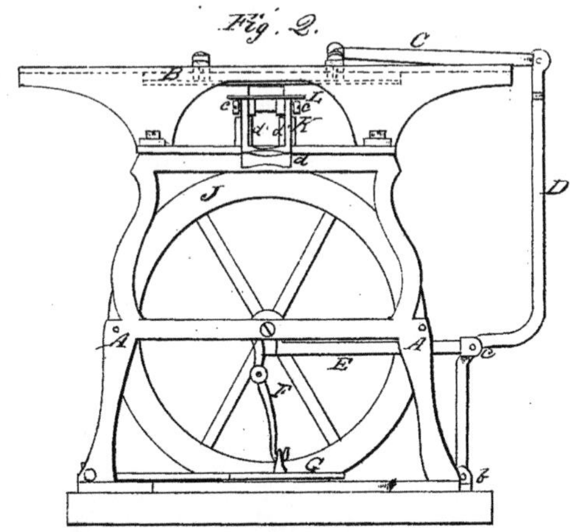

Figure 3.13: 'View 2' [where 'L' marks the position of the daguerreotype plate] from, 'Patent no. 9018: T. Dureya Polishing Plates' , 15 June 1852, Washington D.C. United States Patent Office. National Archives and Records Administration, Maryland.

however, and he soon reverted to his former trade, offering his miners' gold washer for sale from his colonial photography studio on Collins Street in October 1853.[49]

The Duryea name is prominent in histories of colonial photography. Nevertheless, the extent of the Duryea studio's activities has been masked by exhibitions that, in focusing on one state or colony's photographic history, have not had the capacity to reveal the full scope of the studio's trade.[50] Townsend Duryea was involved in studio businesses from 1853 until his last studio was destroyed by fire on 18 April 1875.[51] During this period, he partnered with multiple other photographers. Some, such as Archibald McDonald, his first collaborator in Naarm/Melbourne, and Nicholas Caire, his later pupil in Tarntanya/Adelaide, would go on to develop independent colonial practices. In this sense, the Duryea studio was responsible for spawning a culture of colonial photography bigger than the name itself. Duryea's longest-standing partner, though, was his own brother Sanford, who followed him out from North America. Between 1853 and 1863, together and separately, the Duryea brothers operated studios that spanned the continent. No other colonial studio enterprise, earlier or later in the nineteenth century, achieved quite this breadth of practice.

The success and stretch of the Duryea studio lay in the dexterity with which it negotiated its business in the colonial capitals, while also locking into the sprawling traffic and trade of hinterland districts. Duryea and McDonald, for example, operated two studios simultaneously from November 1853. One was in the heart of Naarm/Melbourne's commercial district and a second was on Yarra Street, Djilang/Geelong, which a young Charles Nettleton joined briefly in 1854.[52] The port at Djilang/Geelong was a funnel for much of the produce from Victoria's wool and raw commodity industries. Pastoralist families such as the Hentys had built storehouses near the docks, for produce awaiting transportation back to England. The studio's proximity to this commercial junction was intended to save prospective portrait customers a trip into the capital, securing their custom before they could visit a rival business.

Figure 3.14: Duryea Brothers Studio, [unidentified family group], c. 1856, half-plate, uncoloured, card-framed, daguerreotype. Art Gallery of South Australia.

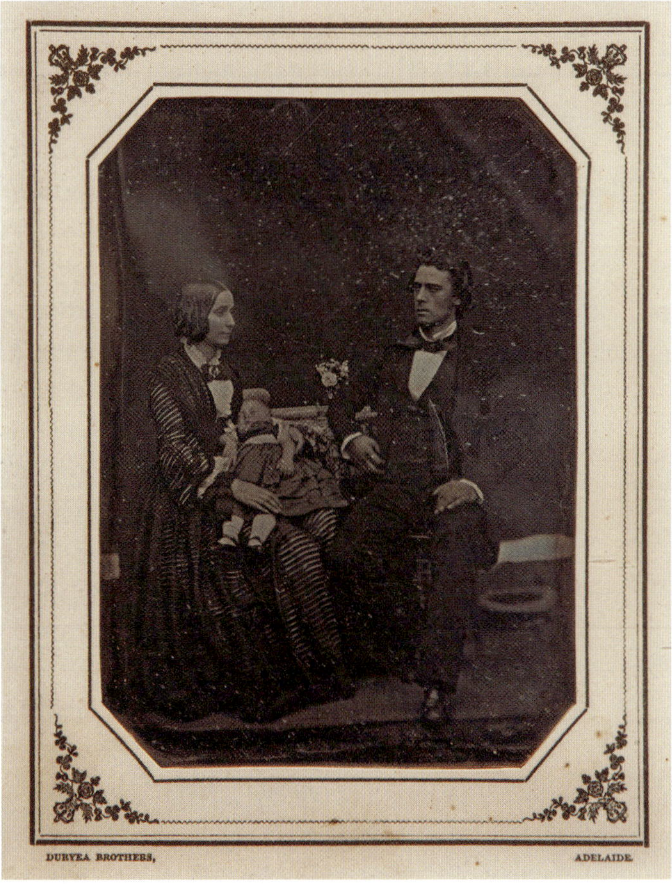

Importantly, Duryea and his partners conceived of the studio in expansive terms, both in relation to the geographies from which it solicited business and who it targeted as patrons. In 1854, Duryea and McDonald extended their studios' presence as far as Launceston in lutruwita/Tasmania, although their partnership later dissolved. In August 1854, Sanford Duryea arrived from New York to join Townsend in the colonial studio scene.[53] The younger brother travelled on to Tarntanya/Adelaide to set up what would become the rooms of the Duryea brothers' next studio, on King William Street. Here the brothers appealed for the custom of colonial men and women, and also that of colonial families.[54] The oldest extant image from any Duryea studio comes from this location, at least two years after Townsend Duryea had begun practising as a colonial photographer. It shows a young couple with their infant child and is composed with some of the hallmarks of a conversation piece (**Figure 3.14**). The man and woman are turned towards each other, placing them in dialogue more with one another than with the photographer, crafting an intimate scene. The angle of the woman's chair ensures that the young child she holds in her lap is on full display to the camera. The infant is almost certainly asleep to facilitate its stillness for the daguerreotype's lengthy exposure. Post-mortem photography was prevalent at this time on account of high infant mortality from infectious diseases.[55] However, here neither parent is dressed in mourning attire. There is a sense that the daguerreotype is as much about the child as about either adult. In the photographer's effort to capture the child still and in full view, other compositional elements have been given less consideration. The posy of flowers on the studio table is partially obscured and awkwardly placed behind the father's elbow, and his hat lies unceremoniously discharged on the floor behind him, but in full view of the camera. Perhaps the daguerreotype was intended to introduce the child to recipients of the portrait who may not have been able to travel. Or perhaps the commission was simply for the parents, in celebration of their growing family.

Families were coveted subjects for colonial photography studios because their patronage meant a larger plate (at considerable expense) or multiple portrait exposures. The Duryea firm is interesting because the unit of the family was also built into the business design. Rather than have both brothers working in the King William Street rooms, often one or both would leave Tarntanya/Adelaide to seek custom from surrounding pastoral districts. Between late 1856 and much of 1857, the Duryea brothers travelled through Kaurna, Meru, Ngadjuri and Ngarrindjeri Country, appealing for commissions from landed colonial families.

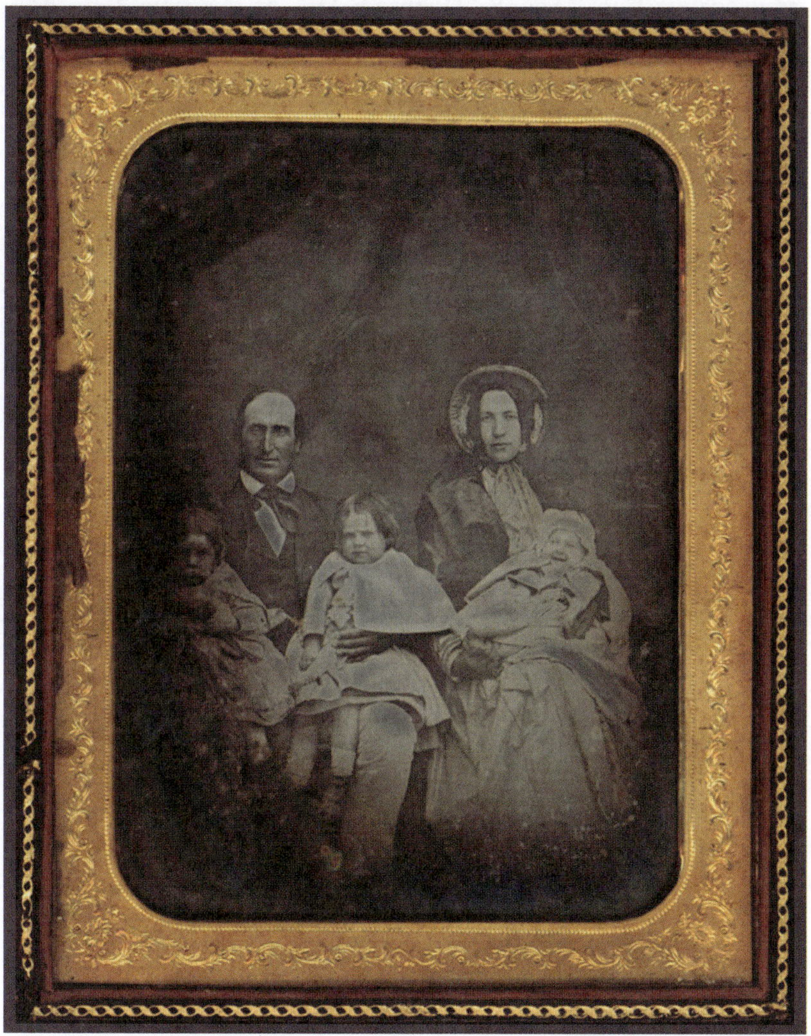

Figure 3.15: Unattributed (likely, Townsend or Sanford Duryea), 'John and Rebecca Ross and three of their five children', 1856–57, half-plate, uncoloured, cased daguerreotype. State Library of South Australia.

Their route zigzagged between the high country and the southern coast, covering the colonial towns of Strathalbyn, Macclesfield, Mount Barker, Woodside, Lobethal, Port Elliot, Goolwa, Milang, Willunga, Aldinga, Burra, Kapunda, Clare and Auburn.[56] At each of these locations, the Duryea studio was without commercial photographic peer or competition. The Duryeas are probably responsible for the portrait of the Ross family dating from 1856–57 (**Figure 3.15**). At this time, John Ross managed the 800-square-mile sheep station of wealthy grazier Charles Brown Fisher, on unceded Ngadjuri Country at Hill River, near Clare.[57] Ross is photographed with his first wife, Rebecca, and the first three of their five children, Sarah, Rebecca and Henrietta.[58] The photographer has commanded the attention of each child, even capturing the youngest infant relatively still but, remarkably, holding a smile. They have, though, struggled with regulating the light. The daughters and their mother have dressed in light-coloured outfits. The capes of the girls' dresses, the swaddling and bonnet of the baby, and even the father's shirt collar, have solarised, an effect in early photographic chemistry where the whites move into the blue spectrum because of an intensity and overexposure of light. This imperfection, rendered in photographic chemistry rather achieved with the application of paint, indicates a strong midday sun high in the sky. It implies the Ross family portrait could have been taken in a provisional outdoor studio the Duryeas assembled from cloth and furniture along their itinerant route.[59]

The Duryea photography studio was intricately implicated in the colony of South Australia's pastoral economy. While on tour, Townsend Duryea used a vacant yard behind his Tarntanya/Adelaide premises to build a 30-foot cutter that would come to have an important role in consolidating his relationship with pastoral communities.[60] At any one time, the Duryeas were only a few days' travel away from the colonial capital, which would have made it possible for Townsend to return to oversee the construction of the vessel. The deck beams were built of Singapore cedar, the keel and stern of Swan River Mahogany, and the deck flooring of American pine.[61] These were important regions for timber but also nodal points for the photography trade generally and, as will become apparent, the Duryeas' studio specifically.

The Duryeas' itinerant photography studio had progressed south to the coastal colonial towns near the Millewa/Murray River estuary by mid-1857. Here, pastoralists around Strathalbyn, Port Elliot, Goolwa and Milang were struggling to sell their grain, due to the lack of available ships to transport their produce to the Tarntanya/Adelaide market. To service the grain trade, the Milang Ploughers Association had commissioned the construction of a large steamer, which was to be launched in August 1857.[62] This was the same month the itinerant Duryea studio was in Milang. Townsend's newly completed cutter, intended to supplement the steamer's service of the grain trade, sailed down from Tarntanya/Adelaide for the ceremony. The 'daguerreotypist's vessel' was a widely anticipated and celebrated addition to the occasion.[63] The cutter symbolises the level of entanglement between the newly sprawling culture of colonial studio photography and the expansion of agrarian colonial commerce. The international materials sourced for its construction demonstrate the extent of the profits generated by the Duryeas' photography business during the mid-1850s, which are otherwise not represented in the quantity of their photographs surviving in Australian public collections today. More than this, though, Duryea's sailing boat highlights how colonial studio photography was not simply a venue for documenting the fortunes of colonial families who followed the extension of the frontier. The profits from studios such as the Duryeas' were actively reinvested back into aspects of the pastoral economy and its logistics of trade.[64]

The financial success of the Duryeas' itinerant studio is further confirmed by the brothers' decision in October 1857 to invest in a new chapter of westward travel. Rather than renewing their Tarntanya/Adelaide rooms after eleven months on the road, they opted to head in the direction of one of Townsend's shipbuilding timber supply lines: the Swan River Colony, on Whadjuk Noongar Country. The next iteration of their rooms opened on St Georges Terrace, Boorloo/Perth, on 26 October 1857.[65] By this time, photography had already been introduced to the colony, but the studio culture was not firmly established. South Australian photographer Robert Hall had offered daguerreotype portraits from the Leeder's Hotel in Boorloo/Perth for eight days during November 1846.[66] Other brief photographic opportunities were represented by ticket-of-leave convict

Edward E. Miller, who advertised his availability in providing instruction in the daguerreotype process 'as practiced in London' during March 1852.[67] There is no evidence Miller was taking commissions for portraits and the short period of his advertisement does not suggest he was successful in recruiting any pupils. A New York daguerreotypist, Samuel Scriven Evans, achieved a slightly more sustained practice operating from hotel rooms, first in Walyalup/Fremantle between mid-March to mid-May 1853, and then in Boorloo/Perth between 9 November 1853 and early January 1854.[68] The Duryea studio would be distinguished from these earlier fleeting studios and photographic endeavours, which had occupied only a transitory role in the Boorloo/Perth colonial portrait market.

It is certainly the Duryea studio that was responsible for the daguerreotype of John Septimus Roe, his wife Matilda, and their three youngest children, Alice, George and Augustus[69] (**Figure 3.16**). The Roes were a prominent colonial family. John and Matilda migrated from England in 1829 for his appointment as surveyor general of the Swan River Colony, established on unceded Whadjak Noongar Country during the same year. This was a position Roe held for over three decades, despite arriving in the colony with imperfect vision resulting from an eye injury sustained during his prior naval career.[70] Roe was active in the town planning of Walyalup/Fremantle but also undertook sixteen surveying expeditions during the 1830s and 1840s, carving out the frontier.[71] As Joanna Gilmour writes, the Roes had thirteen children, all of whom were born in the Swan River Colony.[72]

The half-plate size (10.8 × 14 cm) of the Roes' portrait is typical in its dimensions of the larger format of plates that issued from the Duryea studio. The Ross family portrait (**Figure 3.16**), back in South Australia, is tinged blue where the daguerreotypist struggled to control the exposure, causing some of the whites to solarise and shift beyond the monochrome spectrum. In the Roe family's portrait, by contrast, blue pigment has been purposefully applied to the chequered pattern of the younger boy's frock, Matilda's skirt and the older sister's dress. Additionally, gold paint accents the buttons, belt clasps, ladies' brooches and piping of the legs of John's trousers. These additions show how the Duryeas incorporated a restricted palette of colour-tinting into their business during the late 1850s, well

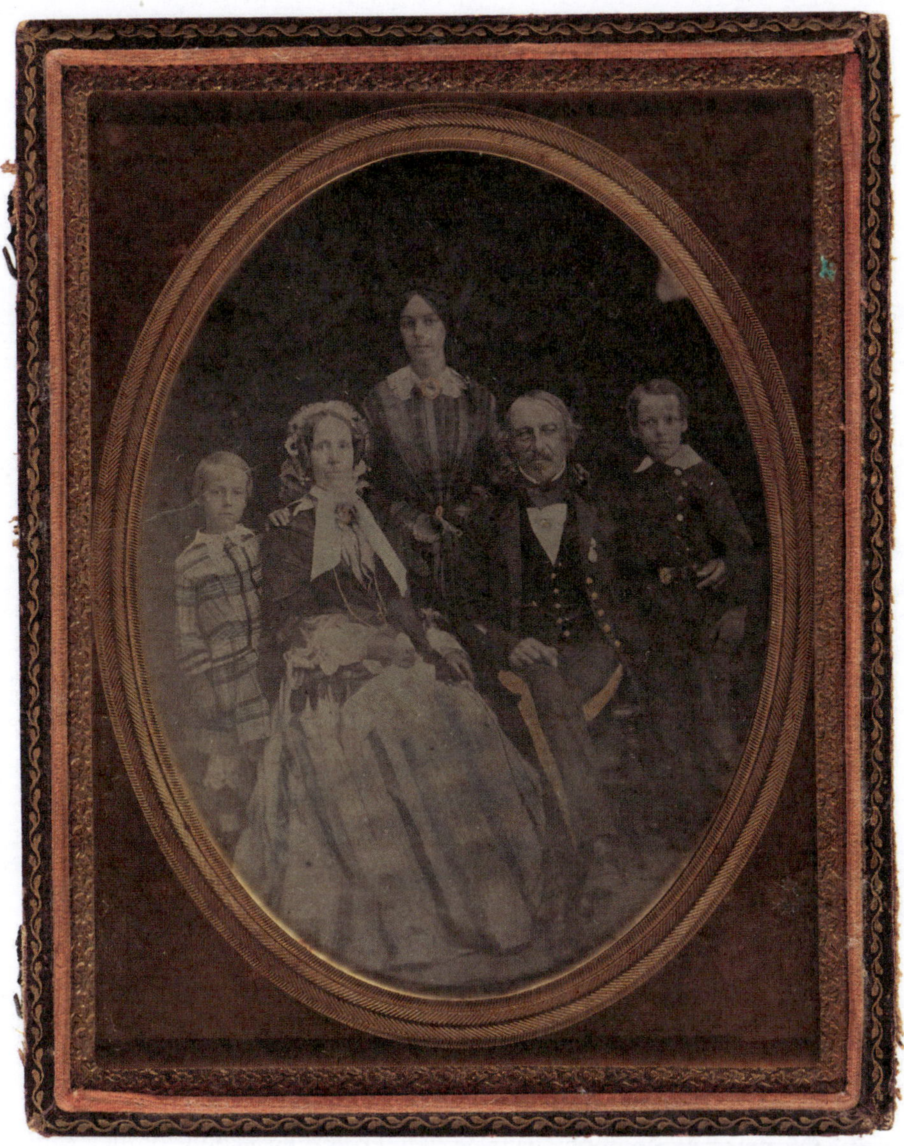

Figure 3.16: Unattributed (likely, Townsend or Sanford Duryea), 'Captain and Mrs J.S. Roe and family', [Captain John Septimus Roe (b. 1797) and Matilda Roe (b. 1805) with Alice (b. 6 August 1845), George (b. 11 June 1848) and Augustus (b. 7 January 1852)], 1857–59, half-plate, colour-tinted, cased daguerreotype. State Library of Western Australia.

after other east coast studios had introduced this practice.[73] The Roes look steadfastly and in unison at the photographer—except for John, whose damaged eye, on our right-hand side, trails off to the side of the camera.

The Duryeas practised photography in partnership in Boorloo/Perth until January 1858, after which time Townsend returned to Tarntanya/Adelaide. Sanford continued the Western Australian arm of the business until September 1859, taking the studio north to Champion Bay, and south-east to connect with pastoral communities in York, Toodyay, Guildford, Bunbury and Vasse. As the York correspondent for the *Inquirer* relayed in May 1858: 'Mr Duryea, the daguerreotypist, is at present in this town, and I observe he gets pretty considerable custom: his portraits are exceedingly good'.[74] The Boorloo/Perth studio operated intermittently between these excursions, with only one rival business: that of part-time schoolteacher Alfred Perkins Curtis, who, from September 1858, offered portraits 'on paper' and 'on glass' by means of the collodion process, in the afternoons.[75] As with the Duryeas' travels around regional South Australia, the entire tenure of their regional Western Australian itinerant studio has until now been represented by only a single portrait. Held in a private collection, it is of Edward and Theodosia Hester and their five young children.[76] Edward came from an extended family of frontier pastoralists and lived on Kaniyang Noongar Country, just outside Bunbury, where he worked as the police magistrate.[77]

One reason for the scarcity of extant daguerreotypes from the Duryeas' first decade of studio practice is that they encouraged clients to send their portraits to relatives overseas. In Boorloo/Perth, for example, Sanford extolled how the cased housing of the daguerreotype portrait was primed for travel through any climate.[78] Like many of the early studios already discussed, the Duryeas did not stamp or emboss their cased portraits with the studio name or brand (they did so only for their card-framed daguerreotypes). There are six half-plate cased daguerreotypes in Western Australian collections that accord with the route of the Duryeas' studio and have identified sitters having come down through colonial family collections.[79] Connecting family history data with knowledge of photographers' itineraries (and products) would most likely attribute a larger body of daguerreotypes remaining in Western Australia today to the Duryea studio. This would still only reflect a small part of what must have amounted to hundreds of commissioned daguerreotypes that helped to keep the studio operational for two years. In September 1859, Sanford Duryea returned to Tarntanya/Adelaide to join his brother's rooms, and in 1863, he left the colonies to venture back to North America. By this time, Townsend Duryea had expanded his business into albumen prints from collodion negatives. The paper nature of this process and the tradition of mounting the prints on card meant that Duryea's portraits were distinguished by an identifiable brand. Imprinted on the reverse of the card is the insignia of his studio and below the photograph itself is Townsend Duryea's name. Printing technologies in the 1860s certainly enabled the Duryea studio to gain traction in the colonial photographic marketplace, but the scale and financial success of the Duryea Brothers earlier partnership is also significant. The proceeds of their daguerreotype studio(s) were substantial enough to fund the construction of a cutter. During this early period, they devised a business around venturing into pastoral districts to connect with agrarian wealth and funnel it into the photography studio. This was a business practice Townsend maintained for the remainder of his colonial career.

Facing the Camera

The corollary of the expanding inland mining and pastoral industries was the forceful and often violent dispossession of Aboriginal people from Country. Across all the studio photography experiences discussed above were Aboriginal encounters with photographers and camera technologies. For example, T. S. Glaister's portraits of wealthy colonists extended to families such as that of Josiah and Eliza Harpur. Eliza was the daughter of Wesleyan pastor William Walker, who worked as a missionary and farmer on unceded Dharug Country.[80] The Harpurs' infant children, Jane and Susanna, were photographed around 1860 in Gadigal Country, Sydney, where Josiah was a merchant and newspaper proprietor. Their portraits were taken with an Aboriginal (possibly Wiradjuri) woman, 'Jerimin Medley', who was indentured in the family's domestic service.[81] Glaister took at least two ambrotypes of the group.[82] During the 1860s, Townsend

Duryea was also responsible for the studio photography of Ngarrindjeri people, probably brought to his expanded sun-lit rooms on Grenfell and King William Streets in Tarntanya/Adelaide. Taken in the new albumen print format, one of these portraits is now held in the South Australian Museum, while others were printed as a photographic insert and illustrative frontispiece to Rev. George Talpin's *The Narrinyeri* [sic] (1874).[83]

As Michael Aird has argued, colonial photographic portraits 'have been used to exclude Aboriginal People from their history and identity', re-enacting the dispossession and displacement acutely experienced firsthand.[84] Such exclusions happened in the moment of composition in the studio, as is the case with Glaister's ambrotype, where 'Jerimin Medley' was configured in relation to her status within the Harpur family, rather than within her own Kin and Country. Townsend Duryea's five portraits of Ngarrindjeri men and women—shown variously bare-chested, in meagre European tunics and, in the case of one man, outfitted in a three-piece suit—were employed to supposedly document the potential of the Ngarrindjeri to become 'civilised'. The sitters did not have their individual identities recorded alongside their portraits and, in the context of Talpin's publication, the images were mobilised ideologically to illustrate his own colonial understanding of the Ngarrindjeri. This disassociation and reconfiguration of Aboriginal identity did not only happen in the colonial studio but also once portraits left these locations. Douglas Kilburn's 1845 portraits of Kulin men and women, taken at his Naarm/Melbourne rooms, show his sitters wrapped in possum skins and displaying their scarification for the camera, as an articulation and inscription of identity. But Kilburn sold a selection of these daguerreotypes to the *Illustrated London News*, where they were translated into engravings for publication. The most pronounced act of representational violence occurred in their translation and reproduction; the engraver covered or reimagined scarification, especially as it appeared on the chests of Kulin men and women.[85]

Toward the end of the 1850s, photographic portraits of Aboriginal people were as likely to be taken by itinerant photographers in provisional studios as in the photography rooms of colonial capitals. During this period, the colonial government of Victoria established six government 'protectorates' for Aboriginal people forcibly removed from Country. Naarm/

Melbourne-based studio photographers visited these protectorates and also toured through the stolen lands that were now pastoral estates. The most documented of the Victorian reserves was Coranderrk Aboriginal Station. Due to its proximity to Naarm/Melbourne, Coranderrk was visited from the early 1860s by several European scientists, artists, and photographers.[86] Studio portraitist Charles Walter used the collodion process to take bust-shot photographs of Elders, adults and children at Coranderrk during the early 1860s. He made small albumen silver prints, which he arranged in groupings in a sectioned frame to show at the Melbourne Intercolonial Exhibition of 1866.[87] The bust-shot format and the presentation of the images in sections with jarring titles like 'Full Blood' underscore the photographers' complicity in the representational violence of the colonial project. However, as Jane Lydon observes, these portraits were also labelled with the names of each Aboriginal sitter, and showed many of the men with parrying shields, painted broad shields and possum cloaks they had brought to Walter's provisional studio.[88] Walter's series is indicative of how multiple registers of meaning, colonial and Indigenous, were at play in photography studio productions.

We see these various registers of meaning, as well as a line of broken Aboriginal custodianship, in the 1850s to early 1860s ambrotype in **Figure 3.17**. This cased image has long been held at the National Science and Media Museum in Bradford, England. It shows eight Aboriginal men and three Aboriginal women. One of the women cradles a baby; another is dressed entirely in light colours with a pulled-back veil as a headdress, indicating this could be the occasion of a marriage (although the photograph does not make clear to which man she could be betrothed). The group is joined by a colonial couple, seated on a chaise longue that is covered with a large possum-skin rug. The group's assemblage, as well as the chaise longue, craft a simulacrum of a generic interior studio set-up, but other props and the photograph's setting mark it out as idiosyncratic. Behind the group is a fence-line entangled with shrubbery, and the logged contours of what looks like a partly constructed hops kiln or grain silo. The setting suggests the location is a pastoral station, rather than a mission station, on account of the absence of any religious symbolism such as books or bibles. The scene and its residents were captured by a

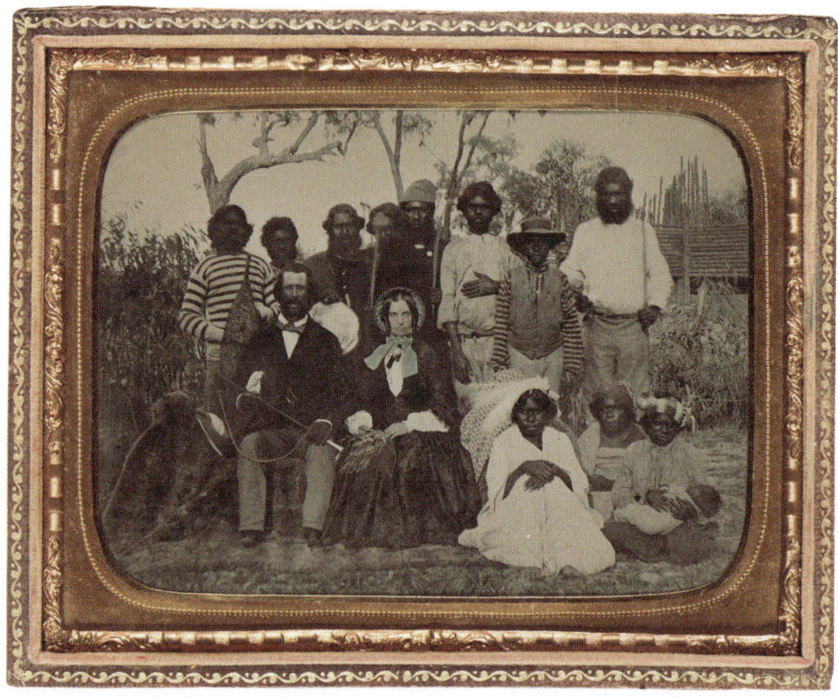

Figure 3.17: Unattributed, late 1850s to early 1860s, half-plate, colour-tinted, cased ambrotype. National Science and Media Museum, Bradford, United Kingdom.

touring or visiting photographer. While the extensive European clothing worn by the Aboriginal men and women imply the level to which their traditional way of life has been upended by their indenture as farm labourers, this is not the only story on display. The man at the left holds an incised broad shield against his body, and two of the men in the centre bear kudgeron/clubs.[89]

This group portrait was commissioned to articulate ideas of property and capital as amassed by the colonial couple in a 'new land'. This consolidation of capital extends to the possum-skin rug, which Fred Cahir has documented were in 'high demand by pastoralists'. Some colonists made their main business of trade the broking of possum-skin rug sales between Wurundjeri Boonwurrung and Wurundjeri Woi Wurrung people and European clients.[90] The colonial couple have laid out the rug to articulate their place as beneficiaries of this trade and have dressed in their finery for the photograph. The man wears suede gloves within which he balances a livestock whip. An unfurled handkerchief cascades awkwardly from his breast pocket and a watch chain loops across the buttons of his three-piece suit. His wife rests one hand in her lap, showing her wedding ring, which has been accented with gold. In her other hand, she holds a fan made of the variegated tail feathers of a lyrebird or black cockatoo. Aside from her wedding ring, the only other gold-accented element of the photograph is a brooch fastened at the hollow of her neck, which contains a portrait (**Figure 3.18**). The likeness held in the brooch is barely perceptible to the naked eye; its diameter within the ambrotype is only a

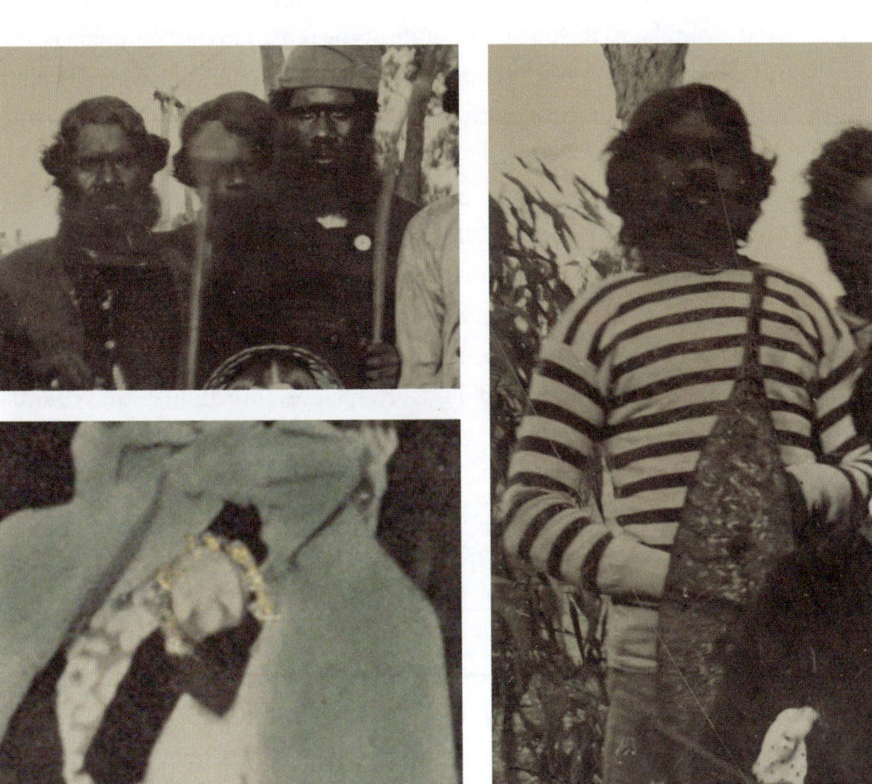

Figure 3.18: [Sections] Unattributed, late 1850s to early 1860s, half-plate, colour-tinted, cased ambrotype. National Science and Media Museum, Bradford, United Kingdom.

few millimetres. Marked out as significant by the gold paint, it could be a valuable family heirloom or portrait of a family member.

The brooch is not the only object to reference people or places beyond the frame, and the colonial couple's story is not the only one on display for the camera. As Wiradjuri/Kamilaroi artist and researcher Jonathan Jones has noted, shields locate their Aboriginal bearers within specific Kin networks. Shield design is a form of shared intergenerational knowledge, crafted through timbers endemic to particular Country. Shields display different Communities' uses of ochre, and practices in mark-making and incised engraving.[91] They are simultaneously defensive weapons and articulations of culture. An example of a broad shield—with the same long tips, curved incised markings and thick horizontal incised band—similar to the one in the ambrotype is held in the National Gallery of Victoria and has been traced to the Millewa/Murray River in eastern Victoria.[92] When I spoke with members of the Wurundjeri Woi Wurrung Cultural Heritage Council, as well as Wurundjeri material culture specialist Jack Norris, they confirmed the shield in the ambrotype was 'certainly south-eastern in style and design', possibly Wurundjeri or Dja Dja Wurrung.[93] However, the photograph's monochrome rendering and the broad shield's partial concealment behind the shoulder of the colonial man, makes it difficult to identify it as the work of a specific Community.

The broad shield and kudgeron/clubs, much like the colonial woman's brooch, articulate genealogies and relationships beyond the frame of the photograph itself. The men who brought these weapons to the makeshift studio may have found comfort and protection in having their ancestral objects with them while standing in front of the unfamiliar apparatus of the photographer's camera. Indeed, the men holding the kudgeron/clubs seem to have moved these slightly during the ambrotype's exposure, which is why they appear a little blurred. The broad shield and kudgeron/clubs' presence in the photograph disrupts a reading of this portrait as only celebrating colonial 'ownership' of land and property. The south-eastern Aboriginal men are communicating a relationship to their Country that predated colonisation and continued in spite of their dispossession on a pastoral station. The international journey of this ambrotype has seen the loss of the names of the Aboriginal men, women and child, *and* the identities of the colonial couple. With the generosity of the Wurundjeri Woi Wurrung knowledge holders and First Nations material culture specialists, we are now able to broadly locate the origin of this group portrait geographically, thinking beyond colonial systems of knowledge. The photographic record of studio and itinerant studio photographers in the mid-nineteenth century documents the totality of colonising agendas Aboriginal people faced when posing for a camera. It also shows, on occasion, how these instances brought forth moments of rare and recorded articulations of identity beyond the colonial predicament.

4

Photographing the Land

Colonial photography of the land and cities is characterised by an articulation of the scale and openness of space. This was both a compositional strategy and a distinct subject of pictures taken outdoors in the colonies—an observation made by Helen Ennis, who identified 'spaciousness' as a key quality of the photographs of Charles Bayliss specifically.[1] Bayliss's iconic 853-centremetre-wide, 23-frame panorama shot from Cammeraygal Country, North Sydney, scanned across the harbour and was dubbed 'the largest photograph' in the world at the Philadelphia Centennial Exhibition of 1876.[2] In this chapter, I extend Ennis's argument to show that colonial photographic practice exhibited a preoccupation with spaciousness even earlier, from the mid-nineteenth century. This was the case even when the material size of the photographic plate or print was not exceptionally capacious. The predilection for expressing spaciousness across different genres of outdoor photography reflected a desire to visualise the land's economic potential and supposed availability, which ran wilfully contrary to an acknowledgement of Indigenous uses and knowledge of Country. Whether taken in urban, pastoral or rural geographies, colonial photography enacted a direct appropriation of Country, performing an erasure of Indigenous sovereignty. Certainly, this appropriation also appears in other forms of colonial art. What sets photography apart is that, as a technology, its functionality and practice was expanding in direct parallel to the construction of colonial cities and towns and the exploration of the inland regions it was being used to visualise.

Photographers had been pushing the optical reach of cameras since the earliest uses of camera equipment in Europe. In 1842, Antoine Claudet, one of London's first commercial photographers, took his camera up the tallest lookout in London, the Duke of York Column in Waterloo Place. From this vantage point, and over successive days, he exposed and developed a series of daguerreotype plates that together showed a 180-degree view over the city. Claudet's panorama, perhaps the earliest photographic panorama, was translated into an engraving and sold to subscribers with the first edition of the *Illustrated London News*.[3] The image, which now survives only as an engraving made after daguerreotypes, is a vision of Dickensian density. Beyond the manicured gardens in the immediate foreground is a scene of cramped industry and urbanisation: terraces adjoining factories, punctuated by billowing smokestacks and the occasional church spire spreading as far as the distant horizon. Claudet's panorama offered a view of a tremendous amount of space but a notable lack of spaciousness. It was captured at the absolute threshold of what the camera could record, with details that the lens could not register added during the engraving process.[4] A colonial practice of photographing the land reacts precisely to this industrially productive, familiar and crowded vision of European cities, but shows its antithesis: the colonising 'opportunity' constructed through spaciousness.

This chapter examines how ways of understanding the landscape aesthetically and economically were intertwined. This entanglement resulted precisely from the diverse professional backgrounds of individuals who practised with photographic technologies outdoors. Certainly, studio photographers, seeking to maximise their profits, photographed buildings and high streets on commission and in proximity to their rooms, from the 1840s. In the next decade, street views were executed by artists and government surveyors in regional towns and rural districts, while cameras were taken out to various frontiers by colonial administrators and their agents. By the early 1860s, 'landscape photography'—images crafted from Romantic notions of the 'empty', pristine wilderness—had begun to circulate and be exhibited, along with photographs that documented 'the raw products of settler expansion'.[5] In this chapter, I highlight how colonial photography fabricated a spaciousness, in images taken in both urban and rural geographies, visually redacting Aboriginal histories of Country.

Vision and Vantage

What is now largely regarded as the oldest extant Australian outdoor photograph—J.W. Newland's daguerreotype of 'Murray Street, Hobart' from 1848—was in fact shot from the window of his second-floor studio rooms in the Stone Buildings (**Figure 4.1**). The Stone Buildings are on the crest of Murray Street at its intersection with Macquarie Street.

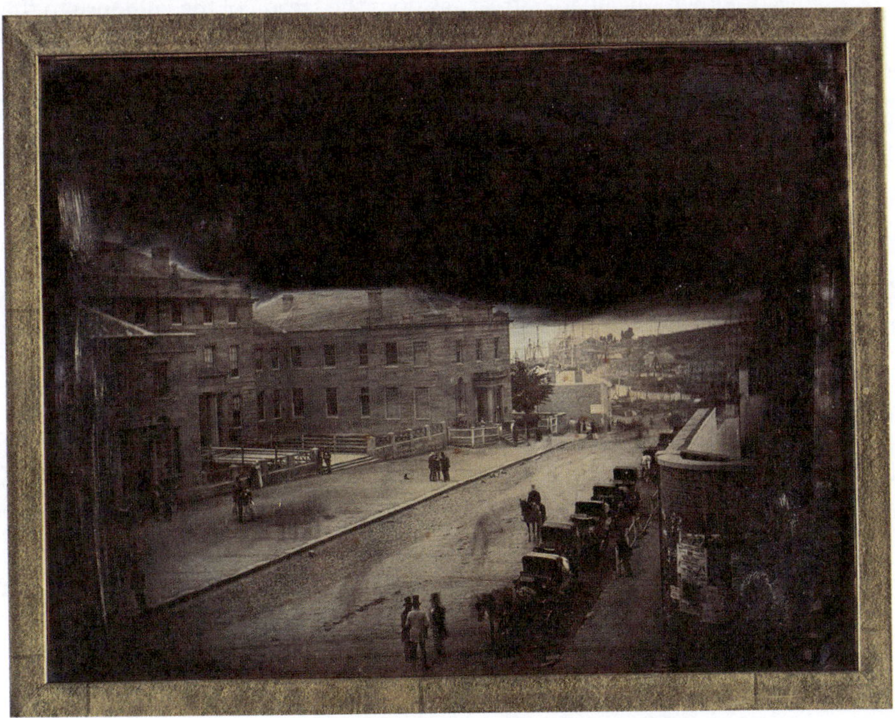

Figure 4.1: J.W. Newland, 'Murray Street, Hobart', 1848, full-plate, uncoloured, framed daguerreotype. Tasmanian Museum and Art Gallery. NB: in the late twentieth century, during a misguided cleaning exercise, detail within the sky was inadvertently erased.

Newland's elevation in the building allowed for a view that extended not only down the colony's main thoroughfare to the ships in the harbour but across the water to the distant shore and mountains. His full-plate daguerreotype was framed and brought down to street level to sit in the window of Miss Hedge's store on the ground floor of the same building.[6] Here it served as an advertisement for the photographer's studio and gallery above, while reflecting the outward-facing scene.

Predictably absent from Newland's view is any reference to the Mouheneenner and their long relationship with this Country. Massacres of the 1820s and 1830s, culminating in the Tasmanian Wars, had decimated Palawa populations across lutruwita/Tasmania, and dispossessed them of the most productive hunting and foraging grounds.[7] While there is a clear line of sight down Murray Street, the monolithic sandstone facade of the Supreme Court at the left in the photograph disrupts any potential vision down Macquarie Street (as does the facade of the jailhouse to the right). Two short blocks behind the court is the site where the Tasmanian Museum and Art Gallery's (TMAG) building would be constructed in 1861, over a substantial shell midden made by Mouheneenner, an ecological and cultural artefact of their long history of custodianship of this land.[8] The institution was established two years before Newland took this photograph, albeit at different provisional premises, and it is in TMAG that the daguerreotype is held today. Newland's daguerreotype put colonial society in conversation with itself, not documenting the violence preceding (and surrounding) its exposure but reflecting its outcome: the coordinated erasure of signs of Aboriginal histories and occupation of Country. As the *Courier*'s journalist noted in a column about the photograph, 'persons standing at the door of the Supreme Court may be recognised'.[9] Those who, in December 1848, subsequently came to peer at these familiar top-hatted figures in the daguerreotype in Miss Hedge's window were doing so from within the photographed scene itself. Herein lies the first primary use for colonial photography of the land: its function as a self-referential tool, fortifying a view of settlement that colonists were at once a part of, and in the process of, constructing.

Newland's street scene runs deep, employing the facades of the buildings to funnel a view that reached beyond the urban centre. Other

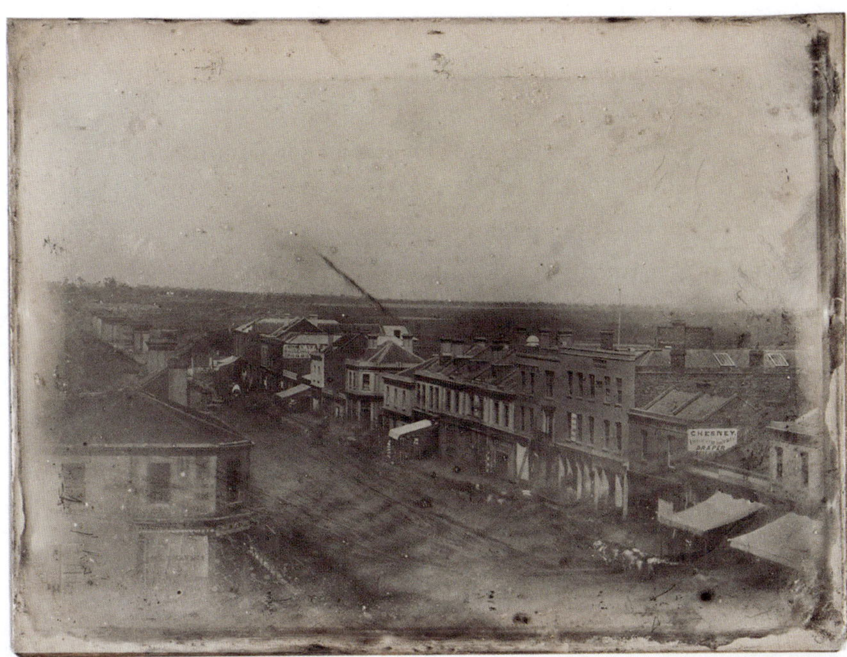

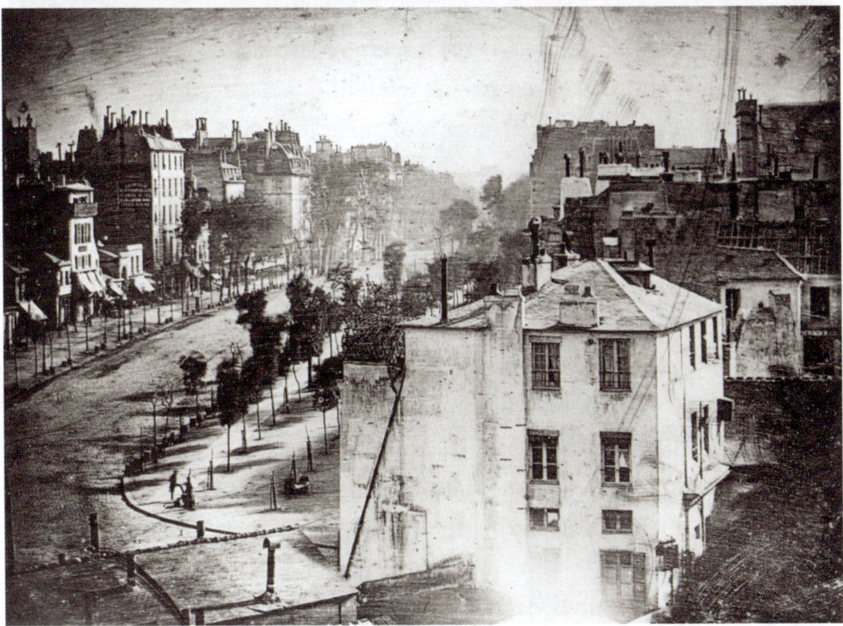

Figure 4.2 (top): Unattributed, 'Swanston Street', 1854–55, full-plate, uncoloured, cased daguerreotype (shown uncased). Powerhouse Museum.

Figure 4.3 (bottom): L.J.M. Daguerre, 'Boulevard du Temple, around noon', 1838–39, full-plate, uncoloured, uncased daguerreotype. Bayerisches Nationalmuseum, Munich.

early photographers sought out a vantage that allowed them to capture the contours of the high street but also see past them. This is evident in the daguerreotype view of Swanston Street, Naarm/Melbourne, shot in 1854–55 from the roof of the first Town Hall (**Figure 4.2**). This plate has previously been attributed to T. S. Glaister, but it was just as likely shot by any one of the seven photographers working with the daguerreotype process in Naarm during this period.[10] The street slices through the centre of the frame. It is a composition distinct from Daguerre's own more famous street scene, 'Boulevard du Temple'(**Figure 4.3**), made over a decade earlier in 1838 (prior to the public announcement of his photographic process) and taken from his studio window in the Diorama Building. Daguerre's boulevard is lined first with small, manicured trees and then framed by dense rows of Parisian terraces. Today, 'Boulevard du Temple' is one of the most discussed street scenes of nineteenth-century photography.[11] Much attention has been given to the eerie absence of people along the thoroughfare. The diffuse renderings of the only two perceptible figures—the shoeshine and their customer—are testament to the protracted nature of early photographic exposures and the necessity for absolute stillness to register clearly within a daguerreotype.

We see, too, the ghostly forms of horses in 'Swanston Street' and, on close inspection, silhouettes in the doorway of the building to the left of Chesney's Draper's, the resolution of which suggests a natural liveliness to the scene. Both daguerreotypes give precedence to the wide street, but in Daguerre's version, this expanse is circumscribed by the densely-packed architecture on its periphery. There is no vision beyond the undulating rooftops crowded with chimneys, or further down the boulevard. By comparison, the colonial photographer has chosen the vantage point of the Town Hall's roof so as not to confine their view to the thoroughfare. 'Swanston Street' shows Princes Bridge arched across Birrarung/the Yarra River, and then the cleared land on the south bank, trailing right back across the horizon.

This unattributed daguerreotype operates as a record of colonial urban development but also as a 'map' of its intended future direction. Swanston Street was named after Charles Swanston, the managing director of the Derwent Bank in lutruwita/Van Diemen's Land. During the 1820s, he had funded the attempts of squatter John Batman to colonise Port Phillip/Boon Wurrung Country by means of grazing. In 1853, engraver and publisher Thomas Ham produced a map dividing unceded Aboriginal land of the newly formed colony of Victoria into the domains of various squatters.[12] Ham made this cartographical impression in his rooms in the Central Land Office at 35 Swanston Street. This is the building approximately halfway down the right-hand side of the street. When looking at this plate with a magnifying glass, we see Ham's own name inscribed above the doorway below the establishment's banner. In 1854, around the time this daguerreotype was taken, Ham engraved and published a cartographic plan for 'The City of Melbourne'.[13] This map neatly squared off the cleared land south of the Birrarung/Yarra River into allotments and defined the perimeter for the proposed site of Government House. There is a synchronicity, then, between the indexical nature of photography and the cartographic engraving occurring just behind the facade of the photograph's Central Land Office building. Each format offers a survey of the land for its colonial uses, whether established or envisaged.

Some early photographers captured street scenes from a height, from rooftops or spires, while others crafted depth for their photographs while remaining at ground level. This flat angled depth is evident in Joseph Turner's 1856 daguerreotype of the laying of the clock tower's foundation stone at Djilang/Geelong (**Figure 4.4**). Turner had begun his photographic career as a studio portraitist on Ryrie Street that same year.[14] His practice's orientation is evident in some elements of the daguerreotype's composition, including the choice of a sixth-plate format, which was much more common for portraits than outdoor views. Turner was working without the aid of a reversing mirror, which both Newland and the Swanston Street photographer used to ensure that the lateral reversal, which naturally occurs when daguerreotyping a scene, was corrected before the image entered the camera. In Turner's scene, the lettered signage on the buildings in the background appears backwards. He stood some distance from the architecture to mask this infidelity. Turner also set up his tripod at a distance from the unfolding ceremonial scene, rather than composing a more intimate 'portrait' of the

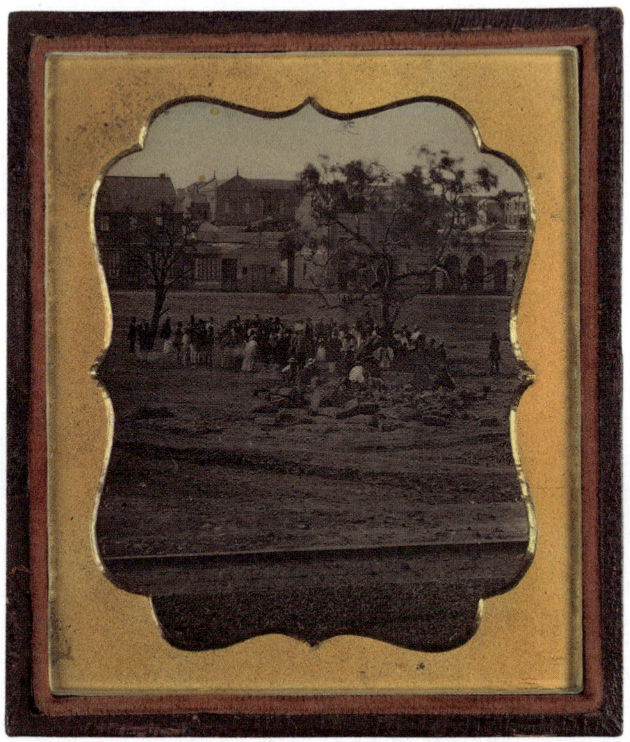

Figure 4.4: Joseph Turner, Untitled [laying the foundation stone of the Geelong clock tower], 1856, sixth-plate, uncoloured, cased daguerreotype. National Gallery of Victoria.

occasion. The spaciousness created through these compositional choices introduces another important subject to the photograph. Prominent in the foreground are the iron rail and paved tracks of a railway line, opened in 1856 and signalling an increased connectivity between Djilang/Geelong and the colonial capital, Naarm/Melbourne. Turner's daguerreotype collapses a few colonial events into the one tiny view. But it is also a photograph of what is not there, the clock tower and the extent of the new railway network, inspiring a certain amount of imaginative conjuring. Two decades later, Turner would extend his engagement with lens-based technologies when he accepted the position of assistant astronomer at the Great Melbourne Telescope. Here, he worked on photographic compositions at even greater distances and produced a large collodion negative of the moon that toured internationally throughout the 1870s.[15]

Compiling the View

Alongside studio portraitists who periodically took or trained their cameras outdoors were well-connected amateurs, artists and government administrators who engaged in photographing examples of colonial construction. These makers thought about photography less in episodic terms and more as a sustained document of a city or region. Collated, sequenced, discussed and displayed, early photographic series constructed a legibility for the land according to its colonial uses. These collections of mid-century colonial photographs were put to work—exhibited and shown to local as well as international audiences. The works by, and attributed to, Robert Tennent, O. (Olaf) William Blackwood and George H. Jenkinson are representative of a new strata and intensity in colonial photographic practice, which emerged alongside and followed the daguerreian street-scene photography described above.

Robert Tennent, the eldest son of a Scottish mercantile and intellectual family, had arrived in the Australian colonies in 1839 without any artistic training. He disembarked the *William Mitchell* in nipaluna/Hobart in June, before sailing north to Boon Wurrung Country, Port Phillip, in October, as part of the squatters' scramble for fertile land.[16] During the 1840s, Tennent consolidated a property portfolio comprising two substantial estates on unceded Dja Dja Wurrung Country in the vicinity of Gnarkeet. He made one trip back to Scotland in 1847–48.[17] By 1849, he was back in the colonies and, in 1850, was appointed as a government magistrate for the greater Port Phillip district and beyond.[18] He sold the last of his pastoral land in 1853 and returned permanently to Edinburgh. This was on the cusp of the photographic boom inaugurated by the gold rushes, and spurred by innovations in collodion processes that consolidated the careers of photographers such as T. S. Glaister and Joseph Turner.

A series of twenty-six salted paper prints attributed to Tennent document his movement across the colony of Victoria and into South Australia. They were not made from collodion glass negatives but as contact prints from paper calotype negatives. Apart from these photographic prints, Tennent's colonial archival trace is scarce, and coalesces around his work in the legal profession and his activities as a grazier. This could be explained by the fact that, unlike other amateurs, such as his contemporary John Hunter Kerr,[19] there is no evidence Tennent met with colonial photographers or exhibited his work at either intercolonial exhibitions or within colonial fraternities. He never advertised his photographic services professionally and his collection very likely left the colonies with him in 1853. As a result, Tennent is absent from anthologies of colonial Australian artists[20] and his images have largely been omitted from catalogues of colonial photography.[21] Despite being among the oldest extant paper photographs produced in an Australian colonial context, they have hitherto sat unmoored from both a Scottish and a colonial history of photography.

Tennent's colonial photographic pursuits were informed by the vigorous uptake of early paper photographic processes in Edinburgh, and his own personal and material connections to this practice. Among the most notable studios in the Scottish capital was that of David Octavius Hill and Robert Adamson, which ran from 1843 until Adamson's death in 1847. Hill and Adamson worked exclusively in the calotype process. During their partnership, they photographed views of the medieval and neo-Classical architecture around Edinburgh and Fife.[22] The partners also produced over 120 salted paper prints of the Newhaven fishing community, which represent one of the earliest instances of social documentary photography.[23] Edinburgh was home to the first amateur photographic society, the Edinburgh Calotype Club. Formed around the time of the inception of Hill and Adamson's studio, the club's founding members included Tennent's younger brother, Sheriff Hugh Lyon Tennent. A salted paper print made by Robert Tennent sits in the club's album, compiled around 1848 and now held in the National Library of Scotland. The print's caption describes how Tennent took the photograph on one of his properties near Gnarkeet, with a provisional camera crafted from a cigar box and fitted with the lens of a telescope.[24] Also in this album is a portrait of Robert Tennent made by Scottish photographer John Adamson in Edinburgh, dated April 1848; and several pages of smaller undated salted paper prints of Edinburgh scenes, and attributed to Sheriff Hugh Lyon and Robert Tennent.[25] This indicates that Robert Tennent connected with the Edinburgh Calotype Club on his brief return to Scotland. He probably showed an early example of his colonial photographic experiments, taking the opportunity to update his technical knowledge and camera equipment.

Tennent may have thought of himself as an emissary for a culture of paper-based photography that was flourishing in Scotland. However, his twenty-six loose colonial salted paper print series, now held in the Scottish National Portrait Gallery, differ in subject matter and aesthetic from those of the Edinburgh Calotype Club or the Hill and Adamson studio. Tennent's colonial series shows open spaces of cleared, cultivated land, such as 'Homestead, South Australia' (**Figure 4.5**). The openness of this location is compositionally enhanced by the large portion of the frame given over to documenting the clear sky. Captured at a distance from the residence, an expansive field of wheat in the foreground is prominent and luminescent, catching the midday sun. The property sits on the

Figure 4.5: Robert Tennent (attributed), 'Homestead, South Australia', 1849–53, salted paper print, 14.7 × 19.4 cm. Scottish National Portrait Gallery, Edinburgh.

cleared ascent of the hill, framed by a perimeter of conifers. Taken on its own, this photograph resembles other extant cased daguerreotypes and ambrotypes of colonial pastoral estates from the 1850s and early 1860s, in which the focus was as much on the residence as it was on the 'productive' and orderly agrarian land surrounding it.[26] In the context of this salted print series, this homestead is part of a story of colonial control the photographer weaves pictorially between Djilang/Geelong and Tarntanya/Adelaide.

The photographic series concertinas the inland regions of south-western Victoria and eastern South Australia into pockets of stable colonial influence. During Tennent's time as a magistrate, he assessed violent conflicts and disputes between colonists, squatters and Aboriginal communities throughout this region. But the photography does not evoke a volatile, violent and isolated frontier. Instead, it presents a view of busy ports, neat streets, and secure mining, grazing and crop-growing estates. As a point of contrast, John Hunter Kerr, who maintained an amateur practice in the mid-to-late 1850s, took photographs of Dja Dja Wurrung alongside mia-mias, north-east of where Tennent was travelling. These photographs, exposed near his station Fernyhurst, show unidentified Dja Dja Wurrung in animal skins and European clothing.[27] Kerr's project was not without an elegiac sentiment, but as Elizabeth Willis notes, it did acknowledge the persistence of a traditional way of life in the face of colonial upheaval.[28]

Although there is no surviving archive of Tennent's correspondence home, or any papers of the Edinburgh Calotype Club, there is a sense that these photographs were compiled with a Scottish audience in mind, if not the club's membership specifically. Many of the salted paper prints have pencilled inscriptions on the verso reading 'salted finish' or 'wet acid'. I think these annotations suggest that Tennent was following either the traditional salted paper printing process, or adding a watered solution of gallic acid or hydrochloric acid to draw out the latent image. He may have been documenting his sensitising and developing techniques so as to discuss his work more fully with colleagues in Scotland.

Tennent also titled some of the prints in relation to European botany, inflecting a colonial scene with a European value. A salted paper print of a single tree on sparse grassland is labelled 'Banksia, the Honeysuckle of Colonists' (**Figure 4.6**). This caption draws a parallel between the celebrated national plant of Scotland and the banksia endemic to the Australian continent, while positioning the tree as colonial property. In the image, the tree dwarfs the scene but is also barely contained in the photographer's frame, its highest leaves slip beyond the upper margin of the paper. Tennent's photographic practice may have been somewhat isolated, but it was not untethered. He negotiated a technical practice of paper-based photography, incubated in Scotland, grafting it onto a colonial context, and later repatriating his examples and efforts. Although Tennent's photographs may seem serene on first inspection, they are a haunting manifestation of genocidal colonial ambition.

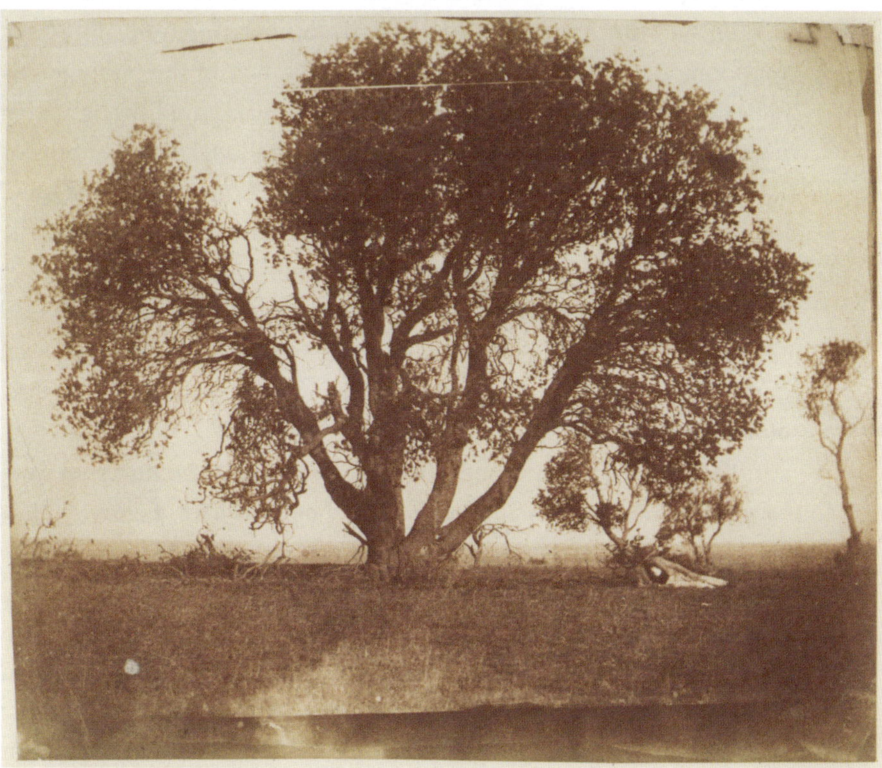

Figure 4.6: Robert Tennent (attributed), 'Banksia. The Honeysuckle of Colonists', 1849–53, salted paper print, 14.4 × 17.30 cm. Scottish National Portrait Gallery, Edinburgh.

Other colonial practitioners thought about photography less as a part of a conversation, local or international, and more in terms of commercial opportunity. By the end of the 1850s, paper-based photographic printing had expanded exponentially—first, with the introduction of wet-collodion glass negatives, which afforded a sharper resolution from which to print; and, second, with the introduction of albumenised paper printing that registered a darker and deeper tonal range. Scottish–Swedish migrant O. William Blackwood took early advantage of these developments.[29] Trained as a painter, Blackwood had spent the mid-1850s working as a colourist for various commercial daguerreotype studios around Warrane/Sydney Cove.[30] However, by 1858, he struck out on his own with a camera. Blackwood did not participate in the scene in which amateur and professional photographers met for photographic excursions, exhibitions or lectures, discussed at more length in Chapter 2.[31] As Gael Newton has noted, Blackwood's business on William Street, Woolloomooloo, was located well beyond the hub of the photography studios that clustered around George Street.[32] Blackwood specialised in views, shot across the harbour and through the inner city. He printed multiple copies and compiled a standardised selection into leather-bound albums. These albums were sold at local booksellers, stationers, and the studio shopfronts of other photographers, including that of Edwin Dalton (for whom he had formerly coloured photographs).[33] While Blackwood utilised the latest photographic technologies and was commercially well connected, he remained artistically independent from an expanding colonial photography scene.

Blackwood was responsible for an early colonial panorama shot from Government House, looking toward Campbell's Wharf (**Figure 4.7**). It was compiled from twelve sequential frames and presented in a leather-bound album in 1858.[34] In the same year, he produced his *Album of Australian Scenery*, fifteen discrete photographic prints taken around Warrane/Sydney Cove and up from the docks, and, in 1859, finished an album of the exterior facades of Sydney banks. Much like Charles Bayliss's panorama a decade and a half later, Blackwood's 1858 panorama, taken from outside Government House, is virtually devoid of any human figures. Certainly, the absence of people is indicative of the difficulty of organising

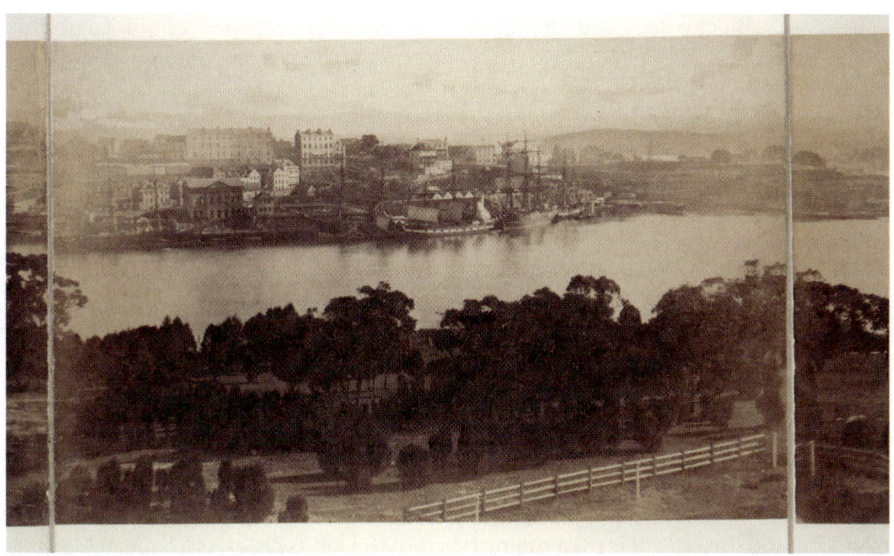

Figure 4.7: O. William Blackwood, [section – frame 4], 'Blackwood's panorama of Sydney & Harbour from Government House', 1858, albumen print(s) concertinaed in leather-bound album, each print approx. 19 × 29.2 cm, overall panorama, 19 × 324.5 cm. State Library of New South Wales.

posed activity in a scene of such breadth. However, it also translates into the compositional choices Blackwood made for his more condensed views of urban Sydney in his *Album of Australian Scenery*. In 'Pyrmont Bridge', he prioritised a lengthy exposure, and used a long lens to capture the detail of the buildings in the background on the easterly shore, all but erasing the mobile foot traffic on the bridge itself (**Figure 4.8**). The exception is a lone top-hatted man who is posed leaning against a bollard. The man's figure functions as an index to the scale of the bridge. This albumen print is also an early example of post-exposure alteration. When fixing the glass collodion negative, Blackwood has painted clouds along the horizon to lessen the stark tonal transition between city and sky, and introduce a sense of atmosphere to the scene.[35] The local intrigue over Newland's daguerreotype a decade earlier in nipaluna/Hobart had been predicated on glimpses of familiarity in the shadowy faces half-turned to the camera. However, a newspaper reviewer implied that the 'artistry' of Blackwood's photographs lay in their elimination of a distracting population, and the omission of anything 'dim or smoky [and] … no hazy outlines'.[36]

Blackwood and his albums sit between cultures of photographic discussion and dissemination. He was distant from the local fraternities and camera clubs, led by people such as William Hetzer, who saw themselves as innovators applying the latest collodion processes to photographing the colonial land. In contrast to Tennent, Blackwood did not contribute to an international conversation on photography that was being conducted among practitioners. Nor did he go on to engage in a more official and emerging culture of colonial exhibition that would advance in the following decade. Rather, Blackwood's photographs were marketed as immediate family keepsakes and objects of extended family exchange. Packaged up in the sentimentalised form of the album but including almost-unpopulated views of the urban landscape, Blackwood's photographs made the sprawling colonial city generic. His customers could 'insert' their own memories into the landscape. As a *Sydney Morning Herald* reviewer noted:

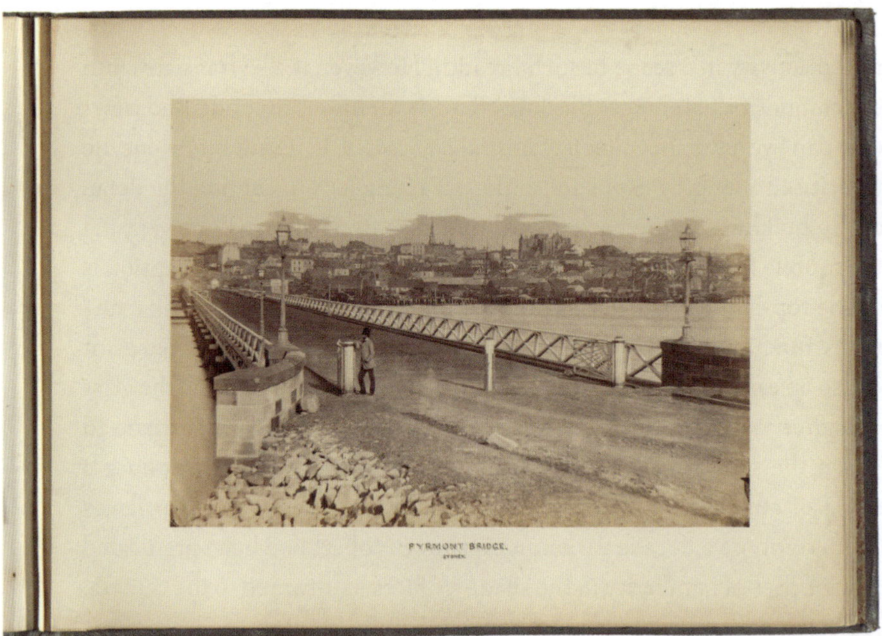

Figure 4.8: O. William Blackwood, 'Pyrmont Bridge, Sydney', 1858, albumen print, 20.6 × 29.2 cm, from *Album of Australian Scenery* (fifteen albumen prints in leather-bound album). National Gallery of Australia.

> Not only will [Blackwood's albums] be a very desirable thing to have by one here, but as a present to those far away … these views of places which are well remembered, or which we have so often to make mention of, will be an invaluable treasure – speaking to us of the past, and full of glad promise and manly hope for the future.[37]

It is hard to imagine what view of a past the reviewer thought Blackwood's photographs could inspire. Certainly, like many of the city's colonial painters,[38] Blackwood had obscured any registration of Gadigal or Cammeraygal connection or claim to their Country, as Conrad Martens had similarly done in his celebrated painting *Campbell's Wharf* of 1857.[39] Blackwood's views in his *Album of Australian Scenery* additionally censored the penal settlement the colony had so recently been built around, omitting barracks and relegating 'old' areas around The Rocks to the background of the picture plane. Priority was given in his albums to recent and in-progress building works. Appearing on the pages around the print of Pyrmont Bridge, which was opened in 1858, is a photograph of St Andrew's Cathedral with the remnants of chiselled sandstone still lying in its yard. Another page shows a trench at Wynyard Square awaiting the construction of the new post office building. A sense of the album's value for posterity is communicated in a copy previously belonging to the Mort family and now held at the State Library of New South Wales.[40] Thomas Sutcliffe Mort (1816–78) was a prominent Sydney businessman to whom Blackwood's far-from-subtle commercial aesthetic evidently appealed. The Mort family's copy has pencil inscriptions on the pages surrounding many of the prints, perhaps made by Thomas or later generations, labelling buildings of personal or familial significance. Blackwood's albums were aimed at a merchant middle class who coveted colonial views they could own, hold, annotate and exchange, with the land's long histories sublimated into their own narrative of its present and future commercial potential. The remainder of Blackwood's relatively short photographic career, which concluded in the mid-1860s, was spent catering to this market by selling smaller albumen print cards (carte de visite) of urban views.

Alongside their retail as collectable items, photographic series occupied increasingly significant roles in the public culture of colonial exhibitions. Within exhibition pavilions and halls, photography sat somewhere between an independent visual art and an installation backdrop, providing geographic context to the commodities on display. Photographs were incorporated into the first colonial exhibitions in 1854–55 in Naarm/Melbourne and on Gadigal Country in Sydney. During the early 1860s, the colonies of Victoria, New South Wales and Queensland all held domestic exhibitions of technology, botany, raw commodities, visual art, and rock and mineral samples. These forums piloted installations that would be sent to the London International Exhibition of 1862. Victoria's exhibition, under the directorship of Supreme Court judge Redmond Barry, focused on displaying the gold wealth of the colony, which had underpinned its economic boom over the preceding decade. Barry solicited data and produce from mining towns, as well as images that represented 'the most striking objects of interest in [each] district'.[41] His requests were discussed on Dja Dja Wurrung Country at the Dunolly Town Council meeting on 6 September 1861. The council's chairman advised that he had approached the only resident photographer, George H. Jenkinson, to take views of Dunolly's major buildings and streets, to be sent to the exhibition, and proposed a £10 fee for this commission.[42]

Jenkinson is now barely remembered as a minor colonial photographer, but his views of Dunolly are extraordinary for the ecosystem of colonial photography they reveal and for their anticipation of future uses of the medium. Born in Belford, Northumberland, Jenkinson's reasons for travelling to the colonies are undocumented.[43] He spent less than two years operating portrait studios in the mining towns of Carisbrook, Maryborough and Clunes, with an assistant named Weekes. At the time of the council meeting, Jenkinson had been in Dunolly two months and his business had gained favourable reviews in the press.[44] He used the ambrotype process for the commission, and framed the plates with gold mats, likely because, as a portrait photographer, these were the materials he had at hand. Twenty-three of Jenkinson's twenty-four ambrotype views taken around Dunolly in September 1861 survive today. When considered in succession, they give the impression of walking around Dunolly,

Dja Dja Wurrung Country, looking over the photographer's shoulder. Jenkinson photographed the high street, Broadway, from north and south vantages, as well as the facades of its businesses: Hislop & Shaw's Manchester and Drapery; Gerrard's Druggists; the Criterion Hotel; A. Martin's Timberyard; the Dunolly branch of the Bank of Australia and James Bell's Dry Goods Store. He also photographed the town's civic and ecclesiastical architecture, such as the Electric Telegraph Office and the Congregational Church. Jenkinson's ambrotypes do not show the open crevasses of Country ravaged by mining but are, instead, a celebratory document of a town developed from mineral wealth. The efficiency and profits of mineral extraction would be communicated elsewhere in the Victorian Exhibition, through a Dunolly-made mining windlass and model imitations of gold nuggets.[45] Jenkinson's photographs open out space otherwise flattened in a colonial lexicon by conventional mapping. His street views presuppose the increasing role that the photography of colonial buildings would have in imperial exhibitions,[46] but also anticipate the twentieth- and twenty-first-century relationship of photography to the systematic recording of urban environments.

The Dunolly ambrotypes are both a topographical survey and a visual census of the town in September 1861. Children and teachers of the Church of England school have emptied out of the schoolhouse and stand in the yard.[47] The telegraph operator and post office clerks have left their desks to meet the photographer (**Figure 4.9**), and the constabulary stand alongside the courthouse or sit astride their stilled horses.[48] Even the patients from the hospital have hobbled out on crutches to stand outside the building or lean out of its open windows.[49] The ambrotypes do not have the candour of early daguerreotyped street scenes, where photographers set up their tripods at a distance from the scene they were documenting. Even the youngest Dunolly residents look directly at the photographer and are conscious of the photographic moment of which they are a part. Neither is there a sense that the residents of Dunolly have been positioned in each frame merely as photographic props, as Blackwood's top-hatted collaborators were. In all twenty-three surviving plates, there is a sense of activity, necessarily paused for the 20-second or so exposure. For example, outside Wilson & Co.'s wine,

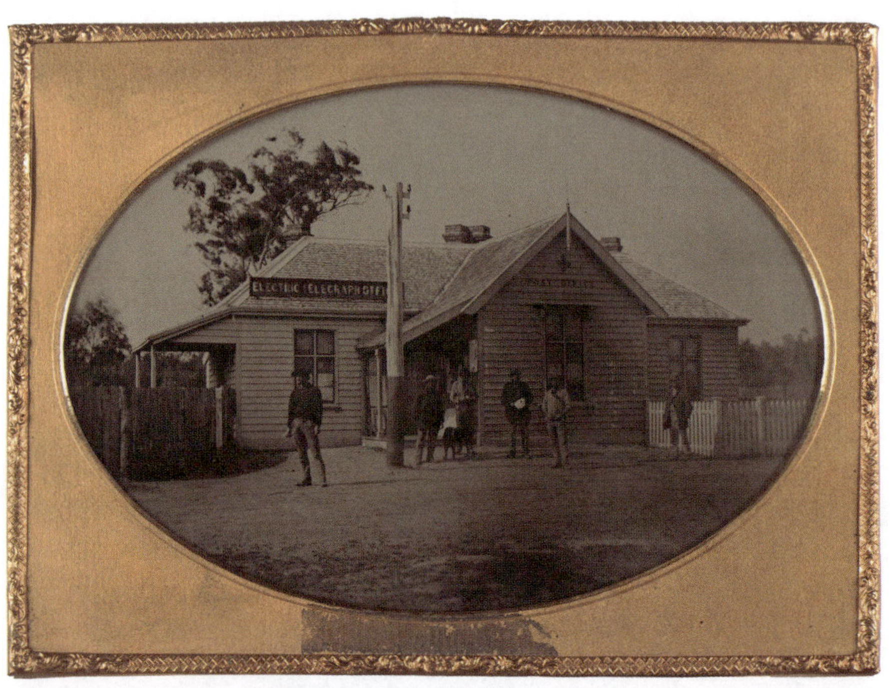

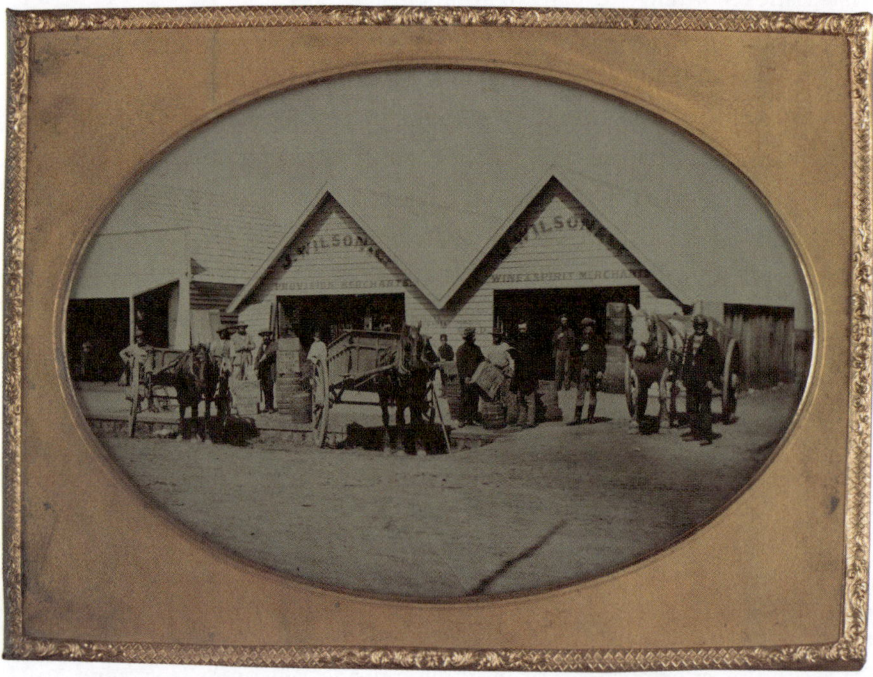
J. WILSON

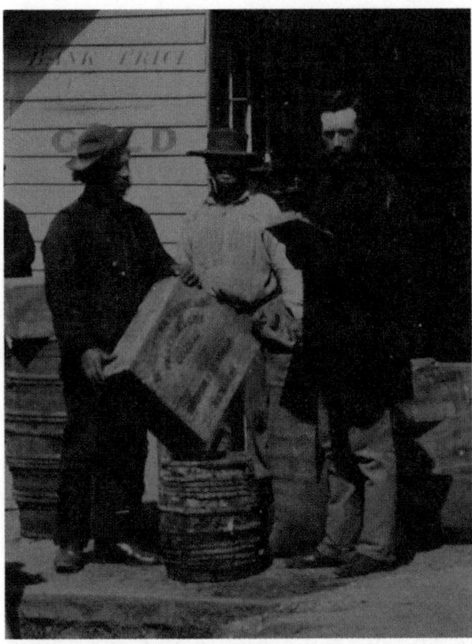

Figure 4.9: G. H. Jenkinson, Untitled [post office and telegraph station, Dunolly], 1861, half- plate, uncoloured, framed ambrotype. State Library of Victoria.

Figure 4.10: G. H. Jenkinson, Untitled [J. Wilson & Co. Provision, Wine & Spirit Merchants], 1861, half-plate, uncoloured, framed ambrotype + section detail. State Library of Victoria.

spirit and provision store, an attendant stands with clipboard in hand, reconciling the crates of cognac being loaded into the cart by the labourer, momentarily turning his gaze to Jenkinson (**Figure 4.10**). In what is a remarkable act of collective photographic collaboration, Jenkinson's series gives the impression that only for an instant has he commanded the attention of the Dunolly colonial population away from the activity naturally unfolding before the camera.

Soon afterwards, this collection of ambrotype views was sent to the Victorian Exhibition in Naarm/Melbourne, which opened in October 1861. Presumably, it was the Dunolly town clerk, Charles Dicker, who deposited the photographs with the exhibition's organising committee, for it is his name that appears alongside them in the catalogue and to whom they were misattributed.[50] They did not receive any of the exhibition's medals, with the more established metropolitan studios, of Archibald McDonald and Richard Daintree, claiming the prizes for photography.[51] Nevertheless, the Dunolly collection was selected to progress to the 1862 London International Exhibition. They appear —without attribution— listed in the inventory of the colony's pavilion.[52] This was not, in fact, their envisaged final destination. At one point, either before the ambrotypes left for the London exhibition, or after the series was returned to Dunolly, international residential addresses were inscribed in ink on the card backings of many of the frames. The surnames of the addressees correlate with the names in the signage of the photographed businesses, strongly suggesting their intended transfer to extended-family members of the colonial proprietors.[53] These ambrotypes had an imagined afterlife as photographs of personal exchange once their function as representative images in colonial exhibitions was served.

This duality of photographing street scenes for government contracts while also retailing the same images as souvenirs for personal collection is apparent in later colonial photographers' businesses. Charles Nettleton, who had trained in the Naarm/Melbourne studio of Townsend Duryea and Archibald McDonald (discussed in Chapter 3), opened his own studio in Naarm in 1858. Peter Cudmore and Joan Kerr note that, although Nettleton maintained a studio business, he was 'best known for his view photographs'.[54] From the late 1850s and into the 1890s, Nettleton was the official photographer for the colonial Victorian government and the City of Melbourne Corporation, a role that saw him document numerous public works and buildings. Nettleton's business emblem, stamped on the card reverse of all his photographs, announced that 'duplicate copies may be had at any time'.[55] The partners, Beaufoy Merlin and Charles Bayliss, toured extensively through Aboriginal land in the colonies of Victoria and New South Wales during 1870–72, creating street-by-street and building-by-building photographic surveys of urban construction. The sun-drenched facade of the Royal Hotel (**Figure 2.8**) is one of thousands of photographs the pair took during this two-year period, leading up to their residency in Hill End, Wiradjuri Country and prior to Bayliss's return to Cammeraygal Country and uptake of panoramic photography. Merlin and Bayliss advertised their street survey in papers such as the *Sydney Morning Herald*. In these forums, they made a perfunctory effort to distinguish themselves from practitioners like Blackwood: 'our negatives are not taken for the mere object of sale', while, like Nettleton, emphasising an extension of their business to general customers: 'copies can be had at all times by or of those parties residing in any part of the colonies'.[56] Precisely because Jenkinson's Dunolly series was never mailed and dispersed, we see in it an early example of an urban photographic survey project that had international exhibition and currency in shaping an image of the colony. What is also evident in the Dunolly series, and repeated in the later upscaled projects of Nettleton, Merlin and Bayliss, is that the colonies were not simply urban, state-sanctioned monoliths but made up of individuals' claims to land and individual ownership of businesses on Aboriginal Country.

Natural History Photography

Photography's use in documenting the land, though, extended beyond its commercial configuration. As John Buckland's 1841 letter to Governor Franklin (described in Chapter 1) relayed, it was anticipated that the indexical nature of photography would enhance both the scientific and artistic study of nature. Buckland may have over-anticipated the reception of photography in these domains, or at least the speed of its absorption into these pursuits. Botanical illustration had been a corollary to the first European encounters with, and invasion of, the Australian continent. Joseph Banks, for example, had recruited Sydney Parkinson and Alexander Buchan as botanical artists on the *Endeavour*'s 1768 Pacific voyage. Beth Tobin has described the tradition of botanical illustration as central to Britain's imperial 'management of information about global resources'.[57] This practice dislodged and decontextualised native specimens from their ecosystems. Artistic studies of plants were often rendered against spacious, non-ornamental, commonly even blank, backdrops.

A practice of botanical illustration continued in the colonies. It is evident in the mid-nineteenth century painted work of Harriet and Helena Scott, who were among the first colonial women professionally employed as illustrators for scientific texts. Important to the genre of natural history illustration was precision colouring. The restricted tinting palettes of commercial colonial photographers were no match for the vitality and spectrum of colours used in botanical painting. But the oldest colonial museum, the Australian Museum in Warrane/Sydney Cove, did employ photographers from the 1860s. Vanessa Finney's study *Capturing*

Nature (2019) highlights the breadth of the Australian Museum's monochrome, largely glass-plate negative collection, compiled from both internal museum work and fieldwork expeditions. We see a range of taxidermied animal carcases and skeletons made into specimens in front of the camera: winched in braces or mounts, photographed next to rulers and placed against the infinite space of blank backdrops. This collection is more weighted to terrestrial fauna but there are maritime elements as well, represented by corals and starfish. Very little is known about how these nineteenth-century photographs were employed in exhibitions or used in collection cataloguing. As Finney explains, 'before 1893, none of the glass plates were dated, indexed or registered … so parts of the history of the making has been lost'.[58] There is, however, evidence of natural history photography occurring outside official museum work—among artists who were tethered to civilian discussions on the natural world and, indeed, in forums like that where Buckland's photographically derived starfish was originally received. Remarkably, it is in this vein of artistic, pseudo-scientific practice that the first instance of a woman working with photographic processes in the colonies can be retrieved.

During the first half of the 1850s, professional colonial artist and sculptor Theresa Walker made photographic salted paper impressions of seaweeds on kanamaluka/the Tamar River in lutruwita/Tasmania. Walker's seaweed photographs were numerous, each specimen spaciously imprinted on a single sheet of photographically sensitised paper. None survive today. Walker was making these photographs at the Launceston harbour master's quarters, where kanamaluka/the Tamar River meets the Bass Strait at George Town. Her first husband, Lieutenant John Walker, had held the position of harbour master for a second term from 1850 until his death in January 1855.[59] Theresa had temporarily stayed on in the accommodation at the invitation of her late husband's successor, Captain Drew. The record of Walker's photographic activity comes from Irish botanist and phycologist (algae specialist) William Henry Harvey, who visited Captain Drew on 3 March 1855. In a letter penned to his sister the following day, now held with his papers at the Gray Herbarium, Harvard University, Harvey recalls meeting Walker and being shown her photographs. He acknowledged her as an artist of 'considerable talent' and attested that her photographic seaweeds were 'remarkably well done'.[60] Walker had hand-coloured at least one photographic study, which Harvey admitted was so realistic, he '[mis]took it at first for a dried specimen'.[61] Harvey's entire description of his morning visit to the harbour master's quarters centres on his interaction with Theresa Walker. This gives the sense he had visited specifically to see her work. Nevertheless, Harvey seemed affronted by Walker herself, who he judged as 'abrupt in manner and so self-opinionated' after she corrected him on the photographic basis of a coloured seaweed study. [62]

We can think about Theresa Walker's seaweed studies as sculptural photographs, which, as contact prints, made 'casts' of seaweeds with light in a manner akin to her practice of casting wax. Theresa was born in Bath, England, in 1807. She received rudimentary training in sketching as a component of her religious schooling. She migrated to Tarantanya/Adelaide in 1836, with her sister Martha and brother-in-law Captain Charles Berkeley.[63] Between her arrival in the colony, her marriage to Captain Walker in 1838, and move to lutruwita/Tasmania in 1850, Theresa's practice centred on low relief bust portraits made from wax. Popularised in the sixteenth century, this process involved carving a profile portrait from a mound of soft wax until the figure sat slightly raised upon the surface of the medallion or backing mount. This mould was then used to make a cast, from which identical wax editions could be issued. In 1841, Walker was the first colonial artist (of any gender) to exhibit at the Royal Academy.[64] She showed medallion busts of Kaurna man and woman Murlawirrapurka and Mukata, feeding an imperial appetite for true-to-life depictions of Indigenous people. Many of Walker's wax portraits were also exhibited in colonial contexts during her lifetime and are now held in Australian galleries.[65] Low relief busts were discussed with much the same vocabulary that would come to be employed for photography. Indeed, her wax profile of Governor George Grey, displayed at Mr Platt's Library in Tarntanya/Adelaide during 1845, was assessed for its truthfulness in verisimilitude, and found by an anonymous press reviewer to be an 'exceedingly clever and correct likeness'.[66]

Although the seaweed studies are Walker's only documented engagement with the medium of photography, they are not an anomaly in her oeuvre. In the 1860s, after her second marriage, to George Poole, Theresa was commissioned to hand-colour hundreds of ichthyological lithographs produced by Arthur Bartholomew for the National Museum of Victoria (now Museums Victoria). The complexity of this task and Theresa's skill in accurately replicating the colouring of the fish saw the payment for the commission revised in her favour, from £10 for 1000 copies to the same amount for 100 iterations.[67] Walker's earlier salted paper photographs were camera-less impressions mediated by light, and created by a direct contact between each seaweed specimen and the photographic paper. The brown-toned silver nitrate did not react to the areas of the paper shielded from the light underneath the specimen, throwing each seaweed's outline into relief. In this way, Walker used light to create a 'cast' of each seaweed, which she then invigorated with colour, as she would go on to do for Bartholomew's natural history lithographs.

Walker's seaweed photographs are additionally related to a botanically focused practice of early camera-less photography in Britain, as well as a culture of scrapbooking fixated on algae. Between 1843 and 1853, amateur British botanist and photographer Anna Atkins completed a three-volume project entitled *Photographs of British Algae*, presented entirely as cyanotypes. This was a similar camera-less photographic process to that which Walker was using, except for the fact that its sensitising chemistry, ammonium citrate and potassium ferricyanide, turned the areas of the paper exposed to light a deep blue. Atkins learned the cyanotype process through her friendship with its inventor, John Herschel.[68] However, her choice in subject matter, seaweeds, was inspired by none other than William Henry Harvey and his 1841 publication *A Manual of the British Algae*. In this publication, Harvey espoused Linnaean nomenclature and taxonomies as the only proper system by which collectors should caption *and* arrange seaweed specimens. In the written frontispiece to the first volume of her project, Atkins described how she annotated her photographs according to Harvey's instruction. But she admitted to tiring of his rigid and bland guidelines for arrangement, crafting a more aesthetic sequencing for her photographed collection.[69] Atkins' photographs, more broadly, gesture to the expanding value of the seaside as a site for British middle-class excursions and leisure time.

Within this context, a whole literature was produced alongside Harvey's manual for seaweed collection and seaweed scrapbooking. In Britain, seaside rambling was a moralised, rational pursuit seen to productively combine mental and physical exercise.[70]

It is possible Walker considered her seaweed studies a contribution to colonial science and society, as they certainly reflected conversations on seaweed underway in the colonies at the time. As Molly Duggins has demonstrated, seaweed albums in the Australian colonies took on a different tone from that of their British counterparts. Mid-century herbarium albums were used to commemorate routes of migration to the colonies, as well as articulate a familiarity with coastal locations of settlement in a 'new' land.[71] However, while place specific, Walker's unbound photographs of seaweed have less of a visual travelogue quality.

This is not to imply that Walker's practice was not place or site specific. Seaweed study permeated not only this moment of Walker's imminent departure from lutruwita/Tasmania, when she was visited by Harvey, but also her artistic milieu during her preceding five-year residence in the colony. In July 1850, Lieutenant Walker was inducted into the Royal Society of Van Diemen's Land, at a meeting where Reverend John Fereday presented on a collection of dried algae he had gathered at George Town.[72] Theresa may have been at this occasion, although, as a woman accompanied by her husband, her name was not recorded.[73] Algae were the topic of discussion at numerous meetings of the society, reflecting the fascination with kelp forests off the coastline. Seaweed represented an untamed aspect of nature that existed in a liminal state. It could only be observed when it washed into the shallows or upon the shore, while, conversely, its intrigue was generated from its origins in a wild maritime ecosystem.[74] During the early 1850s, specimens of lutruwita/Tasmanian seaweed were sent back to the Royal Geographical Society in London for study and publication, and (male) members of the Royal Society of Van Diemen's Land convened for algae-collecting excursions.[75]

Theresa Walker's photographic seaweed studies were exceptional. Independently gathered and executed, they were an extension of a global fascination with algae, and a local colonial compulsion to contain and order elements of the natural world beyond the reaches of agrarian cultivation. Her photographs negotiated amateur cultures of collection and arrangement. Yet, in their indexical, loose-leaf abundance, and with their precision colouring, the photographs resonate with an empirical world of natural history illustration.

Photographic Excursions and Expeditions

Walker's seaweed studies would have been completed in the controlled environment of the harbour master's quarters, after the seaweeds had been dried, rather than at the shoreline. However, increasingly from the late 1850s, colonial photographers took camera equipment out to record their direct encounters with the natural world in situ. It was during this time that the term 'landscape photography' emerged and began to gain traction. In 1858, London-based Royal Geographical Society fellow Joachim Otté published an amateur guide entitled *Landscape Photography*.[76] This technically focused manual canvassed various calotype, wax-paper, collodion and albumenised collodion processes, and the manipulations necessary for executing and developing photographs outdoors. Its frontispiece was illustrated with an engraving of the boxed-knapsack photographic kit required for outdoor excursions (**Figure 4.11**). Inside, it described how the same kit and camera could be affixed with either a single lens or dual lens for stereo exposures. Otté's publication made it to the colonies before 1861. A copy was purchased as part of the Melbourne Public Library's (later the State Library of Victoria) inaugural collection of 3800 texts and is listed in the library's first catalogue.[77]

While a literature on landscape photography was published from Piccadilly, a culture of landscape photography was forged by the application and testing of these methods in the colonial geographies. This is apparent in two successive columns written by a travelling correspondent, Paul Ricochet, for the 28 August and 4 September 1863 editions of the London *Photographic News*. He described his first impressions of Naarm/Melbourne as 'a modern Babylon' or 'miniature London', with the same 'diurnal clatter and roll of wheels; […] every second house [is] a photographic shop, studio or warehouse'.[78] Ricochet confessed that before leaving London, he had carefully packaged photographic

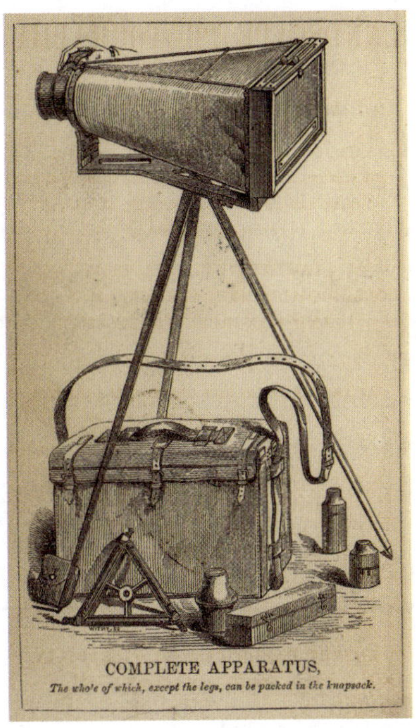

Figure 4.11: Joachim Otté, engraved frontispiece to *Landscape Photography* [...], Robert Hardwicke, London, 1858.

chemicals for sensitising and developing his plates but remarked that this was unnecessary, as 'chemicals by all well-known makers can be bought in Melbourne'. Ricochet lamented that, for all the photographic activity, there was a distinct lack of 'landscape photography going on, even among the amateurs'.[79] Once his journey progressed to nipaluna/Hobart, Ricochet's prose took on a less critical tone. The translucency of the atmosphere in the monumental shadow of kunanyi/Mount Wellington inspired his renewed landscape pursuit. Ricochet relayed to readers his ever-lengthening excursions beyond the city's outskirts and described how the wet-collodion process was untenable on such expeditions. He adopted, instead, dry albumenised collodion plates, which allowed him to do away with his cumbersome developing tent and venture unimpeded inland to leeawuleena/Lake St Clair.[80]

The pair of columns for the *Photographic News* function as part recipe, part manifesto. Ricochet used the dispatches to argue that landscape photography could only be realised well away from colonial cities.

So detailed are his calibrations for sensitising solutions and exposure times that it seems as if he was writing less for the armchair landscape photographer in London and more to entice urban photographers in Naarm/Melbourne to participate in the landscape pursuit.

It has been suggested by several art historians that 'Paul Ricochet' was the pen name for Morton Allport, who sits at the forefront of an Antipodean photographic landscape tradition.[81] Allport was born in England in 1830, and migrated as an infant to lutruwita/Tasmania with his parents. His artistic education began from a young age under his mother Mary Morton Allport, who was one of the colony's first professional miniature painters and lithographers. He chose, though, to follow his father's profession and was admitted to the bar in 1852. Before beginning to practise law, Allport returned to England for a couple of years to refine his sketching practice with John Skinner Prout, who had lived in lutruwita/Tasmania in 1844–48. Five years after his return to the colonies, Allport purchased his first camera in April 1859, from local watchmaker and amateur photographer Charles Abbott.[82] Allport's photographic exploits began in the immediate vicinity of his family home at nipaluna/Hobart.[83] His practice then expanded to fern and rock formations upon kunanyi/Mount Wellington, before culminating in February 1863, with him leading an expeditionary party to leeawuleena/Lake St Clair.[84]

The twenty-four stereo views Allport captured on his expedition to leeawuleena/Lake St Clair present the landscape as 'beautiful, ancient, and empty'.[85] They eschew the histories of Palawa custodianship while reinforcing colonial fantasies of environmental abundance. These are qualities and themes Jarrod Hore has convincingly argued come to define a practice of landscape photography in the colonies bordering the Tasman Sea.[86] All the views from Allport's early 1863 expedition survive as stereo-card albumen prints (**Figure 4.12**) and some are also extant as glass-plate stereo positives. Descriptions of the sites of the exposures are annotated on the photographic prints and outlined in an accompanying letter Allport penned to his brother, Curzon.[87] Only one shot in the sequence includes a reference to people—at a small diggers' camp—who are not part of Allport's travelling party. A fair portion of the photographs are taken in high country, atop summits or along ridges where the view

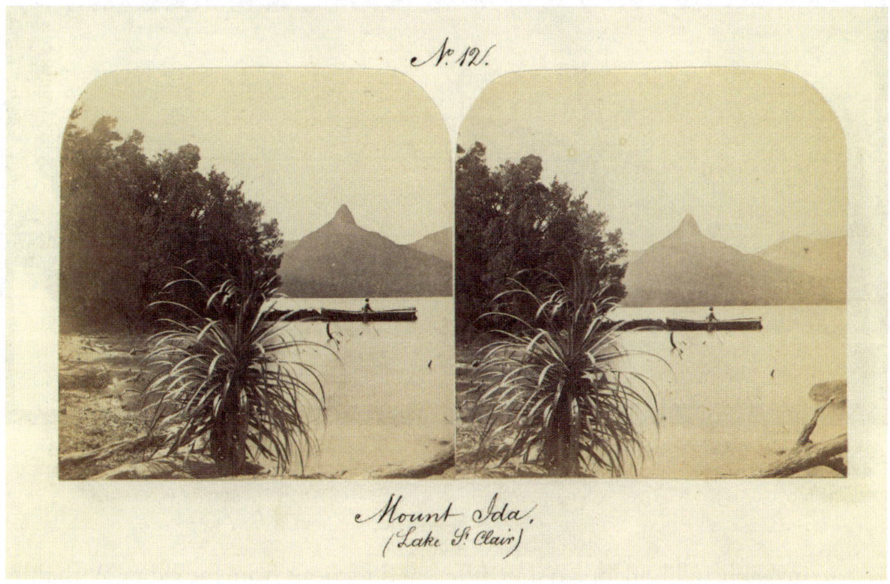

Figure 4.12: Morton Allport, 'No. 12 Mount Ida, (Lake St Clair)', 1863, stereo albumen print, 20.4 × 24.5 cm (approx.), from *Excursion of Lake St. Clair February 1863* album. Allport Library and Museum of Fine Arts.

stretches across rolling mountain ranges towards a distant horizon. Allport demonstrates an aptitude for composition, particularly as it applies to stereo photography. Each shot is configured around multiple depth cues in the fore, mid and background, to aid the simulation of voluminous space when the final images are placed in the stereo viewer. With these high-country exposures, Allport also rekindled a visual trope that had emerged earlier in the century during a Humboldtian era of exploration, where the artist inserted themselves or a surrogate into a scene at a promontory height. This figure's exclusive and aestheticised encounter with the landscape was deployed to represent an all-encompassing sight and imply their mastery over the view.[88] In **Figure 4.13**, Allport evokes this sentiment with his companion in the light-coloured blazer who sits on the ridge's precipice, looking out across the valley in line with the orientation of the camera. But Allport also extends it through the varied placement of his entire party, who, as if configured around some

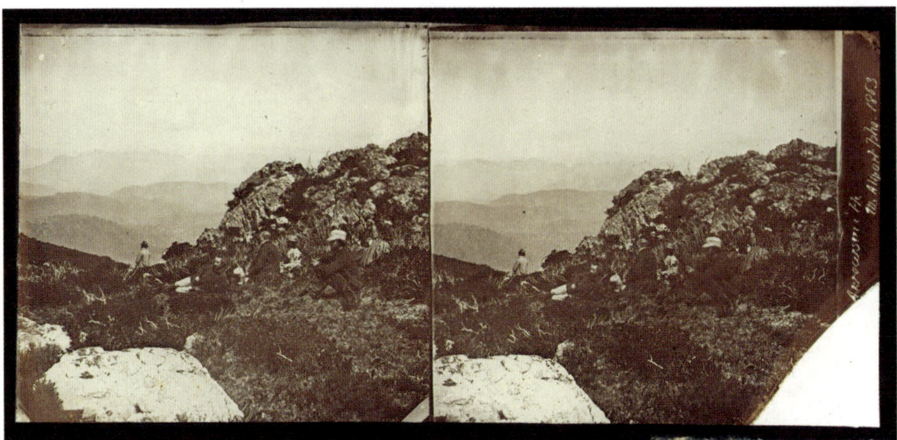

Figure 4.13: Morton Allport, 'Looking Westward from Mt Arrowsmith' [alternative title: 'Mount Byron and the Nine Mountains'], 1863, glass stereo-positive, 7.5 × 14.5 cm. National Gallery of Australia.

invisible radii, all look out in different directions from the ridge. With this, Allport implies photographically a vision of 'emptiness', 'availability' and abundance that is more expansive than the camera can capture.

Allport's photographs present serene, even sublime, visions of nature that simultaneously configure Palawa land as a latent colonial resource. They were almost instantly exhibited on his return to nipaluna/Hobart, at the March 1863 Art Treasures Exhibition. Here, the stereo photographs were praised as 'singularly Romantic [visions] through wild country' and 'truthful delineations', but also valued for the 'extensive quartz formation' they revealed.[89] Morton's photography continued to shuttle between colonial and intercolonial exhibition, and international collections. A selection was included in the Tasmanian Court at the Melbourne Intercolonial Exhibition of 1866, and are possibly the stereo photographs in the large frame jutting out of the central colonnade (**Figure 4.14**). A few of Allport's stereo photographs were also placed in a revolving viewer, through which patrons could experience their virtual simulation of depth and space. Allport had been nominated to oversee the Tasmanian Court, where, as T. Ellis & Co.'s installation shot shows, photography loomed large.[90] Photography served many purposes in intercolonial exhibition contexts—chief among them was providing a visual thread back to sites of extraction for other objects on display, and advertising of the landscapes'

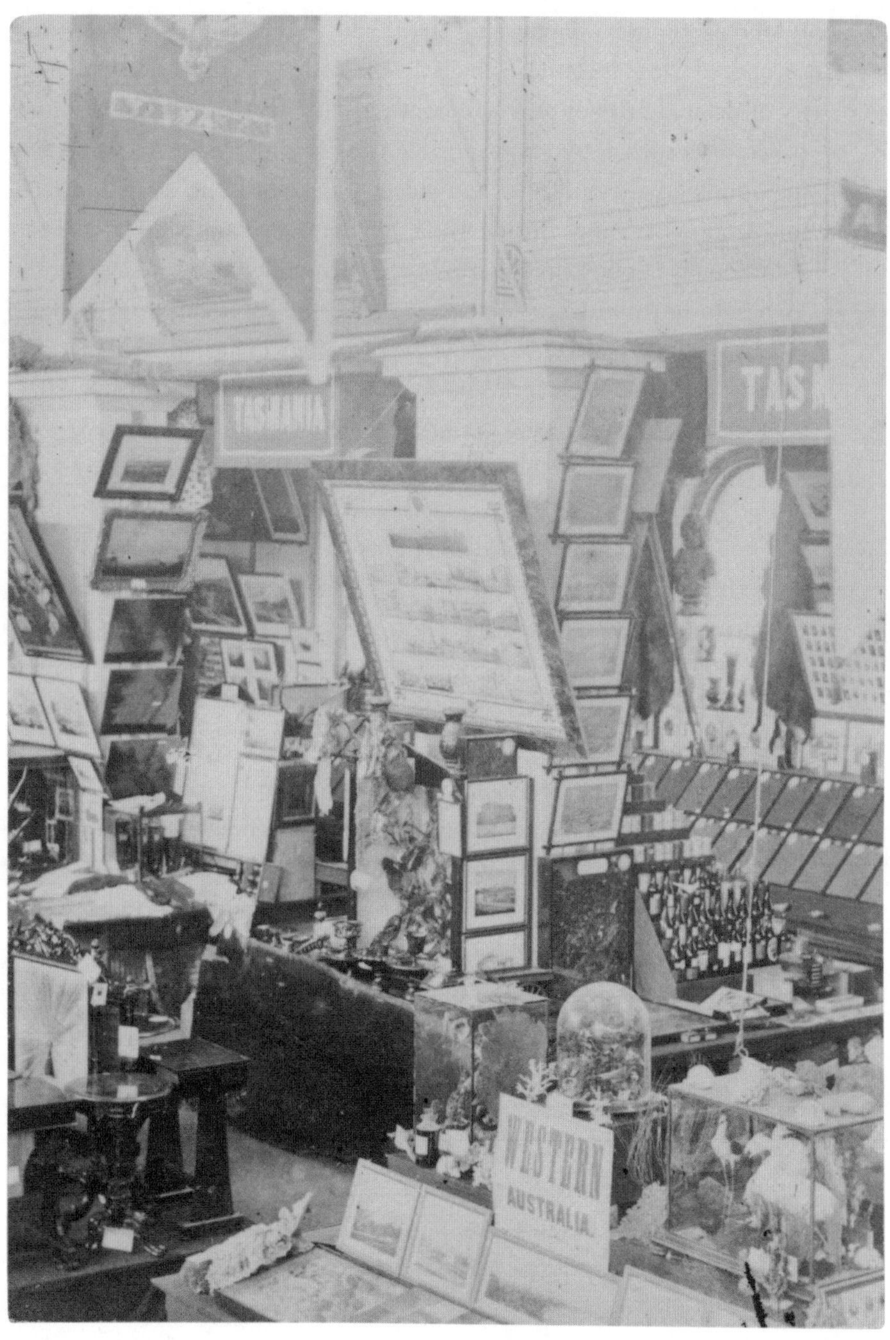

Figure 4.14: T. Ellis & Co., 'Tasmanian Court, Australian Intercolonial Exhibition, Melbourne, 1866-7', card-mounted albumen print, 10.9 × 7.8 cm. National Library of Australia.

resources: timber, minerals and fertile soil, as replete. Allport received a silver medal for his stereos, which the judge thought displayed 'perspicuity of detail, purity of tone and depth of distance'.[91] Other photographs of Allport's, such as two exposures showing colonial-made salmon breeding ponds on a tributary of leeawuleena/Lake St Clair, were translated into wood engravings during 1864, for the *Melbourne Illustrated Post*.[92] Additionally, a photographic print of a fern gully near kunanyi/Mount Wellington, attributed to Allport, was collected by English tourist Helen E. Lambert. It was pasted towards the beginning of her substantial mixed media scrapbook 'Who and What We Saw in the Antipodes' (1868–70).[93] Allport's photographs were premised upon his own romanticised, privileged interaction with the natural world, which he then exhibited and onsold for others to experience vicariously. In this way, he commodified Palawa Country around his own narrative and experiences.

Morton Allport was not the only photographer to contribute to the nascent genre of landscape photography during the late 1850s and early 1860s. Geologist and surveyor Richard Daintree, for example, was hauling his wet-plate collodion kit and camera around Millowl/Phillip Island and along Weariby Yallock/the Werribee River.[94] These expeditions were made in addition to his collaborations with Antoine Fauchery on *Sun Pictures of Victoria*, the contents of which also included some early landscape exposures. These men, and others, sit at the cusp of a technological shift where these first photographic formats, which tethered photographers to the darkroom or darkroom tent, gave way to the new, more mobile possibilities of dry-plate processes. Collodion-albumen and other subsequent negative dry-plate processes allowed photographers to keep their exposed plates for development at a later time. I have argued in this chapter that 'outdoor' colonial photography begins on the windowsills and pavements outside urban colonial studios. Following the outward development of colonial towns and cities—and as photography's chemical components became less volatile—applications for the photographic technology also expanded to become much less exclusively urban.

Nevertheless, there was not a neat linear movement of photographers to the geographic frontiers of colonial control of the land. Paul Ricochet's relief in locating (Palawa) country suitable for his preconceived pursuit of landscape photography relied on his preceding experience of Naarm/ Melbourne's cacophonous urban photographic scene. In the 1870s, studio photographer Charles Walter purchased a landscape photography kit, in a rectangular box identical to that in Otté's 1858 frontispiece illustration. A portrait of Walter with his camera kit strapped to his back was engraved for the December 1873 edition of the *Illustrated Australian News for Home Readers.* The accompanying article, one of several in a series for the paper, outlines a trip 'Our Artist' made to Cape Otway, Gulidjan and Gadubanud Country, on photographic assignment.[95] Colonial cities were not only sites of departure for landscape, or 'wild country' photographic expeditions, but also sites of return. The urban colonial and international exhibition circuit and the pages of large metropolitan colonial periodicals were the spaces where the photographic reproductions of Aboriginal Country, unacknowledged as such, were consumed.

Of course, colonial artists continued to photograph towns and cities for the remainder of the nineteenth century. Just like those first daguerreotypists, Fred Kruger sought out buildings of height from which to capture cityscapes.[96] His 1879 panoramic view of Djilang/Geelong shows the same railway tracks from Turner's sixth-plate daguerreotype slicing across the 80-centimetre length of the photograph. This panorama was exhibited in Kolkata/Calcutta (1883), Amsterdam (1883) and back in Djilang/Geelong (1887).[97] Much like the work of his daguerreian predecessors, Kruger's photography was premised on contradiction. The ostensibly *totalising* vision achieved through such skilled composition provided only ideological renderings of Country, wilfully framed around its immediate colonial uses.

The double consciousness of landscape photography, depicting sites of privileged artistic reverie and documenting untapped natural resources, flourished over the remainder of the nineteenth century. J. W. (John William) Lindt travelled with camera, kit and an assistant in tow along the Boorimbah/ Clarence River in 1875, on assignment for the New South Wales colonial government. Lindt's commission, early in his colonial career, was predicated on illuminating the red cedar resources of the region and documenting the engineering features along the newly completed Newton Boyd Road. As Ken Orchard has outlined, Lindt construed Country according to a German Romantic tradition, presenting the Boorimbah as a languid, safe and 'available' space for artistic contemplation.[98] This series was titled 'Characteristic Australian Forest Scenery', and awarded a gold medal at the Philadelphia Centennial Exhibition of 1876, where Bayliss's gigantic panorama was also hung. Nicholas John Caire trekked through Aboriginal Country in south-eastern Victoria for much of the late 1870s, photographing fern gullies and ancient forests using the albumen processes. As Helen Ennis argues, giant trees served Caire's photographic practice, either dead or alive. One significant vein of his work documented the region's timber's utilitarian use in the construction of picnic shelters and homes.[99] The careers of Bayliss, Kruger, Lindt, Caire, along with an expanding cohort of professional colonial photographers, flooded international and local markets with pictures of Country configured with a colonial, resource-orientated legibility. But the visual vocabularies they drew from, the commodification of Country they enacted, as well as the circuits within which their photographs travelled—both official and familial—were established during this earlier period of practice.

5

Photographic Reproduction and Circulation

Photography's ability to bear witness to a particular moment—seemingly to record and replicate the real—has captivated audiences since the medium's inception. This was keenly felt in a settler colonial context, where populations were distant both from one another, and from a home or family overseas. Consequently, colonists invested photography with a heightened authority and emotional charge as a substitute for firsthand vision. This chapter follows the copying, publication and circulation of a selection of mid-century photographs and photographically based images, where the individual encounter with looking at an image was broadened to a group or communal experience.

The multiplication of a single photographic exposure is most apparent with the introduction of later nineteenth-century photographic innovations and technologies. For example, André-Adolphe-Eugène Disdéri's carte de visite, patented in 1854, exponentially increased the output of commercial photography studios globally from the middle of the 1860s.[1] Carte de visite cameras had multiple lenses that exposed identical portraits on a single glass negative (**Figure 5.1**). The carte de visite format issued standardised albumen prints of 8.9 × 5.4 cm, which were often mounted on card. As Joanna Gilmour notes, '*cartes* were cheap, durable, transportable and, most significantly, collectable'.[2] They opened the photographic portrait marketplace to an expanded class of consumers, extending beyond those middle-class colonials who could afford a daguerreotype from the earliest studios. Two decades later, in the 1880s, halftone printing was refined, and introduced to illustrate publications and newssheets.[3] The halftone method exposed a glass plate photograph through a porous silk screen and onto a printing plate, translating the dark and light areas of the image into a series of black and white dots on the receiving plate. The human eye perceives the arrangement of these black and white dots as producing a tonal range and replicating the original photograph. The economy and speed of the halftone process led to an increased volume of illustrations in journalism, books and literary magazines. This chapter acknowledges the impact that the carte de visite and halftone printing had on the circulation of photographs in the nineteenth century. But it also works to highlight an earlier history of reproducibility these later innovations intersected with and built upon. As Ibbetson's

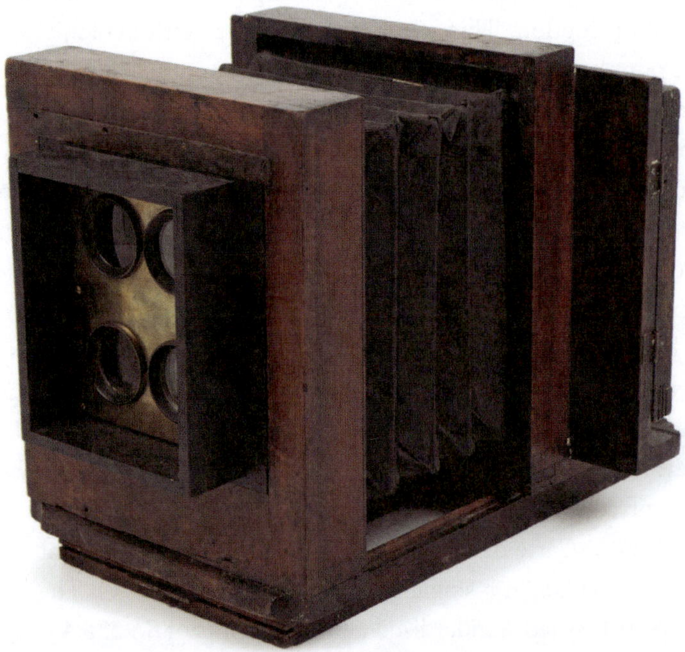

Figure 5.1: E. & H. T. Anthony & Co., carte de visite camera with 'swing back' viewing screen, 1860–80, American made. Powerhouse Museum.

starfish lithograph demonstrated in Chapter 1, the logic of photographic copying is as old as the medium itself, and was first achieved through photography's relationships with other printing and duplicating media.

The reproduction and dissemination of mid-century photography was concentrated around three interesting applications of the medium in a colonial context. Firstly, photographs were used as tools of surveillance and to record the appearance of unlawful characters. A role for photography in policing is commonly understood as beginning in France in the 1880s, with Alphonse Bertillon's division of the paired profile and front-on mug shot as a standardised identification system.[4] Photography intersects with criminality much earlier in the colonies: for example, in documenting bushrangers' capture, prosecution and, sometimes, even death. Significantly, as the discussion of Ben Hall will elucidate, bushrangers also employed photography, to throw the gaze of surveillance back on the authorities. Secondly, photography was deployed to create images of public celebrity for pioneering explorers. Such portraits were commodified as collectable objects, abstracting their subjects, to a degree, from the circumstances and outcomes of their expeditions. The third application of photographic mobility and reproduction was in the consolidation of settler colonial families' portrait collections. Family photographs were exchanged, and individual portraits rephotographed in updated processes, to cement narratives of inheritance and familial identity that were colonially situated. All these uses demonstrate photography's gathering importance within an increasingly complex landscape of colonial vision.

Surveillance and Capture

The figure of the bushranger emerged soon after the British invasion of the Australian continent and has broadly permeated colonial art—not just photography. Bushrangers, as Meg Foster remarks, were criminals who conducted robberies with the threat or orchestration of violence, evading capture 'by concealment in the bush'.[5] Absconding convicts who raided residences and public buildings on the bushland periphery of the first settlements are typically positioned as the first bushrangers. Consequently, the visual 'diagnosis' or identification of bushrangers as criminals dates to this period. For example, bushranger John ('Jack') Donohoe's corpse was sketched in the morgue of Sydney Hospital after he was shot and killed by soldier John Muckleston on 1 September 1830. Donohoe had operated on Dharug Country. He began his unlawful career as a highway robber in 1827, along Richmond Road, with a revolving gang of accomplices. As Grace Karskens has argued, Donohoe was a 'self-conscious outlaw', who executed ambushes in flamboyant attire to give his crimes a 'sense of theatre' and notoriety.[6] Donohoe's post-mortem portrait is ceremonial but, by comparison, austere. In the sketch, which was subsequently lithographed and attributed to Thomas Mitchell, Donohoe is depicted as a cadaver: a naked anatomical subject of study, lying on the mortuary table.[7] He was drawn from the waist up at a blunt profile angle with his neck resting on a support. A plain cloth bunches at his waistline, as if pulled back from the top half of his body in the act of identification, artistically replicated. The artist has configured a physiognomic likeness, stripping back the self-styled trimmings of his bushranger character.

Bushranging crimes peaked in the mid-century through to 1880, correlating with an intensity of prospecting on Aboriginal land in Victoria and New South Wales. Gold mining generated bullion, which was transported to major cities for secure deposit. As historian Mark Finnane notes, the most notorious ambushes by colonial bushrangers were targeted at gold escorts leaving the mining fields.[8] Bushranging extended, though, to vulnerable or loosely guarded cash reserves: taverns, hotels, mail carts and public coaches. It was this more lateral threat of violence to civilians travelling through frontier districts that inspired a generation of colonial artists. S. T. (Samuel Thomas) Gill drew animated scenes of bushranging heists for *The Australian Sketchbook*. Plate 24, dated 1864, shows a band of three men with muskets jumping in front of a passenger-carrying mail coach.[9] Gill gave visual precedence to the startled expressions of commuters, leaving the bushrangers' faces concealed by portraying them as masked or with their backs turned. The sketch is an imaginative rendering, relaying the anxiety of the attack, rather than one that positions Gill himself as an observer to the crime. Colonial sketcher turned South Australian police commissioner George Hamilton may have had more firsthand experience with the criminal activities of bushrangers.

However, his sketches of ambushes, which were exhibited locally in the 1860s, were praised not for their documentary potential but for their artistry and anatomical precision in depicting horses.[10]

In colonial paintings, bushranging was often mythologised at a distance from the ambushes artists set out to document. William Strutt's *Bushrangers, Victoria, Australia 1852* conjures a forlorn scene on St Kilda Road at the bushland extremities of Naarm/Melbourne. A party of respectably dressed travellers sit helpless by the roadside, having been intercepted by a rifle-wielding gang and forced to turn out their pockets. As the date in its title suggests, the scene was crafted with reference to a historic event but, as Andrew Sayers qualifies, Strutt completed the painting in England during 1887, almost forty years after the actual event.[11] Similarly, Tom Roberts' *Bailed Up* shows passengers on a Cobb & Co. coach in Kamilaroi Country, near Inverell, held up by an armed gang of bushrangers. This canvas was completed by Roberts in 1895 at the site of the historic incident, where, as Virginia Spate remarks, Roberts employed local townspeople as in situ models.[12] *Bailed Up* aestheticises a violence that had passed through the region over two decades earlier. The persistence of the bushranging motif into the late nineteenth century speaks to how the white, anti-authoritarian masculine figure of the bushranger (not historically representative of this racially diverse class of criminals) was being reworked into an emerging nationalist narrative.[13]

By contrast, photography intersected more immediately with the economies of surveillance and reporting on bushranging. It was used to substantiate the identities of the criminals, offering up their faces for public consumption and commentary. However, as a practice, photography was evolving rapidly during the mid-century period and bushranging activities inevitably intersected with its more civilian uses.

The complicated collisions between bushranging and photography are demonstrated in the relatively short felonious career of Ben Hall. Hall was born in 1837, the fourth child of Benjamin Hall and Eliza Somers, who had both been transported to the Australian colonies as petty criminals.[14] Their convict sentences concluded in the early 1830s, whereupon they moved to Wonnarua Country, near Maitland, to begin lives as pastoralists.[15] As a young adult, Hall made a living working as a stockman, leasing land near Spring Creek. In 1856, at the age of nineteen, he married Bridget Walsh on Wiradjuri Country, near Forbes.[16] It was probably around this time, or during the first few years of his married life, that Hall began commissioning his own studio portraits. One survives as a sixth-plate ambrotype, and shows Hall in riding boots, loose-fitting jodhpurs and a stockman's dust jacket (**Figure 5.2**). A limited palette of colour tinting, much of which has now dissipated, was applied to his cheeks and lips, necktie and the patterned side-table cloth. Hall appears appropriately stern for his portrait but, especially with the addition of colour, is an image of youthful vitality.

Hall committed robberies during the late 1850s and early 1860s, coinciding with the breakdown of his marriage. He moved into a life of major crime in June 1862, when he joined Frank Christie's (alias Frank Gardiner's) gang for the Eugowra gold escort robbery on Wiradjuri Country. Accounts in the press of Hall's appearance subsequently took on a forensic tone. The *New South Wales Police Gazette* described Hall on 18 November 1863 as:

> [a]bout 28 years of age, 5 foot 9 inches high, stout build, (would weigh about 13 stone 7 lbs) figure erect, respectable appearance, light brown wavy hair, short light beard, thick but darker near his throat and jaws, pleasing expression of countenance, soft grey eyes, handsome nose, inclined to be hooked, and thin compressed lips.[17]

Equally detailed descriptions were given of other high-offending bushrangers during 1863.[18] In August of that year, Fred Lowry, who had also participated in the Eugowra robbery, was shot and apprehended by police sergeant James Stephenson outside Burbong/Goulburn. He died of his wounds on the way to Goulburn jail, and Burbong/Goulburn-based studio photographer George Gregory was called upon to photograph his body. Lowry was pictured in a similar attitude to Donohoe, albeit three decades later, lying on his back with his head resting on a timber support. In his post-mortem portrait, Lowry remains clothed, his straw hat has been pulled back and his face turned toward Gregory's camera.[19] In an act of grim policing publicity, carte de visite prints of Lowry's

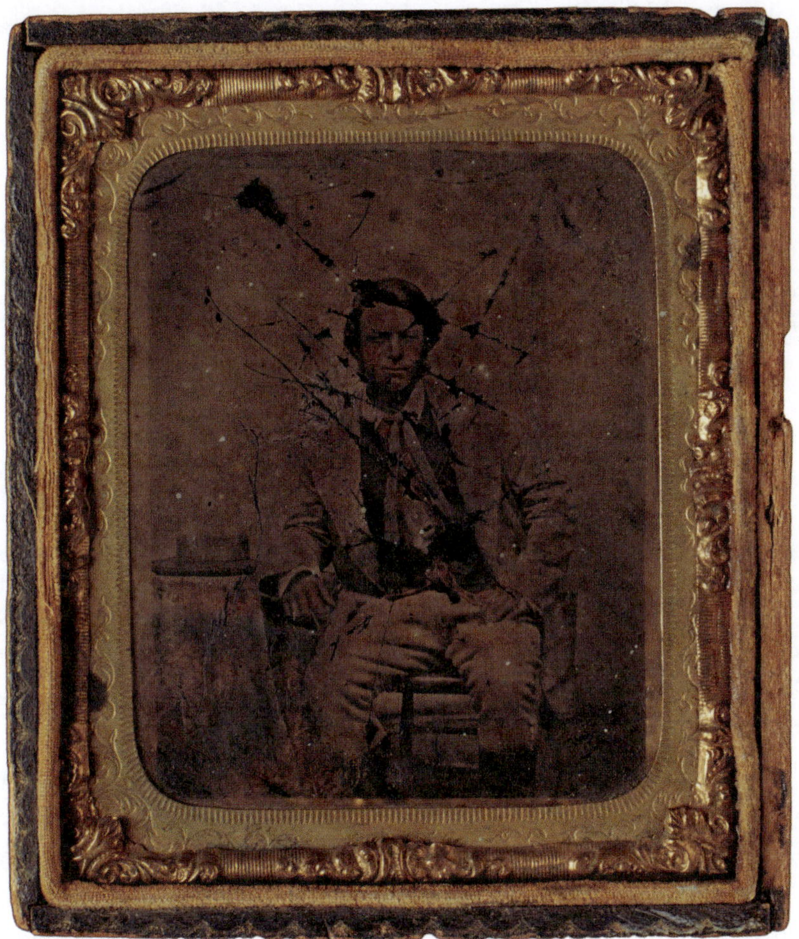

Figure 5.2: Unattributed, 'Ben Hall', c.1861, sixth-plate, colour-tinted, cased ambrotype. Justice and Police Museum/ Museums of History, New South Wales.

post-mortem portrait were publicly retailed and his photograph translated into an engraving for the *Illustrated Melbourne Post,* extending the reach of and expanding the audience for this macabre image.[20] Hall came into possession of a print of Lowry's post-mortem portrait and took to wearing it, as the *Braidwood News* reported in June 1864, 'secured within the lining of the crown of his hat', perhaps as a memento mori.[21]

Hall's criminal career placed him in contact with further civilian uses of photography. In November 1864, he and fellow bushrangers John

Gilbert and John Dunn intercepted and held up a Sydney-bound mail coach on Gundangara Country. The coach had paused at Rossiville, a colonial property on the outskirts of Burbong/Goulburn. A long account of the heist was published in Sydney newspaper the *Empire,* with the journalist quoting at length the eyewitness recollections of Rossiville's unnamed chamber maid. Hall and Gilbert reportedly opened all the mail coach's letters in a search for concealed cash and discovered many of the envelopes enclosed pictorial content:

> [t]here were a number of photographs in the letters all of which they looked at and expressed an opinion ... In one letter there was a photograph of a policeman, whom they apparently recognised, for one of them, pointing his revolver at the photograph said to the other: 'Wouldn't I like to have the original here'.[22]

This revealing passage is suggestive of the quantity of photographs circulating in the postage system by the early 1860s. The felons' violent banter represents an exact mirroring of how the judicial system would come to use photography to document bushrangers' own fatal apprehension.

Ben Hall's own photographic portrait entered public circulation after he was fatally wounded in 1865, at which point it was used to corroborate his criminal identity. Hall was shot multiple times on Wiradjuri Country, near Forbes, on 6 May, when he was ambushed by several police officers. This scene was recast as a dynamic half-page engraving (not photographically derived) and published on the cover of the 25 May edition of the *Illustrated Australian News for Home Readers.* At the time of his death, Hall was reportedly carrying £74, two gold chains, a gold watch and a tiny ninth-plate cased daguerreotype of a woman in his pockets.[23] The daguerreotype is now held at the Forbes and District Historical Museum.[24] It is believed to be of Susan Pryor, to whom Hall was romantically connected. Hall's effects reveal that even bushrangers participated in an emerging culture of photographic exchange (rather than just disrupting its circulation through the post). Hall's body was brought to Forbes Police Station, where it was put on display. A journalist for the *Western Examiner* remarked that hundreds of members of the public came

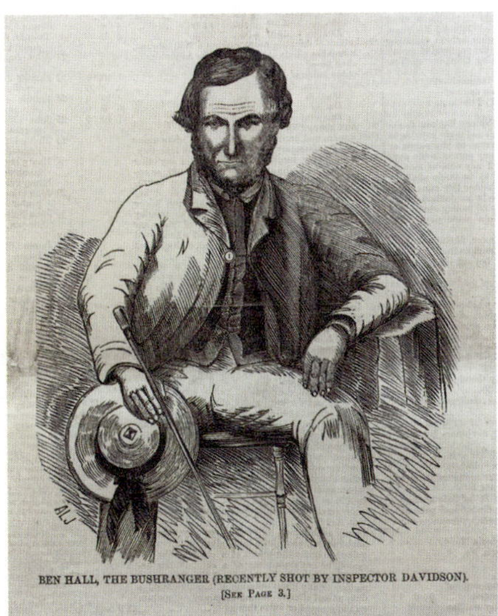

Figure 5.3: Unattributed, 'Ben Hall, (recently shot by Inspector Davidson)', the *Illustrated Sydney News*, 16 May 1865, p. 16.

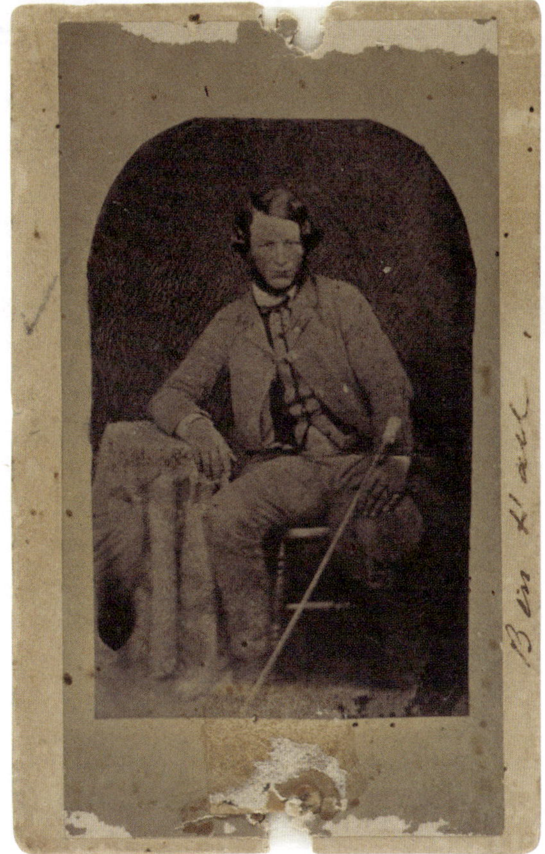

Figure 5.4: Freeman Brothers Studio, 'Ben Hall', 1865, uncoloured carte de visite print mounted on card, 9.9 × 6.4 cm. State Library of New South Wales.

to see Hall's 'handsome face' and commented on his uncanny familiarity: 'I have often seen that face somewhere but cannot tell where'.[25] Around this time, two studio portraits of Hall came into police custody. One is the ambrotype in **Figure 5.2**, discussed above. The second formed the basis of a wood engraving of Hall published in the *Illustrated Sydney News* on 16 May 1865 (**Figure 5.3**). As the accompanying column read, 'Our engraving is from a photograph in the possession of the police department, courteously placed at our disposal by [the inspector-general of the New South Wales police] E. Fosberry [Fosbery]'.[26] The portrait shows Hall seated in the same studio setting as in **Figure 5.2**, in a similar although not identical outfit, holding his hat and riding crop. Before the engraving was made, the Freeman Brothers' Sydney photography studio re-photographed the ambrotype. From their negative, paper carte de visite prints were made, the quantity and circulation of which are now hard to gauge, although (as described earlier) this negative/positive photographic format lent itself to reproduction (**Figure 5.4**).

Rather than being photographed in death, the validation of Hall's capture and demise was presented to colonial audiences through a studio photograph likely of his own commission. Hall's portrait was transformed from a personal keepsake to a seized asset and tool of identification, before finally becoming an object of public collection. Donohoe, Lowry and other bushrangers were portrayed as felons: drawn or photographed as anatomical studies or bullet-ridden cadavers.[27] Conversely, Hall's face and identity were offered up for public consumption from the familiar civilian context of the photography studio. His photograph, its wood-engraved reproduction and carte de visite facsimile offered him some level of respectability entwined with the act of studio portraiture. Although Hall's appearance and 'handsome face' had characterised press descriptions of him since his first crimes, the photograph operated to diminish further the severity of his offences in death.

Hall's portraits emphasise how the temporalities of an offender's photographic documentation and that of their arrest (or death) at the hands of the police did not always align. Photography's authority related to an embodied encounter between photographer and subject. But the photographic exposure did not invariably coincide neatly with the apprehension of the criminal. Hall's portrait(s) were not unique in this regard. We see a similar kind of chronological irregularity in the images of the death of Kelly gang member Joe Byrne, following the June 1880 siege at Yorta Yorta Country, Glenrowan. In the aftermath, J.W. Lindt photographed Byrne's body strung up outside the Benalla Police Station (**Figure 5.5**). Helen Ennis has described this image—'regarded as Australia's first press photograph'—as 'impressive for the legibility of its narrative'.[28] Lindt's photograph is not simply of Byrne, but a photograph of the act of photographing the outlaw. He has composed his shot by positioning the second photographer in the centre of the frame, in front of a party of artists and onlookers who are witnessing the exposure. Lindt's photograph, then, operates to communicate photography's importance in the record and substantiation of Byrne's death.

However, painter and draughtsman Julian Ashton, who was also present at Benalla Police Station, remembered the chronology around the posthumous visual record of Byrne differently. In his autobiography, Ashton recalled how once news of the siege reached Naarm/Melbourne, he was immediately sent by the editor of the *Illustrated Australian News* to Yorta Yorta Country, Glenrowan. Lindt took the first train and, upon

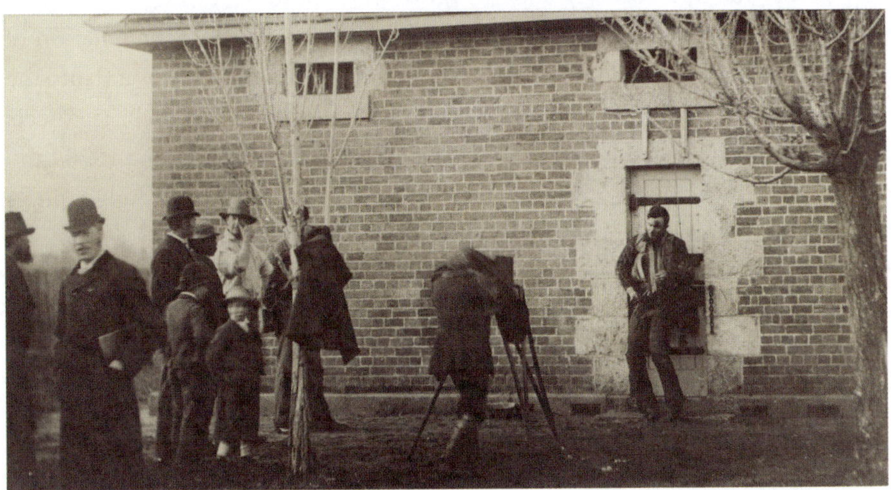

Figure 5.5: J.W. Lindt, [Joe Byrne's body outside Benalla Police Station], 29 June 1880, albumen silver print, 21 × 37 cm. State Library of Victoria.

arrival, was taken to the police station, where Byrne's corpse, having been extracted from the Glenrowan Inn, had rather unnecessarily been placed in a cell. According to Ashton's own recollection, he was the first to visually record Byrne. He completed his sketch of Byrne lying flat 'on the cold cement floor by candlelight'.[29] This sketch was the basis for a wood engraving titled 'Finding Byrne's Body – A Study' published in the 3 July edition of the *News*.[30] Sometime after Ashton's arrival at Glenrowan, a subsequent train delivered 'a number of photographers'.[31] Finding the light in the cell impossible to work with, Lindt requested that Byrne's body be strung up from a pulley in front of the police station. Ashton is also in Lindt's photograph, walking away from the unfolding scene, sketchbook tucked under one arm and looking directly at Lindt.[32] His own sketch of Byrne for the *News* was not just completed (as the photograph suggests) but rendered in a different setting altogether.

Photography's claim to bear witness to a criminal's capture was always contingent on the manufacture of a narrative of colonial criminality. As Susan Sontag famously argued, 'photographs furnish evidence'—as opposed to being evidential of a crime in and of themselves.[33] Certainly, we see this from the caption of Hall's photographically derived wood-engraved portrait, which labels him as a 'bushranger' and notes that he was 'recently shot' (**Figure 5.3**). Studio portraits and studio photographers continued to provide the evidentiary documentation of colonial policing for the remainder of the nineteenth century and into the twentieth century. The first photographically embellished charge sheets were introduced by the New South Wales Police Force in the 1870s and are now held at the Justice and Police Museum .[34] They include a single studio portrait, surrounded by a listing of the height, weight, eye colour, hair colour of the accused and a notation of scars or other distinguishing physical characteristics. This marriage of word and image prompted the reader to calibrate features they could not actually discern fully in the sepia photograph, under the heading of the alleged crime inscribed across the top of each charge sheet. Early twentieth-century glass plate negatives in this collection have names and charge sheet serial numbers scratched into the emulsion, connecting the crime itself to the likeness of the (alleged) offender. Hall's portrait sits at the beginning of these traditions, where the photograph becomes an expression of surveillance and identification of the criminal body.

Exploration and Celebrity

The reproduction and dissemination of colonial photographs was also tied to the business of exploration. Photography was instrumental in mythologising the figure of the colonial explorer. Yet, very rarely were these myths built upon photographs where exploration was actually taking place. Rather, studio photography was mobilised to produce a sense of respectability and heroism for the explorer subject. As James Ryan argues, it was often difficult to take photographic equipment into remote locations: 'photography and exploration remained a demanding combination', he writes, for much of the nineteenth century.[35] Certainly, as Chapter 4 outlined, from the 1860s collodion-albumen processes and purpose-built mobile photography kits made it increasingly possible for colonial photographers to operate in bushland settings. However, as Gael Newton has argued, these individuals can best be classified as 'excursionists'.[36] The careers of Richard Daintree, Morton Allport, J.W. Lindt and the Anson Brothers all show that camera technologies were employed to represent a privileged encounter with nature; but this never occurred too far from colonial settlements. Photography was not employed as a documentary tool of colonial exploration until the end of the century. This is in part a reflection of how amateur technologies, such as those retailed by Kodak, made it possible to carry lighter cameras with film that was able to be stored for longer periods, mitigating the need to develop photographs on location. It is indicative of a shift more generally in the culture of exploration, towards 'scientific' interest, where photography was considered an aid to qualitative research. The Royal Geographical Society in Britain employed its first Official Instructor of Photography, John Thomson, in 1891.[37] In a colonial context, the Horn Expedition of 1894 employed academic scientist Walter Baldwin Spencer as expedition photographer, to document the group's three-month journey through Arrernte Country. Motivated by paternalistic attitudes and what John Morton notes was an 'elegiac context', this was among the first expedition to photograph central desert people on Country occupied in ceremonies and carrying out a range of daily cultural practices.[38] These photographs, taken with the belief that Spencer was documenting a 'dying race', are now valuable not for showing the actual work of the expedition but, rather, for demonstrating the survival of Culture, and as a record of ancestors and Kin.[39]

Before this more integrated employment of photography into expeditions, the medium had long played a part in documenting the profiles of explorers and commemorating their departure. This is evident more broadly in the British imperial world in the portraiture of the expeditionary party that left London in May 1845 to locate an arctic passage between the Atlantic and Pacific oceans. The expedition was led by John Franklin, who had recently concluded his term as governor of Van Diemen's Land. Returning to Britain, Franklin was recruited to head the search for a northwest passage—having already conducted two prior expeditions of the Canadian arctic coast in the early to mid-1820s.[40] Before his party departed the River Thames, daguerreotype portraits of the officers were taken by Richard Beard's studio, on board the expedition's vessels, the *Erebus* and the *Terror*. These daguerreotypes acquired a new significance when the entire expedition fell out of contact. Geoffrey Batchen has outlined how fourteen of the portraits were translated into wood engravings for the *Illustrated London News* in 1851, to accompany reporting on the various search parties sent out after the group.[41] Over the first half of the 1850s, engravings-after-the daguerreotypes of the Franklin party travelled globally, reproduced in the American pictorial press and exhibited at the St Andrews Picture Gallery in Kolkata/Calcutta.[42] Interestingly, it was only once the expedition members were feared deceased that the photographically derived portraits were circulated, as if photography lent something more authoritative and mournfully charged than any other form of representation. The May 1845 departure of the *Erebus* and the *Terror* had initially been visually reported on in the papers by regular wood engravings (not photographically derived).[43] Franklin died midway through his polar expedition on Qikiqtaq/King William Island in 1847, followed shortly after by the remainder of the expeditionary party. By the 1860s, multiple memorials had been erected in Greenwich, England for Franklin's expedition and similarly fated explorers who had gone out in search of the party and the northwest passage. By this stage, Franklin's daguerreotype, and its various facsimiles, had already come to represent his 'heroic' explorer persona internationally.

Franklin's daguerreotypes resonate with the photographic treatment of colonial explorers Robert O'Hara Burke and William John Wills. Burke, a regional police officer, and Wills, a grazier turned assistant astronomer, were appointed by the Royal Society of Victoria and the Victorian colonial government to lead an expedition in 1860 from Naarm/Melbourne, across the continent, to Yulluna/the Gulf of Carpentaria. Neither man had any substantial surveying experience. The expedition was intended to identify interior land suitable for farming, as well as to collect geographic knowledge to aid in the construction of a transcontinental telegraph line. Burke and Wills contracted beriberi, caused by thiamine deficiency. This accelerated the effects of malnutrition and led to their deaths. As Ian D. Clark and Fred Cahir observe, 'Burke's refusal to consult with local Aboriginal people meant that he did not fully appreciate how Aboriginal people prepared nardoo [a native fern] in a way that minimised its effect on thiamine availability'.[44] Only one out of their original group of nineteen, John King, survived the expedition, largely through being cared for by the Yandruwandha People, in south-western Queensland, whose intimate knowledge of Country extended to proper preparation of edible plants.[45]

Burke and Wills sat for individual studio photographs prior to their expedition's departure from Royal Park, Naarm/Melbourne. These portraits were taken at the studio of T.A. (Thomas Adams) Hill.[46] Hill established himself as a photographer in 1855, having taken over the former rooms of Duryea and McDonald (discussed in Chapter 3) when they left for lutruwita/Tasmania.[47] Both portraits are quite standard studio productions. The only hint at an expeditionary motivation for the commission is provided in Wills's ambrotype by the delicate chain that loops around his neck, intersecting with his more prominent pocket watch chain and appearing to support a compass-sized leather pouch (**Figure 5.6**). Hill worked across various photographic formats, offering—alongside daguerreotypes and ambrotypes—calotypes, and collodion and albumen prints.[48] This may explain how rephotographed (and printed) copies of the original cased photographs came to be used by William Strutt on the first page of his album commemorating the expedition (**Figure 5.7**). The album, compiled after the explorers' demise, includes Strutt's own drawings and watercolours. These were interspliced with unattributed documentary photographs, mainly in stereo-print format, some of which show the expedition leaving Royal Park in August 1860 to much fanfare.[49]

Hill collaborated with several engravers, lithographers and publishers, facilitating the transmission of his original photographic portraits of Burke and Wills further afield. The original cased photographs (or, more likely, their rephotographed copies) formed the basis for two large 49 × 38 cm mezzotints of the explorers completed by H.S. (Henry Samuel) Sadd.[50] The photographic genesis of the mezzotints—as seen in Wills's portrait (**Figure 5.8**)—is declared in the inscription that runs along the lower curve of each vignetted image: 'Phot-d by T.A. Hill … Eng-d by H.S. Sadd'. Hill and Sadd had worked on other mezzotints-after-photographs prior to those of the explorers: portraits of elite colonial men that included the second governor of the colony of Victoria, John O'Shanassy.[51] Hill's portraits of Burke and Wills also formed the basis of engravings disseminated in the popular press following news of their death. Draughtsman Eugene Montague Scott copied the portraits for the 22 November 1861 edition of the *Illustrated Australian Mail*, captioning each image 'from a photograph by T.A. Hill'.[52] An unacknowledged artist also used the photographs, or perhaps their already engraved copies, as the basis for two portraits of the explorers in the *Illustrated London News* in February 1862.[53]

These various registers of collection and memorialisation of Burke and Wills's photographs divorced the explorers from the context of their demise. The rich tones and large-scale format of the mezzotints put them in the company of other elite colonial men. The inclusion of Hill's photographs on the front page of Strutt's commemorative album suggested how in death their studio portraits gained a new poignancy (even in comparison to Strutt's own painted representations). The photographs' translation in the colonial and international illustrated press

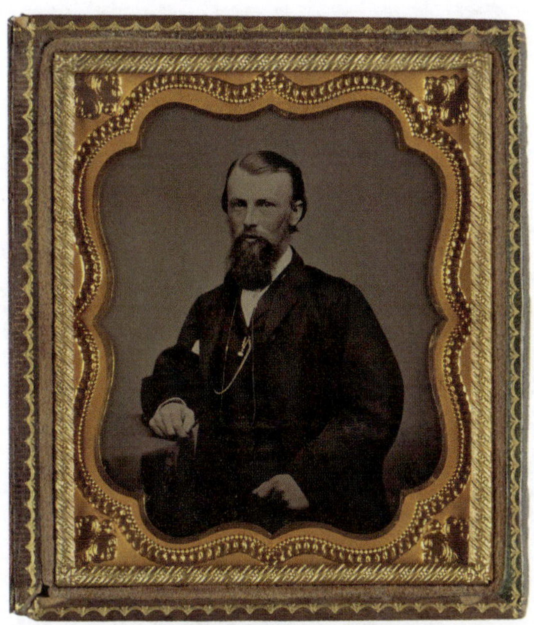

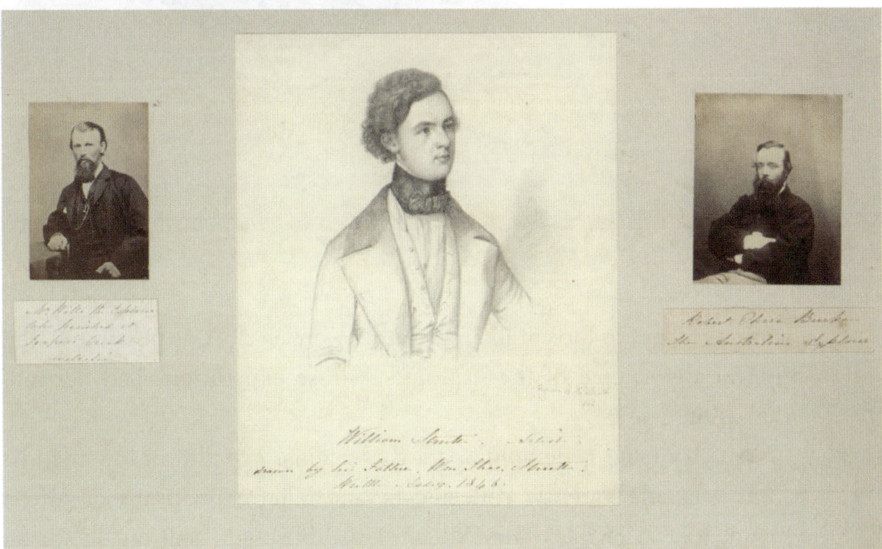

Figure 5.6: T.A. Hill, 'William John Wills', 1860, sixth-plate, gold-accented, cased ambrotype. State Library of New South Wales.

Figure 5.7: William Strutt, 'A collection of drawings in watercolour, ink and pencil by William Strutt R.B.G. F.Z.S. illustrating the Burke and Wills Exploring Expedition Crossing the Continent of Australia from Cooper's Creek to Carpentaria, Aug 1860-June 1861', Vol. 1 [1st series], 1861, p.1. State Library of New South Wales.

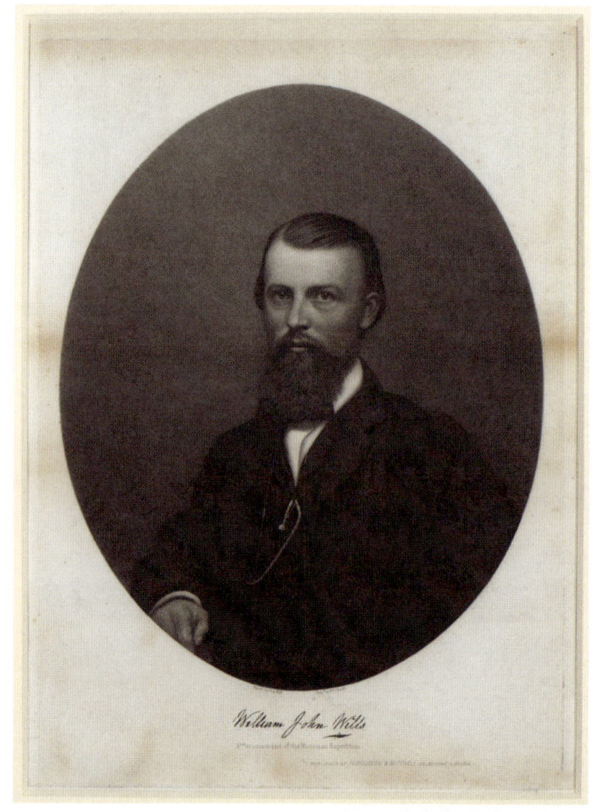

Figure 5.8: H.S. (Henry Samuel) Sadd (engraver) after T. A. (Thomas Adams) Hill (photographer), published by Fergusson & Mitchell, 'William John Wills, 2nd in command of the Victorian Expedition', 1860–61, mezzotint from a photograph, 49 × 38 cm (on paper). National Portrait Gallery, Canberra.

enabled readers to look at likenesses that were as close as possible to the physical appearance of the explorers, whose expeditions had become international news.

Much of the geographic data the original expedition intended to gather was subsequently collected by the relief expeditions of Alfred Howitt, John McKinlay and William Landsborough, sent out in search of Burke and Wills.[54] As discussed in Chapter 2, Landsborough's own expedition was supported by Aboriginal guides, Wamba-Wamba man Jemmy, and Jack Fisherman from the Meeanjin/Brisbane region, who were depicted in the photographically based engraving used as the frontispiece to Landsborough's own published journal. The 1862 Royal

Commission into the Burke and Wills expedition established that Burke was an unfit leader and his decisions to split the party and separate its rations at various stages of their journey were ultimately fatal.[55] But, by this point, photography, alongside other visual media, had played an active role in presenting a heroic persona for the two men. Even before the first statue of the pair was erected in April 1865, on Wurundjeri Country at the corner of Collins and Russell streets in Naarm/Melbourne, photographically derived images had made the figures of Burke and Wills monumental in the public imagination.[56]

Family Photography; Colonial Photography

Mid-century photographic reproduction did not always begin with a photograph and then progress to an engraved or etched copy. Photography was also employed as the method of duplication. We see this use for photography from the advent of the first professional studios. George Barron Goodman's unlicensed daguerreotype rival in nipaluna/Hobart, Thomas Bock, not only recalibrated the early daguerreotype process to accord with the colonial atmosphere and light (see Chapter 2) but also thought innovatively about photography's place within a broader colonial visual economy. For Bock, the camera was both a device for capturing a portrait from life and a tool for copying a portrait already finished in another medium.

Bock arrived in the colony as a shackled convict. In April 1823, he was sentenced to transportation by the judge at the Warwick Assizes, for administering a broth intended to terminate the pregnancy of Ann Yates, whose unborn child he had reportedly fathered.[57] Bock's training as an engraver and skill as a portraitist meant he avoided hard convict labour once he disembarked in lutruwita/Tasmania. In December 1824, the year of his arrival, he was commissioned to engrave a series of note designs for the Bank of Van Diemen's Land's inaugural currency.[58] Between October 1831 and September 1835, Bock was paid by George Augustus Robinson to complete a suite of crayon portraits of Palawa people, who were being systematically dispossessed by Governor Arthur's genocidal 'Black Line' assault.[59] Bock received a conditional pardon in 1832.[60] By the early 1840s, he had completed several sizeable oil-on-canvas portraits for notable colonial families, among them the Wilsons and the Tileys.[61] Bock already had a bevy of portrait clients by the time news of photography's invention arrived in the colony.

Bock's portrait enterprise was not targeted specifically at photographic patrons but at the returning and varied custom of wealthy colonial families. Steve Edwards has argued that in Britain, the need to purchase a licence from Richard Beard to operate a daguerreotype studio (up until the early 1850s) 'created a particular brand of authorship and identity, specific to capital'.[62] As Chapter 2 outlined, Beard licensees were obligated to purchase daguerreotype plates, chemicals, cases and materials of the trade directly from him. This was an investment that focused each studio exclusively on photography and on a particularly homogenised photographic product.[63] Early photography businesses in the Australian colonies were far less regulated. Nevertheless, to ensure a profitable volume of customers, photographers were compelled to travel between cities and towns. Bock's studio practice was different from both of these business models, not least because he infrequently left nipaluna/Hobart and was able to rely on the same clients for repeat commissions. As Chris Long speculates, 'Bock's clientele for his painted portraiture would probably also [have sat] for his photographs'.[64]

This internal circularity of commission, in the service of colonial families, is evident in Bock's portraits of Richard Lewis and his family.[65] Lewis had migrated to nipaluna/Hobart as a free settler in 1815, and established a store and shipping business that transacted with partners in London.[66] In 1823, he was one of the foundational proprietors of the Bank of Van Diemen's Land, which the following year, as discussed above, enlisted Bock to engrave plates for its inaugural currency.[67] By the mid 1840s, Lewis's merchant business had expanded to include his two eldest sons, David and Neil, as partners.[68] Lewis and his family acquired multiple portraits of themselves, reflecting their growing colonial fortune and elevated public profile. Among these pieces were commissions from Bock. Richard Lewis and his wife Isabella were the subjects of large oil-on-canvas portraits completed in the mid-1830s.[69] Isabella sat for Bock again in the early to mid-1850s for a daguerreotype, which he expertly and extensively colour-tinted.[70] In 1851, Richard and Isabella again visited Bock, this time for large-scale portraits of themselves in charcoal and China White.[71] Each of their five sons also sat for a Bock portrait in the same sketched format.[72] The sons' portraits were completed in individual sittings across a period that spanned five years, from 1848 to 1853. Accompanying each commission was the exposure of a daguerreotype, not taken from life but as a capture of the sketched portraits.

An example of this pairing can be seen in Bock's 54.5 × 48 cm sketch of the Lewises' third son, George Richard, completed in 1851 (**Figure 5.9**), and its cased 8.3 × 7 cm sixth-plate daguerreotype reproduction (**Figure 5.10**). In the sketched portrait, Bock used gouache to colour the cravat and lips, and define the eyes, which are rendered in his exaggerated doe-eyed style. China White has been employed to articulate where light fell on the sitter, such as the sheen of the forehead or the bridge of the nose. Bock then tinted his monochrome daguerreotype copy, replicating the coloured and white accenting he had applied to the sketches. He made mobile—or, to return to Gilmour's definition of the later carte de visite, 'transportable'[73]—the relatively immobile large-format framed sketch, by reproducing and packaging a facsimile of each portrait as a compact, cased daguerreotype. Bock employed the photographic technology of the daguerreotype, predicated on the production of a unique image, in the service of providing a reproduction of a portrait in another medium. His mixed-media family portrait amalgams were entrepreneurial. Yet, they were also the product of an unregulated colonial photographic marketplace and reflective of Bock's own diverse skill as a portraitist.

Bock's use of camera technology for copying was exclusive to his own artistic practice. However, by the 1850s, other photography studios were increasingly advertising their services in providing photographic copies of artworks that clients brought to their rooms. Many of the studios discussed in Chapter 3 provided a copying service. T. S. Glaister's promotional pamphlet (see **Figure 3.5**) advertised that 'Views of Buildings, Country Seats, Statuary, Painting, Pictures of all Kinds, Medallions, & co., & co., [were] accurately copied' at his Warrane/Sydney Cove Excelsior

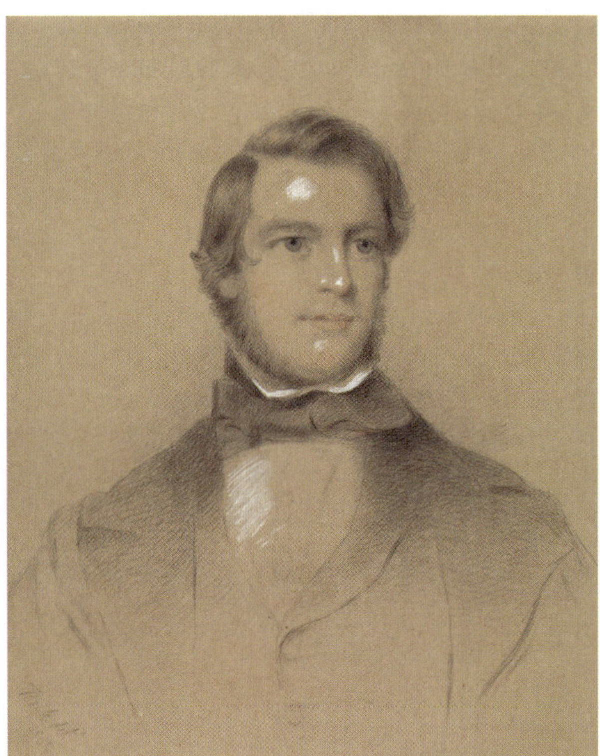

Figure 5.9: Thomas Bock, 'George Richard Lewis', 1851, charcoal, China White and gouache on buff paper, 54.5 × 48 cm (framed, but shown unframed here). Allport Library and Museum of Fine Arts.

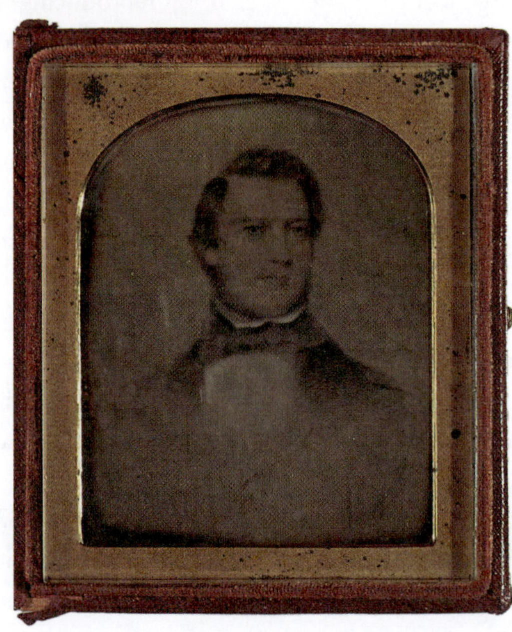

Figure 5.10: Thomas Bock, 'George Richard Lewis', c.1851, sixth-plate, colour-tinted, cased daguerreotype. Tasmanian Museum and Art Gallery.

Galleries. His pupil Edwin Torrens Brissenden, who branched out in 1858 to establish one of the earliest photographic studios in Meeanjin/Brisbane, mimicked his former boss in flagging his own camera-based copying service.[74] The Duryea Brothers notified the Boorloo/Perth public in October 1857 that 'Oil Paintings [could be] Copied' at their city studio.[75] Patrizia Di Bello has argued that photography was primed for reproducing visual art because it used light focused off the original and back into the camera, 'instead of arrangements of pointers, pantographic arms and cutting tools [characteristic of earlier copying devices]', to keep the copy perfectly proportional.[76]

There are examples of early photographically copied artworks in several British and American collections. Antoine Claudet, for instance, was commissioned to photograph displays from the 1851 London International Exhibition as stereo-daguerreotypes. These were not installation shots (although he did shoot those too) but photographs of individual exhibits taken against darkened backdrops, in the style of contemporary museum collection photography. A selection of Claudet's stereo-daguerreotypes are held at the Harry Ransom Center at the University of Texas, Austin. Their subjects included an arrangement of taxidermied birds on a twig mount, a Victorian bust sculpted in the Greek style, and the bronze *Amazone zu Pferde* (1841) by August Kiss.[77] As John Plunkett has noted, stereoscopy 'gave photography a new haptic, material dimension'.[78] Plunkett is here referring to the *illusion* of depth and dimension generated by the stereo format, which is particularly effective when looking at a reproduction of a three-dimensional work of art, such as a sculpture or taxidermied specimen.

In Australian collections, there are very few examples of mid-nineteenth-century photographs of notable public artworks, in stereo format or as single images.[79] The only example I have come across is Louisa How's rephotographed portrait of the dowager countess of Darnley, made from the *Art Journal*'s engraving and preserved within the assemblage in her album (**Figure 2.18**). Even though few examples survive, the copying services of Glaister, Brissenden, the Duryeas and other mid-century studios were advertised for too long to suggest they were not used. Rather, it is far more likely that these photographed images of colonial paintings, medallions and statuary have perhaps not been kept or collected because their value over time was diminished by their status as a copy. The exception to this archival absence of copies comes in the form of the rephotographed photographs of public figures, such as Hall, Burke and Wills, and in the rephotography initiated by colonial families.

Colonial families and family members often commissioned studios to rephotograph pictures of their loved ones originally captured in earlier photographic formats. This was a practice that began in the 1850s, when photography was barely two decades old. Unlike Bock's bespoke reproductions of his large-scale sketches, the rephotographing of existing family photographs was not confined to elite or wealthy customers. Emily Hutchison née Wilson's bid to commission a daguerreotype of her family, and then to have it rephotographed years later, speaks to commonplace uses of the camera as a tool of duplication where family portraits were concerned. Hutchison travelled from London in 1851 through the Assisted Immigration Scheme.[80] She began her time in the colonies as a governess, before marrying Quinbean/Queanbeyan resident Edward Hutchison in 1853.[81] We know much about Emily Hutchison's life in south-eastern New South Wales because she was a fastidious correspondent. Her papers are now a part of the Queanbeyan-Palerang Regional Library collection. Hutchison looked to photography as a panacea for her own homesickness. Her letters recall her reactions to receiving (original) family daguerreotypes in the mail. She commented on a daguerreotype of her mother, writing: 'Your likeness is splendid, and when we looked thro [sic] a magnifying glass it seemed as if it were flesh and blood. If I had a stronger magnifying glass we could see Father's features in your brooch.'[82] Hutchison's response indicates this is a layered portrait, consolidating various registers of intimacy (as was the case in the pastoral estate portrait from **Figure 3.17**). In the daguerreotype, Ann Wilson wears a small brooch—a daguerreotyped, painted or sculpted portrait—to communicate visually her affection for and marriage to her husband (not photographed alongside her). Posting this portrait to her daughter extended that affection to her child and shows the role that colonial photography could play in preserving family bonds.

The receipt of this and other daguerreotypes from her family in England fed Hutchison's desire to commission a photograph of her own family to send in return. In June 1854, she gave birth to a son, Alexander,[83] but it was not until December 1855 that an itinerant photographer visited Quinbean/Queanbeyan. It was probably Lawson Insley who took the Hutchison family daguerreotype, with press advertisements noting that he operated a provisional studio out of Byrne's Hotel at this time.[84] Hutchison was bitterly disappointed with Insley's daguerreotype but mailed it nevertheless. In the accompanying letter to her mother, dated 14 January 1856, she described it as 'very inferior', complaining she had worn her 'silver-grey [dress] with full lace sleeves but you see nothing of this [detail]'.[85] Hutchison did not benefit from the advice that other colonial customers, like Glaister's, were given prior to their portrait sitting, directing them on how to dress for the camera, and what colours and fabrics to avoid.

The Hutchison family daguerreotype took on an increased significance following the premature death of Emily's husband Edward in 1857. Emily had a sophisticated understanding of photography, perhaps precisely on account of her residence in a regional colonial town, and her prior use of the medium as a simulacrum of connection and intimacy. She wrote to her parents in London, asking them to return her family daguerreotype so she could have it copied.[86] It is possible this idea came to her after seeing the copying services of metropolitan photography studios advertised in local newspapers. Hutchison requested her parents send this precious daguerreotype with a family friend travelling to Naarm/Melbourne, rather than by mail.[87] By the time it arrived back in her possession in 1860, the collodion processes had come to dominate the studio photography scene, and it was through this process, and by means of a salted paper print from a collodion negative, that the image was rephotographed and reproduced.[88]

The international relay of Hutchison's daguerreotype underscores the emotion-charged act of duplicating colonial family photographs in the instance of a member's death. Certainly, Hutchison's salted paper print is testament to her grief, where the original daguerreotype was probably invested with a different set of emotions. However, the act of copying also complicates the authority of the camera and the resulting copied photograph as bearing witness to a person, scene or event. A further example of this duplication can be seen in the daguerreotype of William Lawson Snr, taken at Goodman's studio, where, as I argue in Chapter 2, a specifically colonial iteration of photography began. Lawson sat for a daguerreotype between 1846 and 1847 in Goodman's Warrane/Sydney Cove rooms.[89] This daguerreotype is not extant. What is physically preserved at the State Library of New South Wales today is an elaborately gold-framed ambrotype copy (**Figure 5.11**) and a later carte de visite copy (**Figure 5.12**). Lawson Snr passed away in 1850, four years before the ambrotype process was invented in England and a decade before the carte de visite become the portrait format of trade from colonial studios. Much like the Lewises, the Lawsons were early and frequent patrons of photography.[90] They updated the original daguerreotype of their patriarch, as surviving members of the family sought out portrait commissions in the newest format.[91]

The copying of colonial photographs continued well into the twentieth century. The Freeman Brothers' Warrane/Sydney Cove studio, responsible for copying Ben Hall's ambrotype back in 1865, as a carte de visite, were still advertising their services in copying colonial photographs over seven decades later. In a 1938 newspaper advertisement, they invite Sydney customers to have their daguerreotypes copied (**Figure 5.13**). By this point, copying would have involved rephotographing the original daguerreotype as a glass plate negative from which gelatin silver prints could be made. The Freeman Brothers, later Freeman & Co., were the longest-running intergenerational family studio business in the Australian market.[92] Their twentieth-century advertisement declares they were founded in 1848 (as Beard licensees in Bath, England), with James and William Freeman beginning their colonial studio in 1854.[93] The Freemans continued in business until the mid-twentieth century. In 1904, they employed Harold Cazneaux, who went on to become one of the most prominent Australian photographers of his time and a founder of the Sydney Camera Circle.[94] The State Library of New South Wales's acquisition of the Freeman studio negative archive in 1954 was the first substantial acquisition of photography by an Australian collecting

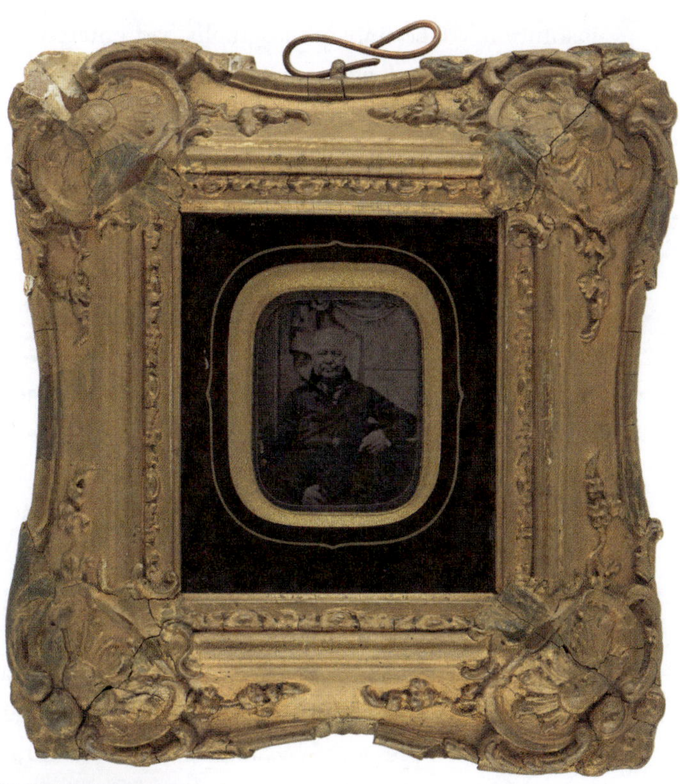

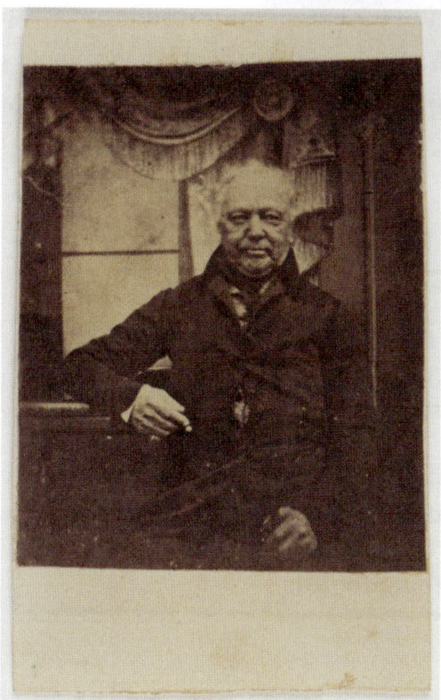

Figure 5.11: Unattributed, 'William Lawson Senior', 1855–60, ninth-plate, uncoloured, framed ambrotype, after a daguerreotype by George Baron Goodman. State Library of New South Wales.

Figure 5.12: Unattributed, 'William Lawson Senior', c.1860-–64, carte de visite, 9.3 × 5.9 cm, after a daguerreotype by George Baron Goodman. State Library of New South Wales.

institution.[95] Certainly, photographs had entered library, museum and historic house collections before this point, largely as a part of family manuscript files.

There was, then, around a century separating the practice of early photography in colonial Australia and the targeted collection of these photographs by Australian institutions. The first librarians and curators of photography were only employed in the second half of the twentieth century: Eric Keast Burke as photographic consultant to the National Library of Australia in 1964; Jennie Boddington as curator of photography to the National Gallery of Victoria in 1972; Gael Newton as curator of photography at the Art Gallery of New South Wales in 1974; Ian North as head of the photography department at the National Gallery of Australia in 1980; and Alan Davies as the photographic librarian at the State Library of New South Wales in 1989 (following his tenure at the University of Sydney's Macleay Museum, where he had worked on the photographic collection since the 1970s). When an active program of collecting Australia's photographic history began at a state and national level, curators and archivists were purchasing photographs that had primarily been preserved by, and passed down through, generations of colonial families. This is the case not just for individual portraits but more broadly for mid-nineteenth-century photography. Many of the images discussed in previous chapters are inflected with their provenance from

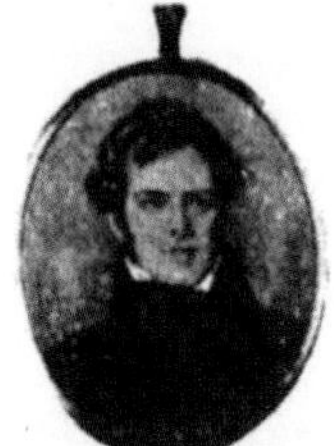

Figure 5.13: The *Methodist*, Sydney, 17 December 1938, p. 23.

colonial families. This is most obvious in the Macarthur family album, which contained Arthur Onslow's portraits of the Menang; Louisa How's album of salted paper prints made on Cammeraygal Country; the Mort family's annotated edition of William Blackwood's *Album of Australian Scenery*; and William Henry Harvey's letter to his sister, describing Theresa Walker's seaweed photographs. In this way, colonial families loom large as the first collectors and 'curators' of foundational Australian photography. As a result, the colonial is reified not only in the content of these images, but the very architecture of the knowledge and cataloguing data gathered around them.

This book contributes to the ongoing project of resituating the oldest photographs in Australian collections as febrile and historically consequential objects, beyond their current material status as delicate and vulnerable artefacts. As Daniel Palmer and Martyn Jolly suggest, 'Colonial Australia grew up with photography and through perpetual re-archiving and re-exhibiting, the nineteenth century is constantly being made anew'.[96] I have argued that we cannot understand the advent of Australian photography—how the medium was discussed, experienced and used—without teasing out photography's various relationships to other visual art, modes of consumption and circulation. This chapter, in particular, has shown that far from being discrete or contained, early photographs were integrated into a broader colonial visual landscape that carried them over greater distances as originals, copies and translations.

Early colonial photographs presented foreign audiences with the first indexical representations of place and people, whether delivered to exhibition halls (as we saw with the Dunolly Street scenes described in Chapter 4), engraved reproductions in the international press (such as the transmutation of Kilburn's daguerreotypes of Kulin men and women, outlined in Chapter 3), or mailed to the residential addresses of extended families (as was the case with the Hutchison family portrait). The history presented here is not one of colonial photography insulated geographically or regionally, but one where a photographic product is constantly in transit. Nevertheless, because the medium's own evolution and history map synchronously onto the implementation and extension of colonial rule in Australia, the technology was also key to building and reinforcing a vision of colonisation at a domestic level for colonial audiences. The archive of collated materials around colonial photographs—the album annotations, diaries, letters and newspaper advertisements—provide a colonial impression of how photography was first used and considered. As such, it is only through reconciling the gendered and cultural silences in the archive, working collaboratively with Aboriginal communities and observing Aboriginal knowledge—what Julie Gough calls 'listening through the dissonance'—that colonial photographs can truly be understood (anew).[97]

Notes

Preface

1 M. Arago, 'Exposé des motifs et projet de loi présentés par M. le minister de l'intèrieur (Séance du 15 Juin 1839)', reprinted in *Historique et Description des Procédés du Daguerréotype et du Diorama,* Alphone Giroux et Éditeurs, Paris, 1839, p. 2.

2 Ibid., p. 1.

3 Helen Ennis, *Photography and Australia,* Reaktion, London, 2008, p. 10.

4 Helen Ennis, 'Other histories: photography and Australia', *Journal of Art Historiography,* No 4. (2011), p. 9.

5 Anne Maxwell and Josephine Croci, Introduction to *Shifting Focus: Colonial Australian Photography 1850-1920,* Australian Scholarly Publishing, Melbourne, 2015, p. xiv.

6 Jane Lydon, 'The Interesting Couple: Simon Wonga in 1857', in Maxwell and Croci (eds), *Shifting Focus: Colonial Australian Photography 1850-1920,* Australian Scholarly Publishing, Melbourne, 2015, p. 58 and p. 63.

7 Ibid., p. 65.

8 See e.g. Jane Lydon (ed.), *Calling the Shots: Aboriginal Photographies,* Aboriginal Studies Press, Canberra, 2014; Jane Lydon, 'Transmuting Australian Aboriginal photographs', *World Art,* Vol. 6, No. 1, 2016, pp. 45–60.

9 Judy Annear, Introduction to *The Photograph and Australia,* Art Gallery of New South Wales, Sydney, 2015, p. 9.

10 Rhiannon Mason, Emma Coffield and Alistair Robinson, *Museum and Gallery Studies,* Routledge, London, 2018, p. 167.

11 Chitra Ramalingam, 'William Henry Fox Talbot (British, 1800-1877) *The Pencil of Nature,* 1844-46, part 4', in Martina Droth et al. (eds), *Britain in the World: Highlights from the Yale Center for British Art,* Yale University Press, New Haven, CT, 2019, p. 125.

12 Chitra Ramalingam, 'Fixing and Fading: narratives of progress, preservation and loss in early photography', *A New Power: Photography in Britain 1800-1850,* keynote address, Weston Library, Bodleian Libraries, University of Oxford, 18 March 2023.

13 Brenda L. Croft interviewed by Larissa Behrendt, 'Naabámi (thou will/shall see): Barangaroo (army of me)', *Speaking Out,* Radio National, ABC Radio, 21 July 2023.

14 Brenda L. Croft, 'Naabámi (thou shall/will see): Barangaroo (army of me)', *The National 4: Australian Art Now*, 2023.

15 Brenda L. Croft, *Naabámi (thou shall/will see) Barangaroo (army of me)*, Washington: Embassy of Australia, 2024, p. 1.

16 Danie Mellor, 'Landstory' (2018) interview for the National Gallery of Australia, 26 June 2019. Recording attached to collection record: Accession no. 2019.1. A-I.

17 Danie Mellor, 'Landstory 2018' [artist statement], *The Landspace: [all the devils are here]*, Tolarno Galleries, Naarm/Melbourne, September 2018.

18 See e.g. Unattributed, '"Jemima" with W.R. Mortlock', c. 1859, quarter-plate, coloured-tinted, cased daguerreotype. Ayers House, Adelaide, 0784.

19 James Tylor with Elisa deCourcy filmed by Jed Cooper, 'How are daguerreotypes made', online resource, for *National Portrait Gallery*, London, 21 June 2023.

20 Natalie Harkin, 'Weaving the Colonial Archive: A Basket to Lighten the Load', *Journal of Australian Studies*, Vol. 44, No. 2, 2020, p. 155.

21 Tiffany Shellam and Joanna Cruickshank, 'Critical Archives: An Introduction', *Journal of Colonialism and Colonial History*, Vol. 20, No. 2, 2019, np.

22 Tony Ballantyne, 'From Colonial Collection to Tribal Knowledge Base: Herries Beattie, Ngāi Tahu Whānui and the many lives of an archive', *Journal of Colonialism and Colonial History*, Vol. 20, No. 2, 2019, np.

23 Brenda L. Croft interviewed by Larissa Behrendt, 'Naabámi (thou will/shall see): Barangaroo (army of me)', *Speaking Out*, Radio National, ABC Radio, 21 July 2023; James Tylor with Elisa deCourcy filmed by Jed Cooper, 'How are daguerreotypes made', online resource, for *National Portrait Gallery*, London, 21 June 2023.

Chapter 1

1 Geoffrey Batchen, 'Antipodean Photography: an itinerant history', in Judy Annear (ed.), *The Photograph and Australia*, Art Gallery of New South Wales, Sydney, 2015, p. 261; Jack Cato, *The Story of the Camera in Australia*, Georgian House, Melbourne, 1955, p. 1; Alan Davies and Peter Stanbury, *The Mechanical Eye in Australia: Photography 1841-1900*, Oxford University Press, Melbourne, 1989, p. 6; Ennis, *Photography and Australia*, p. 13; Jane Lydon, Introduction to *Calling the Shots: Aboriginal Photographies*, Aboriginal Studies Press, Canberra, 2014, pp. 2–3; Gael Newton, *Shades of Light: Photography and Australia 1839-1988*, Australian National Gallery, Canberra, 1988, p. 1; Anne-Marie Willis, *Picturing Australia: A History of Photography*, Angus & Robertson, North Sydney, 1988, p. 7.

2 Willis, *Picturing Australia*, p. 7; Newton, *Shades of Light*, p. 1.

3 Batchen, 'Antipodean Photography', p. 261.

4 Cato, *The Story of the Camera in Australia*, p. 1; Davies and Stanbury, *The Mechanical Eye in Australia*, p. 6; Ennis, *Photography and Australia*, p. 13; Lydon, Introduction, pp. 2–3.

5 See e.g. Helen Ennis, 'Mirror with a Memory', in Helen Ennis (ed.), *Mirror with a Memory: Photographic Portraiture in Australia*, National Portrait Gallery, Canberra, 2000, p. 9; Judy Annear, Introduction, *The Photograph and Australia*, Art Gallery of New South Wales, Sydney, 2015, p. 1.
6 Geoffrey Batchen, *Inventing Photography: William Henry Fox Talbot in the Bodleian Library*, Bodleian Library Publishing, Oxford, 2023, p. 26.
7 Mary Warner Marien, *Photography: A Cultural History*, 2nd edn, Laurence King Publishing, London, 2006, p. 1 and 15.
8 Helmut Gernsheim and Alison Gernsheim, *The History of Photography*, Oxford University Press, Oxford, 1955, pp. 70–1; Marien, *Photography*, p. 15; Batchen, *Inventing Photography*, p. 26.
9 Maria Inez Turazzi, 'Le voyage de l'Oriental-Hydrographe (1839–1840): une expérience transcontinentale', in Christine Barthe and Annabelle Lacour (eds), *Mondes photographiques histoires des débuts*, Musée du quai Branly et Actes Sud, Paris, 2023, p. 308.
10 *Mémoire sur quelques changements á apportes dans l'organisation de la Marine et notamment sur les moyens que la France pourrait employer pour en augmenter le personnel sans augmenter le budget general*, Imprimerie Wittersheim, Paris, March 1839.
11 'Instruction générale addressee aux voyageurs', *Société ethnologique (les procedures)*, Société ethnologique, Paris, 1841; R. Derek Wood, 'The Voyage of Captain Lucas and the daguerreotype to Sydney', *Journal de la Société des océanistes*, Vol. 102, 1996, p. 114.
12 As quoted in Turazzi, 'Le voyage de l'Oriental-Hydrographe (1839-1840)', p. 313.
13 'Nouvelles de mer', *Le Commerce*, Paris, 4 October 1839, p. 7.
14 Turazzi, 'Le voyage de l'Oriental-Hydrographe (1839-1840)', p. 313.
15 Maria Inez Turazzi, 'Viagem do Oriental-Hydrographe (1839-1840) e a Introdução da Daguerreotipia no Brasil', *Acervo*, Rio de Janeiro, Vol. 23, No. 1, 2010, p. 56.
16 Ibid.
17 'Maritima / Salidas Dia 23', *El Mercurio*, Valparaíso, 24 de Junio de 1840, p. 3.
18 R. Derek Wood, 'The voyage of Captain Lucas and the daguerreotype to Sydney', in Annick Foucrier (ed.), *The French and the Pacific World, 17th-19th Centuries*, Ashgate, Aldershot, Hants, 2005, p. 73.
19 'Shipping Intelligence: Arrivals – Monday', *Sydney Monitor and Commercial Advertiser*, 31 March 1841, p. 3.
20 News of *L'Oriental*'s wreck was first published as 'Maritima / Salidas Dia 23', *El Mercurio*, Valparaíso, 24 de Junio de 1840, p. 3. This report was picked up by Antwerp shipping journal *Precurseur* and published as 'Shipwreck of a French Frigate'. The latter was syndicated and reprinted in European, British and colonial papers. See e.g. *Southern Reporter and Cork Commercial Courier*, 15 October 1840, p. 2; *London Evening Standard*, 12 October 1840, p. 4; *La Phare de La Rochelle*, 10 October 1840, p. 1; *Tasmanian Weekly Dispatch*, Hobart, 2 April 1841, p. 2; *Australian*, Sydney, 6 March 1841, p. 2.

21 'The Daguerreotype', *Australasian Chronicle*, Sydney, 13 April 1841, p. 3.

22 'At the stores of Joubert and Murphy', *Australian*, Sydney, 15 May 1841, p. 2.

23 Ibid.

24 The daguerreotype and materials sat dormant in the Bridge Street store of Joubert and Murphy for two years, after which they were advertised for sale once again, this time without the ceremony of a demonstration and as part of the liquidation of Joubert's household. 'Household Furniture', *Sydney Morning Herald*, 20 March 1843, p. 3.

25 Conrad Martens, 'Photogenic Process' and 'Preparation of the Paper', notebook [1835–1856], pp. 16–19. State Library of New South Wales, Sydney, DLMS142. These entries are undated but fall before one for 5 August 1840. For more discussion, see Geoffrey Batchen, *Apparitions: Photography and Dissemination*, Power Publications, Sydney, 2018, p. 15; Newtown, *Shades of Light*, p. 2.

26 From April 1839, positive prints were made through the placement of the negative directly in contact with another sheet of sensitised paper, under a sheet of glass in the sun. Talbot perfected his photogenic drawing recipe in the 1840s, adding acetic and gallic acid to the paper sensitising solution. This iteration was patented as his calotype process. See 'Photographic Pictures, A.D. 1841, No.8842', printed by George Edward Eyre and William Spottiswoode, printers to The Queen, London, 1856. British Library, London; Batchen, *Inventing Photography*, p. 40.

27 Bernard Smith, 'Conrad Martens (1801-78)' in Bernard Smith (ed.), *Documents of Art and Taste in Australia: The Colonial Period 1770-1914*, Oxford University Press, Melbourne, 1975, p. 96.

28 Douglas Dundas, 'Martens, Conrad (1801-1878)', *Australian Dictionary of Biography* online, National Centre for Biography, Australian National University, Canberra.

29 Conrad Martens, 'Notes on Painting', 1835–56, bound notebook, pp. 5–11. State Library of New South Wales, Sydney, DLMS 142.

30 Isobel Crombie, 'Portrait of a Painter: a photograph of Conrad Martens by Freeman Brothers Studio', *Art Bulletin of Victoria*, National Gallery of Victoria, Iss. 30, 1989, p. 37; Conrad Martens, 'A Lecture Upon Landscape Painting', 21 July 1856, Australian Library, Sydney. Reprinted in Smith (ed.), *Documents of Art and Taste in Australia*, p. 100.

31 Conrad Martens, 'Notes on Painting', 1835–56, bound notebook, p. 19. State Library of New South Wales, Sydney, DLMS 142.

32 'G. E. Egerton Warburton, 51st Regiment, Northwich, Cheshire', Statement of Service Register 1837–43, pp. 227–8. The National Archives, Kew, WO 76/350/227; 'Barque, Egyptian, 19 August 1839', p. 95, *Port Officer's Reports of Ships' Arrivals at Hobart*, 3 January 1838 – 29 December 1839. Tasmanian Archives, Hobart, CSO92/1/3.

33 'New Discovery – Drawing by Solar Light. / From Blackwood's Magazine, March', *Launceston Advertiser*, 19 September 1839, p. 1; 'Photogenic Drawing', *Cornwall Chronicle*, Launceston, 19 October 1839, p. 4.

34 George Egerton Warburton, King George Sound, Albany, to Rowland Egerton Warburton Snr, Cheshire, England, 17 April 1841 (transcript from original, privately held), 'Egerton Warburton Family Papers', J. S. Battye Library, State Library of Western Australia, Perth, Acc1179A.

35 Dr William Buckland (Oxford) to Sir John Franklin (Hobart), 5 September 1840. Extract reprinted in 'Daguerreotype', *Tasmanian Journal of Natural Science, Agriculture and Statistics, & c.*, James Barnard, Government Printer, Hobart,1841, p. 71.

36 'Electrotype and Daguerreotype', *Westminster Review*, Vol. 34, June to September 1840, p. 60.

37 Dr William Buckland (Oxford) to Sir John Franklin (Hobart), 5 September 1840. Extract reprinted in 'Daguerreotype', *Tasmanian Journal of Natural Science, Agriculture and statistics, & c.*, James Barnard, Government Printer, Hobart, 1841, p. 72.

38 Three illustrations were sent to Franklin. The other two were: (1) 'a thin section of a Madrepore, drawn with an oxyhydrogen microscope, magnified 12½ times', which is possibly the illustration that appears in *Westminster Review*, Vol. 34, June to September 1840, p. 461; and (2) 'portrait of John Russell engraved on a daguerreotype plate', which is possibly a daguerreotype of a lithograph of Sir John Russell's marble bust, a copy of which is held at the Clark Art Institute, 1978.39. I am thankful to Geoffrey Batchen for sharing with me the second of these two lithographs.

39 Dr William Buckland (Oxford) to Sir John Franklin (Hobart), 5 September 1840. Extract reprinted in 'Daguerreotype', *Tasmanian Journal of Natural Science, Agriculture and Statistics, & c.*, James Barnard, Government Printer, Hobart, 1841, pp. 71–2.

40 Andrew David, *The Voyage of HMS Herald: to Australia and the South-west Pacific 1852-1861 under the command of Captain Henry Mangles Denham*, Miegunyah Press, Melbourne, 1995, p. 28.

41 As noted in Arthur Onslow's diary days later on 7 February 1858. See 'Journal from HMS Herald, 1857-61', in Papers of Captain Arthur Onslow, 1850-1881, Macarthur Family – Papers, 1795-1945, State Library of New South Wales, Sydney, A 4335 [CY 1721].

42 See e.g. George Egerton Warburton (King George Sound, Albany, to his mother (Cheshire, England), 20 April 1853, transcript from original privately held, 'Egerton-Warburton Family Papers', J. S. Battye Library, State Library of Western Australia, Perth, Acc1179A.

43 George Egerton Warburton (King George Sound, Albany, to his mother (Cheshire, England), 25 August 1858, transcript from original privately held, 25 August 1858, 'Egerton-Warburton Family Papers', J.S. Battye Library, State Library of Western Australia, Perth, Acc1179A.

44 As noted in Arthur Onslow's diary days later on 7 February 1858. See 'Journal from HMS Herald, 1857-61', in Papers of Captain Arthur Onslow, 1850-1881, Macarthur Family – Papers, 1795-1945, State Library of New South Wales, Sydney, A 4335 [CY 1721].

45 Discussion between Shona Coyne and Elisa deCourcy, National Museum of Australia, Ngunnawal and Ngambri Country, Canberra, 10 March 2022.

46 Tiffany Shellam and Shona Coyne, 'Objects of mobility: Swan River Colony', in Gaye Sculthorpe et al. (eds), *Ancestors, Artefacts, Empire: Indigenous Australia in British and Irish Museums*, British Museum, London, 2021, pp. 175–6.

47 Isobel Crombie, 'Australian Felix: Douglas T. Kilburn's daguerreotypes of Victorian Aborigines, 1847', *Art Bulletin of Victoria*, Vol. 32, 1991, pp. 21–31; Julie Gough, 'Forgotten Lives – the first photographs of Tasmanian Aboriginal people', in Jane Lydon (ed.), *Calling the Shots: Aboriginal Photographies*, Aboriginal Studies Press, Canberra, 2014, pp. 21–54; Jane Lydon, 'An Interesting Couple: Simon Wonga in 1857', in Anne Maxwell and Josephine Croci (eds), *Colonial Australian Photography, 1850-1920*, Australian Scholarly Publishing, Melbourne, 2015, pp. 58–70.

48 WC Dix and Sara J Meagher, 'Fish Traps in the South-West of Western Australia', in *Records of the Western Australian Museum*, Vol. 4, No. 2, 1976, pp. 171–2.

49 Tiffany Shellam, *Shaking Hands on the Fringe: Negotiating Aboriginal Worlds at King George's Sound*, University of Western Australia Press, Perth, 2009, p. 7.

50 Rebecca Swartz, 'Educating Emotions in Natal and Western Australia, 1854-65', *Journal of Colonialism and Colonial History*, Vol. 18, No. 2, 2017, np; Donna Oxenham, 'Photographing Aboriginal Australians in Western Australia', in Jane Lydon (ed.), *Calling the Shots: Aboriginal Photographies*, Aboriginal Studies Press, Canberra, 2014, pp. 207–29.

51 Batchen, *Apparitions*, 2018, pp. 74–116.

Chapter 2

1 Noel Butlin, *Forming a Colonial Economy, Australia 1810-1850*, Cambridge University Press, Cambridge, 1994, pp. 154– 5.

2 Ross Gibson, 'Ocean Settlement', *Meanjin*, Vol. 53, No. 4, 1994, pp. 666–7.

3 'The Eden', *Unassisted Passenger Index 1842-1855*, Reel 1269, INX-43-81145. State Records Office of New South Wales, Kingsford.

4 Goodman's family and English address are outlined in his marriage notice to Sarah Polack, who he met on his passage to New South Wales: 'Married', *Australian*, Sydney, 6 January 1842, p. 3.

5 'Baptismal register for the Parish of Redgrave 1813-1858', Suffolk, SROI FBI132/D3/2, p. 77. Suffolk Record Office, Ipswich.

6 See an unabridged version of Newland's career in Elisa deCourcy and Martyn Jolly, *Empire, Early Photography and Spectacle: the Global Career of Showman Daguerreotypist J.W. Newland*, Routledge, London, 2021.

7 1841 Census, England, 'St Peters County, Cambridgeshire' HO107, Book 14, District 5, Folio 7, p. 8. National Archives, Kew; '1842 Marriage Register, Melbourn', p. 30, *Ely Diocesan Records*, Cambridge University Library, Cambridge, GBR/0012/MS EDR, Roll 146.

8 'Shipping Intelligence: Arrived', *Melbourne Daily News*, 29 November 1849, p. 2; 'Disposal List of Immigrants for the ship: Royal George', *Register of Assisted Immigrants from the United Kingdom*, 1 February 1849 – 31 October 1851, VPRS 14 / P0000, Box No.4A. Public Records Office Victoria, Melbourne.

9 'Sydney General Trade List: Imports. 7 November, Eden', *Sydney Morning Herald*, 14 November 1842, p. 3.

10 'Daguerreotype Portraits', *Australian*, Sydney, 9 November 1842, p. 2.

11 Steve Edwards, '"Beard Patentee": Daguerreotype Property and Authorship', *Oxford Art Journal*, Vol. 36, No. 3, 2013, pp. 369–94.

12 'Obtaining Daguerreotype Portraits & c. AD 1839 … No 8194', patent document printed by George Edward Eyre and William Spottiswoode, printers to the Queen, London, 1857. British Library, London.

13 'Daguerreotype Portraits', *Australian*, Sydney, 9 November 1842, p. 2.

14 Joseph Fowles, *Sydney in 1848: A Facsimile of the Original Text and Copper-Plate Engravings of its Principal* [sic] *Streets, Public Buildings, Churches, Chapels, etc., from Drawings by Joseph Fowles*, 4th edn?, Ure Smith, Sydney, 1962, p. 50.

15 Ibid., p. 52.

16 'On Monday Mr Goodman Opened His Gallery', *Colonial Observer*, Sydney, 14 December 1842, p. 5; 'The Daguerreotype', *Sydney Morning Herald*, 14 January 1845, p. 2.

17 'Daguerreotype. By Her Majesty's Letters Patent', *Australian*, Sydney, 27 January 1843, p. 1.

18 Data collected by William August Miles, Superintendent of Police, Sydney, 8 June 1842, reprinted in House of Commons, *Parliamentary Papers: Volume 34 Emigration*, H.M. Stationery Office, London, 1843, p. 103.

19 'His Excellency the Governor', *Colonial Observer*, Sydney, 25 January 1843, p. 2.

20 'Mr Goodman', *Australian*, Sydney, 6 February 1843, p. 3.

21 'The Daguerreotype', *Sydney Morning Herald*, 14 January 1845, p. 2.

22 'Daguerreotype', *Sydney Morning Herald*, 4 May 1846, p. 2.

23 'Daguerreotype', *Courier*, Hobart, 25 August 1843, p. 3.

24 Gael Newton, *Shades of Light*, p. 9.

25 Thomas Bock's Notes on Photography, including Talbot's calotype process and daguerreotype manipulations, 17 July 1841 – 31 December 1850, bound paper stitched into a 17 July 1841 edition of the *Athenaeum*. Allport Library and Museum of Fine Arts, Hobart, ALL34-1-1.

26 'To the Editor', *Courier*, Hobart, 6 October 1843, p. 1.

27 Elisa deCourcy, 'Beyond Sentimentality: the family as patron, subject and author of early photography in colonial Australia', *History of Photography*, Vol. 46, No. 2–3, 2022, p. 108.

28 'Daguerreotype, by Her Majesty's Letter Patent – Mr John Flavelle', *Launceston Examiner*, 2 March 1844, p. 1; 'Daguerreotype – Mr Flavelle', *Launceston Examiner*, 4 May 1844, p. 3.

29 'Daguerreotype', *Australian*, Sydney, 11 June 1844, p. 3.
30 'The Daguerreotype', *Sydney Morning Herald*, 14 January 1845, p. 2.
31 'New South Wales, Australia, Convict Registers of Conditional and Absolute Pardons 1788-1870', Reel no: 774. Roll no.: 1250. The State Records Office of New South Wales, Kingswood.
32 Colonial Secretary to George Suttor, Superintendent of Castle Hill Mental Asylum, letter, 12 September 1814, in *Colonial Secretary's Papers, 1788-1825*, Reel no. 6004, pp. 297–8. The State Records Office of New South Wales, Kingswood.
33 John Cobley, 'Bland, William (1789-1868)', *Australian Dictionary of Biography* online, National Centre for Biography, Australian National University, Canberra, 1966.
34 Ibid.
35 'Sworn To No Master, of No Sect Am I', *Sydney Morning Herald*, 13 June 1843, p. 2.
36 See e.g. 'Lands Granted and Reserved by His Excellency Sir Thomas Brisbane from the 24th day of May 1824 to the 1st day of December 1825, New South Wales', *Colonial Secretary's Papers, 1788-1856*. Series NRS 898. The State Records Office of New South Wales, Kingswood.
37 Richard Neville, 'Early Sydney: A Land of Wonder and Delight', Christopher Allen (ed.), *A Companion to Australian Art*, John Wiley & Sons Inc, Hoboken, NJ, 2021, pp. 104–5.
38 Tim Bonyhady, Introduction to Tim Bonyhady and Andrew Sayers (eds), *Heads of the People: A Portrait of Colonial Australia*, National Portrait Gallery, Canberra, 2000, p. 1.
39 'Society for the Promotion of the Fine Arts in Australia', *Sydney Morning Herald*, 2 June 1849, p. 3.
40 'Daguerreotype', *Hawkesbury Courier and Agricultural and General Advertiser*, 26 June 1845, p. 3.
41 'Daguerreotype', *Port Phillip Patriot and Melbourne Advertiser*, 1 August 1845, p. 3.
42 'The Daguerreotype', *South Australian*, Adelaide, 9 January 1846, p. 3.
43 'The Daguerreotype', *South Australian Gazette and Colonial Register*, 24 January 1846, p. 2.
44 Quoted in Gael Newton, *Shades of Light*, p. 8.
45 Melissa Miles, *The Language of Light and Dark: Light and Place in Australian Photography*, McGill-Queens University Press, Montreal, 2015, pp. 5 and 16–18.
46 Helen Ennis, *A Modern Vision: Charles Bayliss, Photographer, 1850-1870*, National Library of Australia, Canberra, 2008, pp. 2–3.
47 'For A Short Period: Newland's Daguerrean Gallery', *Sydney Morning Herald*, 7 March 1848, p. 1.
48 J. W. Newland, unidentified man (New Orleans), 1845, sixth-plate, uncoloured, cased daguerreotype. Bodleian Archives and Manuscripts, University of Oxford. MS. 21206.

49 See competing advertisements: *Daily Tropic,* New Orleans, 24 May 1845, p. 2.

50 For more detail on Newland's travels, see deCourcy and Jolly, *Empire, Early Photography and Spectacle,* pp. 14–57.

51 'Daguerreotipo', *El Mercurio,* Valparaíso, 8 July 1847, p. 4.

52 Beaumont Newhall, *The Daguerreotype in America,* 3rd edn, Dover Publications, New York, 1976, pp. 87–8; Weston J. Naef, *Carleton Watkins in Yosemite,* J. Paul Getty Museum, Los Angeles, 2008.

53 'Arrivals', *The Shipping Gazette and Sydney General Trade List,* 19 February 1848, p. 42.

54 Steven Roger Fisher, *A History of the Pacific Islands,* Palgrave Macmillan, Basingstoke, 2002, pp. 136–9.

55 For more on the Flagstaff War and the broader colonial conflict of which it was a part, see James Belich, *The New Zealand Wars and the Victorian Interpretation of Racial Conflict,* Auckland University Press, Auckland, 1986; John Crawford and Ian C. McGibbon (eds), *Tutu Te Puehu: New Perspectives on the New Zealand Wars,* Steele Roberts Aotearoa, Wellington, 2018.

56 For examples of global reports, see 'Deposition of Queen Pomare by the French', *Illustrated London News,* 24 February 1844, p. 396; 'Late from New Zealand', *Daily Picayune,* New Orleans, 27 July 1845, p. 2; 'War in New Zealand', *Exeter and Plymouth Gazette,* 19 July 1846, p. 4. For journalism and visual ephemera produced in Warrane/Sydney, see e.g 'Under the patronage of his excellency the governor/ Will be published shortly / A View of the Town of Russell', *Sydney Morning Herald,* 12 July 1845, p. 1; 'Kororāreka in the Bay of Islands, New Zealand. Sketched March 10 1845 on the morning before the assault and destruction by Honi Heki / drawn by Captain Clayton, and on stone by W.A. Nicholas. Lithographed and published by E.D. Barlow', lithograph, coloured, 10 × 20 cm inside mount. State Library of New South Wales, Sydney, V7B/ Rus/ 1; 'Heki [sic] and Kawitti [sic]', *Australian,* Sydney, 25 June 1846, p. 3.

57 Polack relocated to Auckland between April and August 1848: see 'Daguerreotype Portraits', *New Zealander,* Auckland, 13 May 1848, p. 1; 'Daguerreotype', *New Zealander,* Auckland, 9 August 1848, p. 4.

58 'For a Short Period: Newland's Daguerrean Gallery', *Sydney Chronicle,* 11 March 1848, p. 1.

59 For more on Queen Pomare IV's image in the imperial space, see Viviane Fayaud, 'A Tahitian Woman in Majesty: French Images of Queen Pomare', *History Australia,* Vol. 3, No. 1, 2006; Patty O'Brien, '"Think of Me as a Woman": Queen Pomare of Tahiti and Anglo-French Imperial Contest in the 1840s Pacific', *Gender and History,* Vol. 18, No. 1, 2006.

60 'Daguerreotype', *Launceston Examiner,* 10 December 1845, p. 3. 'We have seen some excellent daguerreotype portraits of Aboriginals, by Mr Goodman, now in Melbourne. They exceed in execution any of Mr Goodman's productions in this colony, who we hear had considerably improved his apparatus'.

61 For a more extended discussion on Kilburn's daguerreotypes, see Jane Lydon, 'Photographing Kooris: Photography and Exchange in Victoria', in Lydon (ed.), *Calling the Shots: Aboriginal Photographies*, Aboriginal Studies Press, Canberra, 2014, pp. 107–9.

62 Fayaud, 'A Tahitian Woman in Majesty', p. 123. See e.g. C. B. Hoare, 'H.M. Queen Pomare IV', c. 1877, albumen silver photograph from the album: Tahiti, Samoa and New Zealand Scenes compiled between 1885 and 1900. Museum of New Zealand Te Papa Tongarewa, Wellington. 0.041297; 'Pomare – from a photograph', *Illustrated Times*, London, 17 March 1860, p. 162.

63 deCourcy and Jolly, *Empire, Early Photography and Spectacle*, p. 66.

64 *Coach and Horses*, Cumberland and Essex streets (1836) NRS 14401[4/67] reel 5053; *The Rainbow*, Clyde Street (1838) NRS 14401 [4/69] reel 5054; *The Hunter River Hotel*, Sussex Street (1843) NRS 14401 [4/75], *'Publicans' licenses index, 1830-1861*, State Archives of New South Wales, Kingswood.

65 Cecil Scott Bennett, *Biographical register of the Tasmanian Parliament, 1851-1960*, ANU Press, Canberra, 1980, p. 101.

66 'Exhibition of Dissolving Views', *Maitland Mercury and Hunter River General Advertiser*, 9 August 1848, p. 2.

67 deCourcy and Jolly, *Empire, Early Photography and Spectacle*, pp. 85–9.

68 'Shipping Intelligence: Arrived', *Melbourne Daily News*, 29 November 1849, p. 2.

69 'Disposal List of Immigrants for the ship: Royal George', *Register of Assisted Immigrants from the United Kingdom*, 1 February 1849 – 31 October 1851, VPRS 14 / P0000, Box No.4A. Public Records Office Victoria, Melbourne.

70 Isobel Crombie, 'Louisa Elizabeth How: Pioneer Photographer', *Australian Business Collectors Annual*, 1984, p. 82.

71 See e.g. HOW, Robert, *Depasturing Licenses Index 1837-1851*, District: Liverpool Plans, License: 60, Year: 1839. Series: NRS 14363. Item No. 4/92. Index No. 67. The State Records Office of New South Wales, Kingswood; 'Transfer of Runs', *New South Wales Government Gazettes*, Sydney, 9 July 1851, 1071.

72 See e.g. HOW, Robert, 'No. 5 Whaling Allotments at Neutral Harbour, Parish of Willoughby', *Court of Claims (Land) Index*, 26 May 1842. Item No. 2/2370. Index No. 54. The State Records Office of New South Wales, Kingswood.

73 Isobel Crombie, 'How, Louisa Elizabeth (1821-1893)' in Joan Kerr (ed.), *The Dictionary of Australian Artists: Painters, Sketchers, Photographers and Engravers to 1870*, Oxford University Press, Melbourne, 1992, p. 375.

74 'Philosophical Society of New South Wales', *Empire*, Sydney, 10 September 1857, p. 4.

75 Ibid.

76 'Australian Nature and the Art of the Photographer', *Photographic News*, 19 July 1859, pp. 244–5; 'Australian Nature and the Art of the Photographer', *Photographic News*, 28 July 1859, pp. 232–3; 'Australian Nature and the Art of the Photographer', *Photographic News*, 19 July 1859, pp. 280–1.

77 'Philosophical Society of New South Wales – List of contributors and contributions at the Photographic Exhibition', *Sydney Morning Herald*, 22 December 1859, p. 4.
78 The argument for Louisa How having received instruction at a commercial studio is put forward by Barbara Hall and Jenni Mather in *Australian Women Photographers: 1840-1960*, Greenhouse Publications, Richmond, Vic, 1986, p. 8.
79 Isobel Crombie, 'Louisa Elizabeth How: Pioneer Photographer', p. 82.
80 'De La Rue & Co.' is embossed in small gold lettering on the inside of the cover, below the seam of the endpapers. 'Chatto and Hughes: Stationery and Books Just Landed on *Star of Peace*', *Sydney Morning Herald*, 22 February 1858, p. 6.
81 See e.g. Helen E. Lambert, 'Who and What We Saw at the Antipodes', 1868–70, mixed-media scrapbook, National Gallery of Australia, Canberra, 83.25.1-210.
82 Geoffrey Batchen, *Negative/Positive: A History of Photography*, Routledge, Abingdon, Oxon, 2021, p. 189.
83 Jan Brazier (curator), 'The Business of Photography: the 19th Century studio in New South Wales', Chau Chak Wing Museum, Warrane/Sydney, 18 November 2020 – 22 August 2021; Jack Cato, *The Story of the Camera in Australia*, Georgian House, Melbourne, 1955, p. 17.
84 Isobel Crombie, 'Louisa Elizabeth How: Pioneer Photographer', pp. 82–5.
85 Ibid., p. 83.
86 This portrait is now held by the Tate: Sir Thomas Lawrence, 'The Countess of Darnley', c. 1825–30, oil paint on canvas, 69 × 56.5 cm. Tate, London. N00324.
87 Robert Hunt, 'On the Applications of Science to the Fine and Useful Arts: Photography on Glass Plates', *Art Journal*, London, 1850, pp. 38–40. T.A. Malone, 'Photography on Paper and on Glass', *Art Journal*, London, 1850, pp. 261.
88 T. A. Malone, 'Photography on Paper and on Glass', *Art Journal*, London, 1850, pp. 261.
89 Gwen Trundle, 'Landsborough, William (1825-1886)', *Australian Dictionary of Biography* online, National Centre for Biography, Australian National University, Canberra, 1977.
90 William Landsborough, *Journal of Landsborough's Expedition from Carpentaria, in search of Burke and Wills, with map showing his route*, F.F. Baillière, Melbourne, 1862.
91 'Station in Leichhardt District / For Sale', *Empire*, Sydney, 26 July 1859, p. 8.
92 William Landsborough, Notebook 2 (24 June 1859); Notebook 3 (28 June – 6 July 1859); Notebook 4 (7–9 July 1859); Notebook 6 (15–19 July 1859); Notebook 7 (19–22 July 1859); Notebook 8 (25 July – 2 August); Notebook 9 (6–11 August 1859); unpublished papers. State Library of Queensland, OM69-17. In Landsborough's diary from this time, there is mention of 'Chinang Bobby' a 'tall, powerful young Aboriginal': William Landsborough (diary), 9 July 1856 – 7 June 1859, unpublished manuscript, State Library of Queensland OM69-17-1.
93 Peta Jeffries, 'William Landsborough's Expedition of 1862 from Carpentaria to Victoria in search of Burke and Wills: exploration with native police troopers and

Aboriginal guides', in Ian D. Clark and Fred Cahir (eds), *The Aboriginal Story of Burke and Wills: Forgotten Narratives*, CSIRO Publishing, Collingwood, Vic, 2013, p. 343.

94 Frontispiece to *Journal of Landsborough's Expedition from Carpentaria [...]*, stipple engraving after Unattributed, 'W. Gleeson, Jemmy, W. Landsborough, Jack Fisherman, and unidentified man', 1862, albumen print studio photograph, 20.5 × 28.5 cm (mounted). State Library of Victoria, Melbourne, H2013.284/52.

95 Louisa How, 'Mr William Landsborough, "Tiger" and J.L. [John Landsborough], 1858–59, salted paper print from a collodion negative, 11.5 × 15.9 cm (print). Art Gallery of New South Wales, Sydney. 208.1989.

96 Jane Lydon, 'Photography Across Cultures', in Judy Annear (ed.), *The Photograph and Australia*, Art Gallery of New South Wales Press, Sydney, 2015, p. 118.

97 Ibid.

Chapter 3

1 David Campany, *On Photographs*, Thames & Hudson, London, 2020, p. 8.

2 Paul Sendziuk and Robert Foster, *A History of South Australia*, Cambridge University Press, Melbourne, 2018, p. 46.

3 Ibid.

4 'A daguerreotype has been sent to the colony, and is in the hands of Mr Gill, the artist', *South Australian Register*, Adelaide, 8 November 1845, p. 2.

5 'Local Intelligence', *Adelaide Observer*, 14 August 1847, p. 5; 'Kooringa–The Burra township'; 'Opening of Lode in Stock's air-hole, in the mine'; 'Interior of the mine'; 'Burra Burra Mines – the surface operations', *Illustrated London News*, 2 December 1848, p. 339.

6 Ron Appleyard, 'Hall, Robert (c.1821-1866)', in Joan Kerr (ed.), *The Dictionary of Australian Artists: Painters, Sketches, Photographers and Engravers to 1870*, Oxford University Press, Melbourne, 1992, pp. 340–1.

7 'Daguerreotype', *Adelaide Observer*, 23 January 1847, p. 8; 'Mr Hall's Daguerreotype Establishment', *South Australian Register*, Adelaide, 23 February 1848, p. 1.

8 Jane Messenger makes this argument, but she also factors in the German practitioners Schohl and Hesseltine, whose studio in Tarntanya/Adelaide had closed by 1847, as had George Barron Goodman's, discussed in the previous chapter. See Jane Messenger, 'Daguerreotype portraits, 1840s-c.1860', in Julie Robinson and Maria Zagala (eds), *A Century in Focus, 1840s-1940s: South Australian Photography*, Art Gallery of South Australia, Adelaide, 2008, p. 28.

9 Chris Evans and Louise Miskell, *Swansea Copper: A Global History*, Johns Hopkins University Press, Baltimore, 2020, p. 125.

10 Fionn Montell-Boyd, Articles of Silver: the material and industry of photography's emergence in Britain, unpublished PhD thesis, 2024, University of Oxford,

Oxford, Chapter 3. For more on the intersection between mining and photography, see Siobhan Angus, *Camera Geologica: An Elemental History of Photography*, Duke University Press, 2024.

11 Evans and Miskell, *Swansea Copper*, p. 124.

12 'Inward Overseas Passenger Lists: British and Foreign Ports', October to November 1852, pp. 275–6. Public Records Office, Victoria, Melbourne, VPRS 947/P0000.

13 Marcel Safier, 'Glaister, Thomas Skelton (1824-1904)' in John Hannavy (ed.), *Encyclopedia of Nineteenth-Century Photography*, Routledge, New York, 2008, p. 594–5.

14 'Daguerreotype Gallery, Meade Bro. and Co.', *Banner*, Melbourne, 18 July 1854, p. 16.

15 Ibid.

16 See e.g. Unattributed, (Swanston Street, Melbourne), c. 1853, full-plate, uncoloured cased daguerreotype. Powerhouse/Museum of Applied Arts and Sciences, Sydney, H6786-1/1; Unattributed, 'Portrait and George Walker Johnson and family', c. 1855, full-plate, uncoloured, framed daguerreotype. State Library of New South Wales, Sydney, MPG/230; Unattributed, (Group portrait of unidentified men, possibly members of the Presbyterian Church), c. 1852, full-plate, uncoloured, cased daguerreotype, State Library of South Australia, Adelaide, SRG 123/348/292; Unattributed, 'Actors of the Adelaide Stage', c. 1850, full-plate, colour-tinted, cased daguerreotype. State Library of South Australia, Adelaide, B46371; J. W. Newland, 'Murray Street, Hobart', 1848, full-plate, uncoloured, framed daguerreotype. Tasmanian Museum and Art Gallery, Hobart, ISPH1867.

17 Arline Meyer, 'Re-dressing Classical Statuary: The Eighteenth-Century "Hand-in-Waistcoat" Portrait', *Art Bulletin*, Vol. 77, No. 1, 1995, pp. 45–63. I am thankful to Laura Jocic for drawing my attention to this resemblance in pose and its history.

18 A 'Mr Gilbert' also briefly offered daguerreotypes from his home at Eastern Hill during 1845. See 'Daguerreotype', *Port Phillip Patriot and Morning Advertiser*, 25 November 1845, p. 3.

19 J. Manton Junior, 22 Collins Street (1851); J. Barling, Greater Bourke Street (1853); Mr Nott, 3 Swanston Street (1854); Duryea and MacDonald, 3 Greater Bourke Street (1853–54); Mr Scarlett, Central Melbourne (1854); Meade Bros. & Co., Greater Collins Street (1854–55); W Robinson, Collins Street (1855); GW Perry, Collins Street (1855); JC Alexander, Elizabeth Street (1855); T. Burrows, Tarraville (1855); Woodbury, Homington Road, North Melbourne (1855); Batchelder, Collins Street (1855); Acley, Tarraville (1855); Ostler and Jackson, Castlemaine (1855).

20 'Profitable Employment at the Diggings', *Argus*, Melbourne, 23 March 1855, p. 8.

21 Further supported by their notice of marriage: 'Notice of Births, Marriages and Deaths', *Argus*, Melbourne, 25 April 1854, p. 4.

22 See 'Crown Reserves Correspondence', State Records Office of Victoria, North Melbourne, VPRS 242/P0000; 'Obituary', *Kyabram Union*, 23 October 1891, p. 2.

23 W. L. Ross (printer), *Glaister's Excelsior Photographic Galleries*, four-page pamphlet, 1856 or 1857, p. 2, State Library of New South Wales, Sydney, MLMSS 9487.

24 Anon., 'Extracts, Photography', *Sydney Magazine of Science and Art*, James W. Waugh, George Street, Sydney, December 1857, p. 156.

25 'Register of baptisms, burials and marriages', Vol. 1, Reel 5001. State Records Office of New South Wales, Kingsford, NRS-12937.

26 'KING, Thomas, Ship: Scarborough', *Convict Indents Index 1788-1801*, State Records Office of New South Wales, Kingsford, INX-77-14258.

27 '764. Thomas King', *Proceedings of the Old Bailey*, 29 October 1783, p. 1068.

28 '1011. Thomas King', *Proceedings of the Old Bailey*, 20 October 1784, p. 1353.

29 Michael Flynn, *The Second Fleet: Britain's Grim Convict Armada of 1790*, Library of Australian National History, North Sydney, 1993, p. 241.

30 Unattributed, 'Rose Cottage, Pyrmont, residence of Thomas and Jane Day', 1860s, hand-coloured albumen print mounted on card, 14.6 × 18 cm. State Library of New South Wales, Sydney, SPF/420.

31 'Collodiotypes', *Sydney Morning Herald*, 14 November 1857, p. 7; 'Important Notice', *Sydney Morning Herald*, 4 September 1858, p. 2.

32 Edwin Dalton, 'Eleanor Elizabeth Stephen', c. 1854, sixth-plate, hand-coloured, cased daguerreotype. State Library of New South Wales, Sydney, MIN 194.

33 John McPhee, *The Painted Photograph in Tasmania: 1850-1900*, Queen Victoria Museum and Gallery, Launceston, 2017, pp. 7–8 and 10.

34 See e.g. T. S. Glaister, [Jane Henriette Kidd Harpur, Susanna Matilda Australia Harpur and Jerimin ('Medley') Harpur], c. 1860, quarter-plate, hand-painted, cased ambrotype. National Gallery of Australia, Canberra, 2018.813; T. S. Glaister, [Cape Family Children], four ninth-plate ambrotypes, colour-tinted, package side by side across a quarter-plate case. National Library of Australia, Canberra, PIC P763 LOC C11; T. S. Glaister, 'Professor John Smith (first professor of Experimental Philosophy at the University of Sydney)', c. 1858, hand-coloured stereo-daguerreotype in a Mascher case. Tasmanian Museum and Art Gallery, Hobart, Q185.

35 There are two further hand-coloured ambrotype portraits of the Day family taken by Glaister in the library of the Australian Society of Genealogists, Sydney. See T. S. Glaister, 'Jane Day and her daughters, Jane, Mary and Eliza', 1859, full-plate, hand-coloured, framed ambrotype, 14.2 × 19.5 cm (image) 35.7 × 40.5 cm (framed). Australian Society of Genealogists, Sydney, 15/000020; TS Glaister, 'Jane Day', 1860s, mammoth-plate, hand-coloured, framed ambrotype, 29 × 23.7 cm (image) 42.5 × 37.5 cm (framed). Australian Society of Genealogists, Sydney, 15/000019.

36 Ennis, *Photography and Australia*, pp. 13–14.

37 'KAY, Mr', *Unassisted Immigrants Index 1842-1855*, State Records Office of New South Wales, Kingsford, INX-43- 105369.
38 'Albion Gold Mining Company, Register, Avoca', *Avoca Mail*, 9 July 1870, p. 3.
39 See e.g. Unattributed, 'George Taylor and his wife Ann (neé Collis Pratt)', 1850s, quarter-plate pair of colour-tinted, cased ambrotypes. Art Gallery of South Australia, Sydney, 20102Ph6; Unattributed, 'James Lawrence Oliver Stapleton, and Sophie Stapleton and Marguerite Aurelie', c. 1860, sixth-plate pair of gold-tinted and lightly colour-tinted, cased ambrotypes. State Library of South Australia, Adelaide, B 19711; Unattributed, 'Unidentified woman and child, and unidentified man', 1860s, half-plate pair of colour-tinted, cased ambrotypes. Powerhouse/Museum of Applied Arts and Sciences, Sydney, 96/73/1.
40 Nigel Lendon and Joan Kerr, 'Merlin, Henry Beaufoy (c.1830-1873)', in Joan Kerr (ed.), *The Dictionary of Australian Artists: Painters, Sketches, Photographers and Engravers to 1870*, Oxford University Press, Melbourne, 1992, p. 530.
41 Alan Davies and Peter Stanbury, *The Mechanical Eye in Australia: Photography 1841-1900*, Oxford University Press, Melbourne, 1985, p. 62; 'View of Hill End', *Australian Town and Country Journal*, Sydney, 30 March 1872, p. 17.
42 Newton, *Shades of Light*, p. 53.
43 'Hill End, From Our Correspondent', *Sydney Morning Herald*, 31 October 1872, p. 6.
44 Charles Bayliss, 'Panorama of Sydney Harbour and suburbs from the north shore', 1875, twenty-three albumen silver prints from a corresponding twenty-three mammoth-plate collodion negatives, knitted together to form an unbroken panorama. National Gallery of Australia, Canberra, 82.1159.1-23.
45 American and Australasian Photographic Company, and others, Untitled [B.O. Holtermann with gold nugget], mounted collage image (albumen print, ink and watercolour), 36.7 × 27.4 cm. State Library of New South Wales, Sydney, PXD 762 no. 9.
46 Marcel Safier claims Townsend and Sanford were both employed at a studio on 140 Grand Street, Williamsburg, Brooklyn, but I have been unable to locate in primary source material this studio or the Duryeas' employment. See 'Duryea, Townsend (1823-1888) and Sanford (1833-1904)', in John Hannavy (ed.), *Encyclopedia of Nineteenth-Century Photography*, Routledge, New York, 2008, p. 457.
47 'Patent no. 9018: T. Dureya Polishing Plates', 15 June 1852, Washington D.C. United States Patent Office. National Archives and Records Administration, Maryland.
48 'Inward Overseas Passenger Lists: British and Foreign Ports', August to December 1853, p. 13. Public Records Office of Victoria, North Melbourne, VPRS 947/P0000.
49 'Important to Miners – A Gold Washer', *Argus*, Melbourne, 18 October 1853, p. 3.
50 See e.g. Julie Robinson and Maria Zagala (eds), *A Century in Focus, 1840s-1940s: South Australian Photography*, Art Gallery of South Australia, Adelaide, 2008.

51 RJ Noye, 'Dureyea, Townsend (1823-1888)', *Australian Dictionary of Biography* online, National Centre for Biography, Australian National University, Canberra.
52 'Daguerreotypes', *Banner*, Melbourne, 15 November 1853, p. 2.
53 'Inward Overseas Passenger Lists: British and Foreign Ports', July to September 1854, p. 69. Public Records Office, Victoria, VPRS 947/P0000.
54 'Daguerreotypes', *Adelaide Times*, 15 February 1855, p. 1.
55 Audrey Linkman, *Photography and Death*, Reaktion, London, 2011, p. 18.
56 Route outlined in 'Daguerreotypes', *Adelaide Observer*, 20 December 1856, p. 8.
57 G.W. Symes, 'John Ross (1871-1903)', *Australian Dictionary of Biography* online, National Centre for Biography, Australian National University, Canberra.
58 The children are born in January 1853 (Sarah), March 1854 (Rebecca) and July 1855 (Henrietta), according to *South Australian Births Index of Registrations 1842-1906*, South Australian Genealogy and Heraldry Society, Adelaide, 1997, pp. 2577–8.
59 The State Library of South Australia catalogue record identifies the children as the Rosses' three eldest, Sarah, Rebecca and Henrietta, and attests that the photograph was taken in 1856 at Stanley Flat near Clare. It is unclear how this provenance data was gathered, but the location is on the Duryea studio's itinerant route. It is also possible, although less likely, that the young family travelled to Tarntanya/Adelaide and the blue solarisation has occurred in the Duryeas' sky-lit studio.
60 'Overland Voyage', *Adelaide Times*, 27 August 1857, p. 3.
61 'Cutter for the Lake and Murray Trade', *South Australian Register*, Adelaide, 21 July 1857, p. 2.
62 'Milang Ploughing Match', *South Australian Register*, Adelaide, 21 August 1857, p. 3.
63 'Cutter for the Lake and Murray Trade', *South Australian Register*, Adelaide, 21 July 1857, p. 2.
64 Townsend Duryea also bought unceded Ngarrindjeri land along the Millewa/Murray River at the conclusion of the studio tour but there is no evidence he worked it himself: 'Sales of Crown Lands', *Adelaide Observer*, 10 October 1857, p. 8.
65 'Daguerreotypes. Duryea Brothers (from Adelaide)', *Inquirer and Commercial News*, 28 October 1857, p. 2.
66 Arrival: 'Shipping Intelligence', *Inquirer*, Perth, 11 November 1846, p. 2; Departure: 'Shipping Intelligence', *Perth Gazette and Western Australian Journal*, 28 November 1846, p. 1; Advertisement: 'Notice. Open Eight Days Only. Daguerreotypes', *Inquirer*, Perth, 11 November 1846, p. 2.
67 'Situation Wanted', *Perth Gazette and Independent Journal of Politics and News*, 5 March 1852, p. 2.
68 'Local Intelligence', *Inquirer*, Perth, 9 March 1853, 2; 'Daguerreotype', *Inquirer*, Perth, 9 November 1853, p. 2.

69 The genders and relative ages of the children in this daguerreotype indicate that they are the Roes' three youngest offspring. Two sons, in succession, preceded by a sister who is older by several years, occurs only at the end of Matilda's pregnancies: Sophia (female) b. 1829; Matilda (female) b. 1831; James (male) b. 1833; Eliza (female) b. 1834; John (male) b. 1836; Frances (female) b. 1837; Jessie (female) b. 1839 d. 1839; Ellen (female) b. 1840; William (male) b. 1842; Frederick (male) b. 1843; Alice (female) b. 1845; George (male) b. 1848; Augustus (male) b. 1852. Genders and birth dates sourced from birth announcements placed in the *Inquirer* (Perth) and the *Perth Gazette and Independent Journal of Politics and News.* Names and dates confirmed in the Western Australian Birth Registry Online Index, sourced through the National Library of Australia.

70 Malcolm Uren, 'John Septimius Roe (1797-1878)', *Australian Dictionary of Biography* online, National Centre for Biography, Australian National University, Canberra.

71 Jillian Barteaux, 'Urban Planning as colonial marketing strategy for the Swan River Settlement, Western Australia', *Australian Historical Archaeology*, Vol. 34, 2016, pp. 24–6.

72 Joanna Gilmour, *Husbands and Wives*, National Portrait Gallery, Canberra, 2010, p. 31.

73 'Daguerreotypes! Duryea Brothers', *Inquirer and Commercial News*, Perth, 28 October 1857, p. 2.

74 'York', *Inquirer and Commercial News*, Perth, 5 May 1858, p. 2.

75 'Photography', *Inquirer and Commercial News*, Perth, 8 September 1858, p. 2.

76 Anne Gray, *Out of the West: Western Australian Art 1830s to 1930s*, National Gallery of Australia, Canberra, 2011, p. 34.

77 Anne Harse, *The Hester Story: 1829-1945, A History of the Hester Family in Western Australia and the Early Development of the Bridgetown District*, self-published, Fremantle, 2014, pp. 48–50.

78 'Is now at hand for procuring a correct and durable likeness', *Inquirer and Commercial News*, Perth, 17 November 1858, p. 2; 'Ladies and Gentleman, Send Your Portrait', *Inquirer and Commercial News*, Perth, 12 January 1859, p. 1.

79 See e.g.'Three Daughters of Francis and Emma Lochee', 1858, half-plate, colour-tinted, cased daguerreotype. Royal Western Australian Historical Society (RWAHS), Perth, P1999.7299; 'George Burnie', pre-1860, half-plate cased daguerreotype. RWAHS, Perth, P1999.7298; 'Walter Padbury', pre-1860, half-plate cased daguerreotype. RWAHS, Perth, P1999.7300; 'Unnamed man', 1858, half-plate cased daguerreotype. Bridgetown Historical Society, Bridgetown; 'Daguerreotype of an unidentified man', 1850–60, half-plate, colour-tinted, cased daguerreotype. State Library of Western Australia, Perth, BA2003.

80 S.G. Claughton, 'William Walker (1800-1855)', *Australian Dictionary of Biography* online, National Centre for Biography, Australian National University, Canberra.

81 The Aboriginal woman is referred to, by alternate names, on each catalogue: T.S. Glaister, 'Untitled [Jane Henrietta Kidd Harpur, Susanna Matilda Australia Harpur and Jerimin (Medley) Harpur]', c. 1860, quarter-plate, heavily coloured, cased ambrotype. National Gallery of Australia, Canberra, 2018.813; T. S. Glaister, 'Group portrait of Old Sally (nurse) with Eliza's children Janie and Susie', c. 1860, quarter-plate, heavily coloured, cased ambrotype. State Library of New South Wales, Sydney, MIN 567.

82 T.S. Glaister, Untitled [Jane Henrietta Kidd Harpur, Susanna Matilda Australia Harpur and Jerimin (Medley)], c. 1860, quarter-plate, hand-coloured, cased daguerreotype. National Gallery of Australia 2018.813.

83 Full title: George Talpin, *The Narrinyeri* [sic]*: An account of the tribes of South Australian Aborigines inhabiting the country around the Lakes Alexandrina* [sic], *Albert, and Coorong, and the lower part of the River Murray: their manners and customs, also, an account of the mission at Port Macleay*, J.T. Shawyer, Adelaide, 1874.

84 Michael Aird, 'Aboriginal People and Four Early Brisbane Photographers', in Jane Lydon (ed.), *Calling the Shots: Aboriginal Photographies*, Aboriginal Studies Press, Canberra, 2014, p. 153.

85 *Illustrated London News*, 26 January 1850, p. 53.

86 Jane Lydon, 'The experimental 1860s: Charles Walter's images of Coranderrk Aboriginal Station, Victoria', *Aboriginal History*, Vol. 26, 2002, p. 78. I acknowledge Jane Lydon, who also shared with me her knowledge and opinion on Figure 3.17 ambrotype's location and the details within the photograph.

87 Carl (Charles) Walter, 'Portraits of Aboriginal Natives Settled at Coranderrk, near Healesville, about 42 miles from Melbourne. Upper Yarra. Also Views of the Station & Lubras Basket-Making', 1866, 106 albumen-silver prints approx. 10 × 6.7 cm laid down in panels to form a girded presentation 101.2 × 146.8 cm. State Library of Victoria, Melbourne, H91.1/1- 106.

88 Lydon, 'The experimental 1860s', p. 118.

89 'Kudgeron' is a term for club I was advised to use by Wurundjeri cultural artefacts specialist Jack Norris.

90 Fred Cahir, 'Dallong – Possum Skin Rugs', *Provenance* online (journal of the Public Record Office of Victoria), No. 4, 25 March 2020, p. 9.

91 Jonathan Jones, Murruwaygu: following in the footsteps of our ancestors, PhD dissertation, University of Technology, Sydney (UTS), 2018, pp. 2 and 125–6.

92 Now unknown maker, Broad shield, early-to-mid-nineteenth century, earth pigments on wood, can and pipeclay. 23.3 × 87 cm. National Gallery of Victoria, Melbourne, 2011.123. I am thankful to Stephen Gilchrist for drawing my attention to this shield.

93 Conversation between the author, Garrick Hitchcock, Jack Norris and Colin Hunter Sr, Wurundjeri Woi-wurrung Cultural Heritage Aboriginal Corporation, 12 February 2024.

Chapter 4

1 Helen Ennis, *A Modern Vision: Charles Bayliss, 1850-1897*, National Library of Australia, Canberra, 2008, p. 1.

2 Charles Bayliss, 'Panorama of Sydney Harbour and Suburbs from the North Shore', 1875, twenty-three albumen prints from collodion negatives, overall image: 52.2 × 853.2 cm. National Gallery of Australia, Canberra, 82.1159.1.1-23; 'The Largest Photograph in the World', *Oakland Tribune*, California, 8 June 1876, p. 1.

3 Geoffrey Batchen, *Apparitions: Photography and Dissemination*, Power Publications, Sydney, 2018, pp. 74–5.

4 Ibid.

5 Jarrod Hore, *Visions of Nature: How Landscape Photography Shaped Settler Colonialisation*, University of California Press, California, 2022, pp. 10–11.

6 A second plate of the same view also remained in Newland's Daguerreian Gallery upstairs and travelled with him when he moved on to Kolkata. See Elisa deCourcy and Martyn Jolly, *Empire, Early Photography and Spectacle: the Global Career of Showman Daguerreotypist J.W. Newland*, Routledge, London, 2021, pp. 84–6.

7 Lyndall Ryan, *Tasmanian Aborigines: A History Since 1803*, Allen & Unwin, Sydney, 2012, pp. 67 and 143–6.

8 Joseph Pugliese, 'Disjunctive Traces' in Julie Gough (ed.), *Tense Past*, 2nd edn, Tebrikunna Press, nipaluna, 2021, pp. 95–6.

9 'View of the Metropolis', *Courier*, Hobart, 9 December 1848, p. 2.

10 The following daguerreotype photographers were operating in Naarm/ Melbourne during 1854–55: Mr Nott, 3 Swanston Street (1854); Duryea and MacDonald, 3 Greater Bourke Street (1853–54); T. S. Glaister, Meade Bros. & Co., Greater Collins Street (1854–55); W. Robinson, Collins Street (1855); G.W. Perry, Collins Street (1855); J.C. Alexander, Elizabeth Street (1855); Batchelder, Collins Street (1855). This plate has previously been attributed to T.S. Glaister, but Glaister was known for his technical skill, and this daguerreotype was not properly fixed and, as a result, has substantially faded.

11 See e.g. Geoffrey Batchen, *Burning with Desire: the conception of photography*, MIT Press, Cambridge, MA,1999, pp. 133–6; Jennifer Green-Lewis, 'At Home in the Nineteenth Century: Photography, Nostalgia and the Will to Authenticity', *Nineteenth-Century Contexts*, Vol. 22, No. 1, 2000, pp. 53–4; 'Steffen Seigel, 'Cat in the Window? A Closer Look At How People Try to Have a Closer Look', in Amos Morris-Reich and Margaret Olin (eds), *Photography and Imagination*, Routledge, New York, 2019, pp. 1–12.

12 Thomas Ham, 'Ham's squatting map of Victoria (carefully corrected to this date from colonial government surveys)', 1853, 46 × 71.5 cm. National Library of Australia, MAP NK 10059.

13 Thomas Ham, 'Plan of the city of Melbourne embracing, Collingwood, South Melbourne and Sandridge, shewing part of Richmond, Prahan & St Kilda', 1854, 61 × 46 cm. National Library of Australia, MAP RM 1303.

14 Candice Bruce and Gael Newton, 'Turner, Joseph', in Joan Kerr (ed.), *The Dictionary of Australian Artists: Painters, Sketches, Photographers and Engravers to 1870*, Oxford University Press, Melbourne, 1992, p. 813.
15 Daniel Palmer and Martyn Jolly, *Installation View: Photography Exhibitions in Australia 1848-2020*, Perimeter Editions, Melbourne, 2022, pp. 50–1 and 55.
16 'Shipping Intelligence', *Colonial Times*, Hobart, 18 June 1839, p. 4; 'Shipping News: Arrived', *Port Phillip Patriot and Melbourne Advertiser*, 14 October 1839, p. 7.
17 'Port Phillip / Cleared Out', *Australian*, Sydney, 16 February 1847, p. 2.
18 'Colonial Secretary's Office Announcements', *New South Wales Government Gazette*, Sydney, 18 June 1850, p. 915.
19 Elizabeth Willis, 'Overlooked and Forgotten: Representations of Aboriginal Pastoral Workers in Nineteenth-Century Victoria', in Anne Maxwell and Josephine Croci (eds), *Shifting Focus: Colonial Australian Photography 1850-1920*, Australian Scholarly Publishing, North Melbourne, 2015, pp. 47–9. John Hunter Kerr, [Full-length portrait of Dja Dja Wurrung women wearing animal skins and one Dja Dja Wurrung man in European clothes], 1850s, printed later by George W. Priston, c. 1865–c. 1875, albumen silver print, 14.6 × 20.1 cm. State Library Victoria, Melbourne. H30158/10.
20 See e.g. Joan Kerr (ed.), *The Dictionary of Australian Artists: Painters, Sketches, Photographers and Engravers to 1870*, Oxford University Press, Melbourne, 1992.
21 See e.g. Judy Annear (ed.), *The Photograph and Australia*, Art Gallery of New South Wales Press, Sydney, 2015; Cathy Leahy et al. (eds), *Colony Australia, 1770-1861, Frontier Wars*, National Gallery of Victoria, Melbourne, 2018; Julie Robinson (ed.), *A Century in Focus: South Australian Photography 1840s-1940s*, Art Gallery of South Australia, Adelaide, 2007.
22 Stephen Monteiro, 'Hill, David Octavius (1802-1870) and Adamson, Robert (1821-1848)', in John Hannavy (ed.), *Encyclopedia of Nineteenth-Century Photography*, Routledge, New York, 2008, pp. 657–60; the two most sizeable collections of Hill and Adamson salted paper prints are housed at the Scottish National Portrait Gallery and the University of Glasgow.
23 Featherstone et al., 'A Pictorial Partnership: The Photographs of Hill and Adamson' in *Hill and Adamson: Photographs from the J. Paul Getty Museum*, J. Paul Getty, Los Angeles, 1999, p. 72.
24 Roddy Simpson, *The Photography of Victorian Scotland*, Edinburgh University Press, Edinburgh, 2012, pp. 50–1.
25 'Edinburgh Calotype Album', Vol. 1, c. 1848, 206 salted paper prints from calotype negatives. National Library of Scotland, Edinburgh. Phot.med.33.
26 See e.g. Unattributed, [Carfrae property 'Ledcourt', Kobram/Stawell, Victoria], c. 1857, quarter-plate, cased daguerreotype, with colour accenting. National Gallery of Australia, Canberra. 2008.954; Unattributed, [View of an Australian homestead with three men in leather caps and two dogs and two drovers with

cattle in the background], c. 1860, half-plate uncoloured cased ambrotype. National Gallery of Australia, Canberra. 2010.354; Unattributed, [The Store and residence of John Bourne Crego and his partner, Henry Wilshire Webb], 1863, quarter-plate uncoloured cased ambrotype. Art Gallery of New South Wales, Sydney. 229.1989; Unattributed, 'Sandford, the home of John Henty, Portland Region, Victoria', 1850s–60s, quarter-plate, uncoloured, cased ambrotype. National Library of Australia, Canberra. PIC 11 #P727.

27 John Hunter Kerr, [Full-length portrait of Dja Dja Wurrung women wearing animal skins and one Dja Dja Wurrung man in European clothes], 1850s, printed later by George W. Priston, c. 1865 – c. 1875, albumen silver print, 14.6 × 20.1 cm. State Library of Victoria, Melbourne. H30158/10.

28 Willis, 'Overlooked and Forgotten', p. 48.

29 W. Wickman and B. Groom, 'Blackwood, Olaf William', in Joan Kerr (ed.), *The Dictionary of Australian Artists: Painters, Sketches, Photographers and Engravers to 1870*, Oxford University Press, Melbourne, 1992, pp. 70–1.

30 'Notice: Photographic Colouring', *Sydney Morning Herald*, 12 May 1857, p. 8; 'Mr Insley's Photographic Skylight Gallery', *Sydney Morning Herald*, 3 August 1857, p. 1.

31 See e.g. 'Philosophical Society of New South Wales – List of contributors and contributions at the Photographic Exhibition', *Sydney Morning Herald*, 22 December 1859, p. 4.

32 Gael Newton, *Shades of Light: Photography and Australia 1839-1988*, Australian National Gallery, Canberra, 1988, p. 26.

33 'Blackwood's Views of Sydney', *Sydney Morning Herald*, 4 October 1858, p. 8.

34 Frederick Frith and John Mathieson Sharp together and separately took earlier panoramas in nipaluna/Hobart. See Frederick Frith and John M. Sharp, 'Panorama of Hobart, in five pieces, taken from the Domain', 18 January 1858, five-plate panorama, salted paper prints from collodion negatives. Tasmania Archives and Heritage Office, Hobart. NS2960; John M. Sharp, 'Hobart Town from the Domain', 1857, five-plate panorama, salted paper prints from collodion negatives, overall image 15 × 95.2 cm. State Library of Tasmania, Hobart. Crowther Collection C5674.

35 Gael Newton identified this painterly addition of clouds across other Blackwood photographic prints. Newton, *Shades of Light*, p. 27.

36 'The Fine Arts', *Sydney Morning Herald*, 4 August 1858, p. 5.

37 Ibid.

38 Rebecca Edwards, '"A Delightful and Difficult Art"', Cathy Leahy et al. (eds), *Colony Australia, 1770-1861, Frontier Wars*, National Gallery of Victoria, Melbourne, 2018, p. 180.

39 Elspeth Pitt, 'Conrad Martens / Campbells Wharf 1857' in Leahy et al. (eds), *Colony Australia, 1770-1861, Frontier Wars*, National Gallery of Victoria, Melbourne, 2018, p. 192.

40 O. William Blackwood, 'Album of Australian Scenery', 1858, fifteen albumen prints, appox. 21.5 × 29.5 cm in a leather-bound album. Mort Family Collection, State Library of New South Wales, Sydney. PXD 955.
41 Quoted in Annear (ed.), *The Photograph and Australia*, p. 280.
42 'Dunolly Town Council. September 6.', *Maryborough and Dunolly Advertiser*, 11 September 1861, p. 3.
43 1871 England Census, Northumberland, Belford (town), Ecclesiastical District 23. The National Archives Kew, London. Class RG10; Piece 5177; Folio 23; p. 11.
44 'Photography', *Maryborough and Dunolly Advertiser*, 3 July 1861, p. 3.
45 *Catalogue of the Victorian Exhibition of 1861: with prefatory essays indicating the progress, resources, and physical characteristics of the colony*, John Ferres, Government Printer, Melbourne, 1861, pp. 112 and 258.
46 Palmer and Jolly, *Installation View*, pp. 30–55.
47 G.H. Jenkinson, [Church of England School, Dunolly], 1861, half-plate, uncoloured, framed ambrotype. State Library of Victoria, Melbourne. H261126.
48 G.H. Jenkinson, [Police Court, Dunolly], 1861, half-plate, uncoloured, framed, ambrotype. State Library of Victoria, Melbourne. H26135.
49 G.H. Jenkinson, [Dunolly Hospital], 1861, half-plate, uncoloured, framed, ambrotype. State Library of Victoria, Melbourne. H26128.
50 *Catalogue of the Victorian Exhibition of 1861*, p. 267; Alan Davies and Peter Stanbury, *The Mechanical Eye in Australia: Photography 1841-1900*, Oxford University Press, Melbourne, 1985, p. 42.
51 *Catalogue of the Victorian Exhibition of 1861*, pp. 291–2.
52 'Victoria and the Great Exhibition / The following report and catalogue have been forward by Mr J.G. Knight, Victoria Department, International Exhibition, London May 25', *Argus*, Melbourne, 11 July 1862, p. 7.
53 For example, Simpson's Hotel has an address to a John Simpson in Cambridgeshire; the Dunolly branch of the Bank of Australia, for which Walter Wilson Duke was manager in 1861, is addressed to William Duke in Sussex. G.H. Jenkinson, [Simpson's Bendigo Hotel, Dunolly], 1861, half-plate, uncoloured, framed, ambrotype. State Library of Victoria, Melbourne. H26125; G.H. Jenkinson, [Bank of Australia, Dunolly], 1861, half-plate, uncoloured, framed, ambrotype. State Library of Victoria, Melbourne. H26115.
54 Peter A. Cudmore and Joan Kerr, 'Nettleton, Charles (c.1825-1902)', in Joan Kerr (ed.), *The Dictionary of Australian Artists: Painters, Sketches, Photographers and Engravers to 1870*, Oxford University Press, Melbourne, 1992, p. 567.
55 See e.g. Charles Nettleton, Untitled [Bourke St, North], 1867–74, carte de visite, 6.3 × 10 cm. Art Gallery of New South Wales, Sydney. 436.2014.
56 Davies and Stanbury, *The Mechanical Eye in Australia*, p. 62.
57 Beth Fowkes Tobin, 'Imperial Designs: Botanical Illustration and the British Botanical Empire', *Studies in Eighteenth-Century Culture*, Vol. 25, 1996, p. 265.

58 Vanessa Finney, *Capturing Nature: Early Scientific Photography at the Australian Museum*, NewSouth Publishing, Sydney, 2019, p. 111.
59 Julianne Roughley, 'Walker, Theresa Susannah Eunice Snell, née Chauncy (Mrs Poole) (1807-1876)', in Joan Kerr (ed.), *The Dictionary of Australian Artists: Painters, Sketches, Photographers and Engravers to 1870*, Oxford University Press, Melbourne, 1992, p. 830.
60 William Henry Harvey (Port Arthur, Tasmania), to Hannah Harvey Todhunter, 4 March 1855, Gray Herbarium, Harvard University, Cambridge, MA, manuscript file: GH-2-39-C-LF.
61 Ibid.
62 Ibid.
63 'Emigration to South Australia', *Australian*, Sydney, 17 February 1837, p. 3.
64 Jane Lennon, 'Theresa Walker's South Australia', in Tim Bonyhady and Andrew Sayers (eds), *Heads of the People: A Portrait of Colonial Australia*, National Portrait Gallery, Canberra, 2000, p. 5.
65 Jane Hylton, *Colonial Sisters: Martha Berkeley & Theresa Walker, South Australia's First Professional Artists*, Art Gallery of South Australia, Adelaide, 1994, p. 78; 'Kartamiru (first born male), also known as Murlawirrapurka, King John and Onkaparinga Jack of South Australia', c. 1840, cast wax medallion, 9.2 cm (diameter) (framed 19.8 cm x 19.8cm), National Gallery of Australia, 79.2244A; 'Mukata, wife of King John, commonly known as Pretty Mary of South Australia', c.1840, wax medallion, 9.2cm (diameter) (framed 19.8 cm x 19.8cm), National Gallery of Australia, 79.2244B; 'Mrs Grey (Lady Eliza Lucy Grey)', c. 1845, cast wax medallion, 19 cm diameter (framed), National Portrait Gallery, Canberra 1999.52.2; 'Sir John Franklin', c. 1846, cast wax medallion, 22.3 cm diameter (framed), National Gallery of Victoria, Melbourne, 1995.723; 'Portraits of South Australian Residents', early 1840s, twelve low relief wax busts and four medallions mounted, Art Gallery of South Australia, Adelaide, S153.
66 'Portrait of Governor Grey', *South Australian Gazette and Colonial Register*, Adelaide, 25 October 1845, p. 2; Theresa Walker, 'Sir George Grey', [Inscription: The Ports of South Australia Declared Free / July 3rd 1845] low-relief wax medallion bust, 1845. Framed 18.8 x 18.8cm. National Portrait Gallery, Canberra. 1999.52.1.
67 See: Arthur Bartholomew and Theresa Poole, 'Reef Ocean Perch, Helicolenus percoides', lithographic ink, vanish and water colour on paper, 1861, Museums Victoria, PZ 33.3. Later inserted in: *Frederick McCoy, National History of Victoria: Prodromus of the Zoology of Victoria; Figures and Description of the Living Species of All Classes of the Victorian Indigenous Animals,* John Ferres, Government Printer, Melbourne, 1878, Plate 33.
68 Meredith Key Soles, 'Atkins, Anna Children (1799-1871)' in John Hannavy (ed.), *Encyclopedia of Nineteenth-Century Photography*, Routledge, New York, 2008, p. 93.

69 Introductory page of Anna Atkins, *Photographs of British Algae: Cyanotype Impressions*, Part I, 1843, National Science and Media Museum, Bradford, 1937-403.

70 Molly Duggins, 'Pacific Ocean Flowers: Colonial Seaweed Albums', in Steve Mentz and Martha Elena Rojas (eds), *The Sea and Nineteenth-Century Anglophone Literary Culture*, Routledge, London, 2016, pp. 120–1.

71 Ibid.

72 'Royal Society of Van Diemen's Land (from *The Courier*)', *Launceston Examiner*, 17 July 1850, p. 8.

73 Walker knew the Feredays. In 1855, she completed a wax bust of the reverend's wife and watercolourist, Susan Fereday. This portrait was still in Walker's possession when Harvey visited her in March 1855, and he commented on it favourably in his letter to his sister; Correspondence, William Henry Harvey to Hannah Harvey Todhunter, Port Arthur, Tasmania, 4 March 1855, Gray Herbarium, Harvard University, Cambridge, MA, manuscript file: GH-2-39-C-LF.

74 Ann Christie, '"An Imitation of Seaweed": Nature and Design in a Late Eighteenth-Century Printed Cotton', in Kathleen Davidson and Molly Duggins (eds), *Sea Currents in Nineteenth-Century Art, Science and Culture: Commodifying the Ocean World*, Bloomsbury, London, 2023, p. 237.

75 See e.g. 'Royal Society of Van Diemen's Land', *Courier*, Hobart, 15 February 1853, p. 2; 'Royal Society of Van Diemen's Land', *Adelaide Observer*, 26 November 1853, p. 1.

76 Joachim Otté, *Landscape Photography or, A Complete & Easy Description of the Manipulations and Apparatus Necessary for the Production of Landscape Pictures, Geological Sections, etc. by the Calotype, Wet Collodion, Collodio-albumen, Gelatine, and Wax-Paper Processes by the Assistance of Which an Amateur May at Once Commence the Practice of the Art*, Robert Hardwicke, London, 1858.

77 *Catalogue for the Melbourne Public Library for 1861*, printed by Clarson, Shallard & Co., Melbourne, 1861, p. 326. State Library of Victoria, Melbourne, RARELT 018.1 M48C.

78 Paul Ricochet, 'Photography in Australia', *Photographic News*, London, 28 August 1863, pp. 412–13.

79 Ibid., p. 413.

80 Paul Ricochet, 'Photography in Australia', *Photographic News*, London, 4 September 1863, pp. 425–6.

81 Anne-Marie Willis, 'Allport, Morton (1830-1878)', in Joan Kerr (ed.), *The Dictionary of Australian Artists: Painters, Sketches, Photographers and Engravers to 1870*, Oxford University Press, Melbourne, 1992, p. 16; Tony Brown and Gillian Winter, *First Views of Lake St Clair: John Skinner Prout (1845) and Morton Allport (1863)*, Pear Tree Press, Hobart, 2011, p. 95. As Brown and Winter point out, there is no record of a 'Paul Ricochet' in any of the immigration or shipping manifests for Naarm/Melbourne or nipaluna/Hobart in the early 1860s.

82 As recorded in the diary of Charles's brother, Alfred Abbott, 1 August 1858 – 21 July1861. Allport Library and Museum of Fine Arts, Hobart, ALL 6/1/1.

83 See e.g. Morton Allport, 'Elizabeth Allport with Baby in Garden of *Fernleigh*, Davey Street', c. 1856, card-mounted stereo print, 8 × 16 cm (approx.). Allport Library and Museum of Fine Arts, Hobart, AP 17.

84 Brown and Winter, *First Views of Lake St Clair*, p. 92.

85 Jarrod Hore, *Visions of Nature: How Landscape Photography Shaped Settler Colonialism*, University of California Press, Oakland, 2022, p. 6.

86 Ibid.

87 Morton Allport to Curzon Allport, 'Excursion to Lake St Clair, February 1863', compiled March 1863, Hobart, one album of twenty-four albumen silver stereographic prints sequenced and captioned, accompanied by a letter, all leather-bound. Allport Library and Museum of Fine Arts, Hobart, Mss Box 11 Folder 7.

88 Mary Louise Pratt, *Imperial Eyes: Travel Writing and Transculturation*, 2nd edn, Routledge, London, 2008, pp. 200–1.

89 'Art Treasures' Exhibition', *Mercury* (Hobart), 25 February 1863, p. 3; 'Art Treasures Exhibition', *Walch's Literary Intelligencer and General Advertiser*, No. 47, Vol. 4, March 1863, p. 136.

90 *Catalogue of the Contributions Made by Tasmania to the Intercolonial Exhibition of Australia at Melbourne in 1866*, James Barnard, Government Printers, Hobart, 1866(?), p. 20.

91 *Intercolonial Exhibition of Australasia, Melbourne 1866-67: official record containing introduction catalogues, reports and awards of the jurors and essays and statistics on the social and economic resources of the Australasian colonies*, Blundell & Co. Printers, Melbourne, 1867, pp. 350–1.

92 NB: These are not in stereo, nor from the February 1863 expedition. 'The Salmon-Breeding Ponds on the River Plenty, Tasmania – [Photographed by G. M. Allport, esq]'; 'A Rapid on the River Plenty, near the Breeding Ponds – [Photographed by G. M. Allport, esq]', *Illustrated Melbourne Post*, 26 August 1864, p. 12.

93 Helen E. Lambert, 'Who and What We Saw in the Antipodes', 1868–70, leather-bound album containing photography, collage and coloured drawing. National Gallery of Australia, Canberra, 83.25.24.

94 See e.g. Richard Daintree, 'The "Nobby", Phillip Island', c. 1858, albumen print, 19 × 24 cm. State Library of Victoria, Melbourne, PCLTAF 994; Richard Daintree, [View on the River Werribee], c. 1861, glass wet-plate collodion negative, 20 × 25.2 cm. State Library of Victoria, H36562.

95 See: 'A Trip to Cape Otway (By Our Travelling Photographer)', *Illustrated Australian News for Home Readers*, Melbourne, 31 December 1873, p. 212; Tim Bonyhady, *The Colonial Earth*, Miegunyah Press, Melbourne, 2000, pp. 190–3.

96 Isobel Crombie, *Fred Kruger: Intimate Landscapes 1860s-1880s*, National Gallery of Victoria, Melbourne, 2012, p. 1.

97 Ibid., pp. 13–17.

98 Ken Orchard, 'J.W. Lindt's "Characteristic Australian Forest Scenery" (1875) and the Construction of an Emblematic Australian Landscape', in Anne Maxwell and Josephine Croci (eds), *Shifting Focus: Colonial Australian Photography 1850-1920*, Australian Scholarly Publishing, North Melbourne, 2015, pp. 88–99.

99 Helen Ennis, *Photography and Australia*, p. 59.

Chapter 5

1 Although André-Adolphe-Eugène Disdéri patented the carte de visite in Paris during 1854, its commercial uptake in the colonial portrait studio markets begins from 1859. Gael Newton (*Shades of Light*, p. 27) identifies O. William Blackwood (discussed in Chapter 4) as being the first to practise with the carte de visite, in late 1859.

2 Joanna Gilmour, *Carte-O-Mania*, National Portrait Gallery, Canberra, 2018, p. 9.

3 Mary Warner Marien, *Photography: A Cultural History*, 2nd edn, Laurence King Publishing, London, 2006, p. 165.

4 Ibid., pp. 222–4.

5 Meg Foster, *Boundary Crossers: The Hidden History of Australia's Other Bushrangers*, NewSouth Publishing, Sydney, 2022, p. 1.

6 Grace Karskens, *The Colony: a history of early Sydney*, Allen & Unwin, Sydney, 2010, pp. 303–5.

7 Thomas Mitchell (attributed), 'Donahoe [sic]', 1830, lithograph, 21.8 × 27.8 cm. State Library of New South Wales, P2/361.

8 Mark Finnane, 'Law and Regulation', in Alison Bashford and Stuart Macintyre (eds), *The Cambridge History of Australia, Vol. 1: Indigenous and Colonial Australia*, Cambridge University Press, Cambridge, 2015, p. 411.

9 S. T. Gill, 'Attacking the Mail', 1864, coloured lithograph, 17.5 × 25 cm. Plate 24 from *The Australian Sketchbook*. National Gallery of Victoria, 3049.25-4. Thank you to Alisa Bunbury for drawing my attention to this lithograph.

10 Mary Mackay, 'Hamilton, George (1812-1883)', in Joan Kerr (ed.), *The Dictionary of Australian Artists: Painters, Sketches, Photographers and Engravers to 1870*, Oxford University Press, Melbourne, 1992, p. 344.

11 Andrew Sayers, *Australian Art*, Oxford University Press, Oxford, p. 61.

12 Virginia Spate, *Tom Roberts*, Lansdowne Press, East Melbourne, 1978, p. 94.

13 Foster, *Boundary Crossers*, p. 170; Wayne Tunnicliffe, 'Bailed Up' in Anne Gray (ed.), *Tom Roberts*, National Gallery of Australia, Canberra, 2015, p. 215.

14 R. B. Walker, 'Bushranging in Fact and Legend', *Historical Studies: Australia and New Zealand*, Vol. 42, No. 11, 1964, p. 201–2.

15 'Biography of Ben Hall', *Maitland Mercury and Hunter River General Advertiser*, 18 May 1865, p. 2.

16 Edgar F. Penzig, 'Ben Hall (1837-1865)', *Australian Dictionary of Biography* online, National Centre for Biography, Australian National University, Canberra, 1972.

17 'The following description of offenders is published for the general information of the police', *New South Wales Police Gazette and Weekly Record of Crime*, Sydney, 18 November 1863, p. 350.

18 Ibid.

19 A copy of Lowry's photographic post-mortem portrait was pasted in an unnamed amateur's scrapbook, now held at the National Portrait Gallery, Canberra: Unattributed, 'Lowry', c. 1863 (print), albumen silver print, 5 × 8.5 cm. National Portrait Gallery, Canberra. 2008.4.AB.

20 Alan Davies, 'Gregory, George (1843-1914)', in Joan Kerr (ed.), *The Dictionary of Australian Artists: Painters, Sketches, Photographers and Engravers to 1870*, Oxford University Press, Melbourne, 1992, p. 322. A second portrait showing Lowry alive but not photographically based was engraved for the *Post* by Samuel Calvert for the 20 October 1863 edition.

21 'More Sticking Up', *Braidwood News and Southern Goldfields Advertiser*, 4 June 1864, p. 3.

22 'Sticking up of Rossiville and Robbery of the Sydney Mail by Hall, Dunn and Gilbert', *Empire*, Sydney, 16 November 1864, p. 3.

23 'Ben Hall's Death [From a Forbes Correspondent]', *Burrangong Argus*, 13 May 1865, p. 2.

24 Unattributed, [unidentified woman, possibly Susan Pryor], ninth-plate, colour-tinted, gilt-framed cased daguerreotype. Forbes and District Historical Museum.

25 'Death of Ben Hall (From the Forbes Correspondent of the 'Western Examiner')', *Sydney Morning Herald*, 13 May 1865, p. 7.

26 'Ben Hall, the Bushranger', *Illustrated Sydney News*, 16 May 1865, p. 3.

27 For a further example, see the posthumous carte de visite of Daniel (Mad Dog) Morgan at Pechelba Station: Hermann Pohl, 'Daniel Morgan, bushranger, shot a Pechelba Station, April 9th 1865', 1865, carte de visite, 11 × 7 cm. State Library of Victoria. H13188.

28 Ennis, *Photography and Australia*, p. 30.

29 Julian Ashton, *Now came still evening on*, Halstead Press, Sydney, 1941, pp. 31–2.

30 'Finding Byrne's Body – A Study' (initialled with J. R. A.), *Illustrated Australian News*, Melbourne, 3 July 1880, p. 105.

31 Ashton, *Now came still evening on*, p. 32.

32 As identified by Newton, *Shades of Light*, p. 44.

33 Susan Sontag, *On Photography*, 4th edn, Picador, New York, 1979, p. 5.

34 See e.g. 'Charge sheet for James "Jim", aka Wilson, brother of Ned Kelly', New South Wales Police, 1878, paper, albumen photograph and ink, 30.5 × 25 cm. Justice and Police Museum / Museums of History New South Wales, Sydney, JP86/417.

35 James Ryan, *Photography and Exploration*, Reaktion, London, 2013, p. 13.

36 Newton, *Shades of Light*, p. 46.

37 Ryan, *Photography and Exploration*, p. 14.

38 John Morton, 'Old Pictures, New Frames: Introducing the Photographs of Baldwin Spencer and Frank Gillen', in Batty et al. (eds), *The Photographs of Baldwin Spencer*, Miegunyah Press, Melbourne, 2005, p. xiii.
39 Ibid., p. xiv.
40 B. A. Riffenburgh, 'Franklin, Sir John', *Oxford Dictionary of National Biography* online, 2022.
41 Geoffrey Batchen, *Apparitions: Photography and Dissemination*, Power Publications, Sydney, 2018, pp. 78–9; 'Portraits of Sir John Franklin and his crew', *Illustrated London News*, 13 September 1851, pp. 329–30.
42 See Boston illustrated periodical *Gleason's Pictorial Drawing Room Companion*, 18 October 1851, p. 1 (the *Gleason*'s engravings may have been second-generation copies of photographically derived engravings) and reporting on Franklin's engraving being exhibited at the St Andrews Picture Library in Calcutta/Kolkata in 1854. Both are discussed in Batchen, *Apparitions*, p. 80; deCourcy and Jolly, *Empire, Early Photography and Spectacle*, p. 118.
43 'Departure of the 'Erebus' and 'Terror' on the Artic Expedition', *Illustrated London News*, 24 May 1845, p. 328.
44 Ian D. Clark and Fred Cahir, '"I suppose this will end in our having to live like the blacks for a few months": reinterpreting the history of Burke and Wills', in Ian D. Clark and Fred Cahir (eds), *The Aboriginal Story of Burke and Wills: Forgotten Narratives*, CSIRO Publishing and State Library of Victoria, Melbourne, 2013, p. 366.
45 Ian D. Clark, 'The members of the Victorian Exploring Expedition and their prior experience with Aboriginal Peoples', in Ian D. Clark and Fred Cahir (eds), *The Aboriginal Story of Burke and Wills: Forgotten Narratives*, CSIRO Publishing and State Library of Victoria, Melbourne, 2013, p. 44.
46 There is a daguerreotype of Burke in the State Library of New South Wales's collection that is likely by Hill, and was likely rephotographed (and printed through the albumen process) to form the basis for later engraved reproductions, which, like Sadd's, are captioned as originally from a photograph by Hill. Burke's folded arms, the tuft of hair escaping from behind his ear, the direction of his gaze and identical nature of his outfit are carried across this and other photographically derived reproductions. See 'Portrait of Robert O'Hara Burke', 1860, sixth-plate, cased uncoloured daguerreotype. State Library of New South Wales, SAFE/D 179/ Item 1.
47 'Trade and Professional Directory … Photographic Artists', *Age*, Melbourne, 11 December 1855, p. 3. The trade directory lists Hill as based at 3 Bourke Street East, which is the same address kept by Duryea and McDonald in Naarm/Melbourne.
48 Alan Davies and Joyce Thomson, 'Hill, Thomas Adams', in Joan Kerr (ed.), *The Dictionary of Australian Artists: Painters, Sketches, Photographers and Engravers to 1870*, Oxford University Press, Melbourne, 1992, p. 364.

49 William Strutt, 'A collection of drawings in watercolour, ink and pencil by William Strutt R.B.G. F.Z.S. illustrating the Burke and Wills Exploring Expedition Crossing the Continent of Australia from Cooper's Creek to Carpentaria, Aug 1860-June 1861', Vol. 1 [1st series], 1861, approx. twenty-five mixed media illustrative leaves. State Library of New South Wales, DL PXX 3.

50 The State Library of Victoria, Melbourne, the National Gallery of Australia, and the National Portrait Gallery, Canberra, hold identical copies of the Sadd mezzotints made of Burke and Wills after photographs by T.A. Hill and published by Fergusson & Mitchell.

51 H. S. Sadd and T. A. Hill, 'Portrait of Sir John O'Shanassy / dautpe. by T.A. Hill, engd. By H.S. Sadd', c. 1859, mezzotint, 16.7 × 12.1 cm. National Library of Australia, PIC Drawer 7821 S8395. Further collaborations between Sadd and Hill include H.S. Sadd and T.A. Hill, 'Portrait of W. Mackay, L.L.D / engraved by H.S. Sadd from a Daguerreotype by T.A. Hill', c. 1855, mezzotint, 28 × 21 cm. State Library of Victoria, H90.159/12; HS Sadd and TA Hill, 'J. Everard Esq. M.L.A. for Rodney / dautpe. by T.A. Hill, engd. By H.S. Sadd', c. 1855, mezzotint, 25 × 18 cm. State Library of Victoria, H90.159/13. Sadd collaborated with other colonial photographers around this time too: see e.g: H. S. Sadd and G. Perry, 'Sir Charles H. Darling K.C.B. Govenor of Victoria / Phot-d G. Perry … Eng-d H.S. Sadd', 1860s, mezzotint, 32.07 × 25.72 cm. State Library of New South Wales, DG P2/22; H. S. Sadd and Perez Mann Batchelder, 'The Very Reverend H.B. Macartny, Dean of Melbourne / engraved by H.S. Sadd from a Daguerreotype by Batchelder', c. 1855, mezzotint, 37 × 26 cm. State Library of Victoria, H90.159/6.

52 As quoted and reproduced in Richard Neville, *Faces of Australia: Image, Reality and the Portrait*, State Library of New South Wales Press, Sydney, 1992, p. 80.

53 'The Burke and Wills Australian Exploring Expedition', *Illustrated London News*, 1 February 1862, p. 127.

54 Kathleen Fitzpatrick, 'Robert O'Hara Burke (1821-1861)', *Australian National Dictionary of Biography* online, National Centre for Biography, Australian National University, Canberra, 1969.

55 TS Pratt, Matthew Hervey, EPS Sturt, Francis Murphy, JF Sullivan, *Burke and Wills Commission. Report of the Commissioners Appointed to Enquire into the Report Upon the Circumstances Connected with the Sufferings and Death of Robert O'Hara Burke and William John Wills, the Victorian Explorers. Presented to Both Houses of Parliament by His Excellency's Command*, John Ferres Government Printer, Melbourne, 1862.

56 'The Burke and Wills Monument', *Age*, Melbourne, 22 April 1865, p. 6.

57 'Warwick Assizes', *Oxford Journal*, 19 April 1823, p. 4.

58 Jocelyn Hackforth-Jones, *The Convict Artists*, Macmillan, South Melbourne, 1977, p. 20.

59 Gaye Sculthorpe, 'Thomas Bock and the mystery of Trukanini's shell necklace', in Jane Stewart and Jonathan Watkins (eds), *Thomas Bock*, Ikon Gallery, Birmingham, 2018, pp. 50–1.

60 'Entry 113, Bock, Tho', Convict Department Conduct Registers of Male Convicts Arriving in the Period of the Assignment System', Vol. CON31/1/1 – 'Convict Surnames Beginning with A and B 1 Jan 1803–31 Jan 1830', Tasmanian Archives and Heritage Office, Hobart.
61 Diane Dunbar, 'Thomas Bock: Society Portraitist, the Oil Paintings', in Diane Dunbar (ed.), *Thomas Bock: Convict engraver, society portraitist*, Queen Victoria Museum & Art Gallery, Launceston, 1988, pp. 42–3 and 55.
62 Steve Edwards, ''Beard Patentee': Daguerreotype Property and Authorship', *Oxford Art Journal*, Vol. 36, No. 3, 2013, p. 387.
63 Ibid.
64 Chris Long, 'Thomas Bock as a photographer', in Diane Dunbar (ed.), *Thomas Bock: Convict engraver, society portraitist*, Queen Victoria Museum & Art Gallery, Launceston, 1988, p. 63.
65 An earlier version of the discussion of the Lewis portraits was published in Elisa deCourcy, 'Beyond Sentimentality: The Family as Patron, Subject and Author of Early Photography in Colonial Australia', *History of Photography*, Vol. 46, No. 2–3, 2022, pp.110–13.
66 Richard Lewis travels from London to Sydney on the *Eliza*, and from Sydney to Hobart on the *Spring*. See '1822 Hobart Town Muster' HO10/18', File 18, Reel 65, p. 17. Records from the Home Office, London. Held in reproduction at the National Library of Australia, Canberra; 'Mr Richard Lewis', *Sydney Gazette and New South Wales Advertiser*, 2 September 1815, p. 2. I am thankful to research librarian Steve Pearsall, Launceston Library, for helping me track Lewis's journey across collections and archives.
67 Hubert C. Lewis, 'Richard Lewis (1789-1867)', *Australian Dictionary of Biography* online, National Centre for Biography, Australian National University, Canberra, 1967.
68 'Local / Foundational Stone', *Courier*, Hobart, 25 January 1845, p. 2.
69 Thomas Bock, 'Richard Lewis Esq', c. 1835, oil on canvas in original Huon Pine frame with gilt slip, 98 × 86 cm (framed). Allport Library and Museum of Fine Arts, Hobart, FA1355; Thomas Bock, 'Mrs Isabella Lewis (née Makellar)', c. 1835, oil on canvas in original Huon Pine frame with gilt slip, 98 × 86.5 cm (framed). Allport Library and Museum of Fine Arts, Hobart, FA1352.
70 Thomas Bock, 'Isabella Lewis', c. 1853, cased, coloured sixth-plate daguerreotype. Allport Library and Museum of Fine Arts, Hobart, FA1358.
71 Thomas Bock, 'Richard Lewis Esq', 1851, charcoal, China White and gouache on buff paper, in Huon pine frame, 53 × 46.7 cm (framed). Allport Library and Museum of Fine Arts, Hobart, FA1354; Thomas Bock, 'Mrs Isabella Lewis', 1851, charcoal, China White and gouache on buff paper, in Huon pine frame, 54.5 × 48.5 cm (framed). Allport Library and Museum of Fine Arts, Hobart. FA1357.
72 Thomas Bock, 'Thomas Lewis', 1848, charcoal, China White and gouache on buff paper, in Huon pine frame, 55 × 48.5 cm (framed). Allport Library and Museum

of Fine Arts, Hobart, FA1356; Thomas Bock, 'Charles Lewis', 1853?, charcoal, China White and gouache on buff paper, in Huon pine frame, 54.3 × 47.7 cm. Allport Library and Museum of Fine Arts, Hobart, FA1349; Thomas Bock, 'Neil Lewis', 1853, charcoal, China White and gouache on buff paper, in Huon pine frame, 55.5 × 48.5 cm (framed). Allport Library and Museum of Fine Arts, Hobart, FA1353; Thomas Bock, 'David Lewis', 1853?, charcoal, China White and gouache on buff paper, in Huon pine frame, 54.7 × 48.5 cm (framed). Allport Library and Museum of Fine Arts, Hobart, FA1348.

73 Gilmour, *Carte-O-Mania*, p. 9.

74 'Brissenden's Excelsior Photographic Gallery, George Street Brisbane', *Moreton Bay Courier*, 27 January 1858, p. 1.

75 'Daguerreotypes!', *Inquirer and Commercial News*, Perth, 28 October 1857, p. 2.

76 Patrizia Di Bello, Introduction to 'The Sculptural Photograph in the Nineteenth Century – Special Issue', *History of Photography*, Vol. 37, No. 4, 2013, p. 386.

77 Antoine Claudet, 'An Arrangement of Stuffed Birds at the Great Exhibition', 1851, uncased stereo-daguerreotype, Harry Ransom Center, University of Texas, Austin, 964.0865.0004; Antoine Claudet, 'A Victorian Bust in the Greek Style', 1851, uncased stereo-daguerreotype, Harry Ransom Center, University of Texas, Austin, 964.0865.0005; Antoine Claudet, 'Amazone zu Pferde (Kiss)', 1851, uncased stereo-daguerreotype, Harry Ransom Center, University of Texas, Austin, 964.0865.0007.

78 John Plunkett, ''Feeling Seeing': Touch, Vision and the Stereoscope', *History of Photography*, Vol. 37, No. 4, 2013, p. 389.

79 The Powerhouse Museum in Sydney has an unattributed negative (Object no. 85/1286-443) taken between 1895 and 1923 that reproduces the framed painting of WC Piguenit's 'The Flood in the Darling 1890', 1895, oil on canvas, 122.5 × 199.3 cm, held at the Art Gallery of New South Wales, 6105.

80 'Assisted Immigration Index 1839-1896', 1852, Reel 2463, [4/4923]. New South Wales State Archives and Records, Kingswood.

81 'Marriages', *People's Advocate and New South Wales Vindicator*, Sydney, 20 August 1853, p. 2.

82 Emily Hutchison, Queanbeyan, to Ann Wilson, London, 24 April 1854. Article 6 of 57. Queanbeyan-Palerang Regional Library, LH 994.47/HUT.

83 'Births', *Sydney Morning Herald*, 20 June 1854, p. 8.

84 'Queanbeyan, Daguerreotype Likenesses', *Goulburn Herald and Country of Argyle Advertiser*, 8 December 1855, p. 3.

85 Emily Hutchison, Queanbeyan, to Ann Wilson, London, 14 January 1856. Article 36 of 57. Queanbeyan-Palerang Regional Library, LH 994.47/HUT.

86 Emily Hutchison, Queanbeyan, to Ann and Thomas Wilson, London, 15 November1857. Article 49 of 57. Queanbeyan-Palerang Regional Library, LH 994.47/HUT.

87 Emily Hutchison, Queanbeyan, to Ann Wilson, London, 16 March 1858. Article 52 of 57. Queanbeyan-Palerang Regional Library, LH 994.47/HUT.

88 See reproduction in Errol Lea-Scarlett and Tim Robinson, *First Light on the Limestone Plains: Historic photographs of Canberra & Queanbeyan*, Hale & Iremonger, Sydney, 1986, p. 19.

89 We can attribute this now-lost daguerreotype to Goodman's studio sometime in 1846–47 because this is the period in which he began using faux studio backdrops: 'Daguerreotype', *Sydney Morning Herald*, 13 April 1846, p. 1. An identical studio backdrop appears in the surviving daguerreotype of Charles Windeyer held at the National Portrait Gallery in Canberra (2009.116). This backdrop is replicated in Lawson Snr's copy portraits.

90 deCourcy, *Beyond Sentimentality*, pp. 104–5.

91 See the extensive collection of Lawson and Icely nineteenth-century family photographic portraits at the State Library of New South Wales.

92 Alan Davies, *Freeman Studio in the Picture Gallery*, State Library of New South Wales, Sydney, 2003, p. 6.

93 Iris Burke and Keast Burke, 'James Freeman (1814-1870), *Australian Dictionary of Biography* online, National Centre for Biography, Australian National University, Canberra, 1972; Davies, *Freeman Studio in the Picture Gallery*, p. 3.

94 Helen Ennis, Introduction to *Harold Cazneaux: The Quiet Observer*, National Library of Australia, Canberra, 1994, p. 2; Newton, *Shades of Light*, p. 88.

95 In 1954, Valentine Waller, the owner of Freeman Studios, donated 400 early glass plate negatives to the Mitchell Library, State Library of New South Wales. In 1968, William Pooley donated 60,000 Freeman portrait negatives, on glass and acetate film. With successive owners' donations to the library, the collection has swelled to over 100,000 negatives. For further information, see the State Library of New South Wales record compiled by Alan Davies, 'Freeman Studio, Sydney, studio portraits – 1855-', 13 Vols. Reference Code: 825450.

96 Daniel Palmer and Martyn Jolly, *Installation View: Photography Exhibitions in Australia (1848-2020)*, Perimeter Books, Melbourne, 2022, p. 9.

97 Julie Gough, 'The Process of Disclosure', in Julie Gough (ed.), *Tense Past*, Tebrikunna Press, nipaluna, 2021, p. 272.

Index

Page numbers in **bold** indicate illustrations.

THE MIEGUNYAH PRESS

This book was designed by Pfisterer + Freeman and Megan Ellis
The text was typeset by Megan Ellis
The text was set in 11.5 point Arno Pro Regular
with 15 points of leading
The text is printed on 80 gsm woodfree
This book was edited by Sarina Rowell